AN ANGLE OF VISION

CLASS : CULTURE

SERIES EDITORS
Amy Schrager Lang, Syracuse University, and Bill V. Mullen, Purdue University

AN ANGLE OF VISION

Women Writers
on Their Poor and Working-Class Roots

Edited by
LORRAINE M. LÓPEZ

The University of Michigan Press / Ann Arbor

Copyright © by the University of Michigan 2009
All rights reserved
Published in the United States of America by
The University of Michigan Press
Manufactured in the United States of America
⊚ Printed on acid-free paper

2012   2011   2010   2009   4   3   2   1

A CIP catalog record for this book is available from the British Library.

Library of Congress Cataloging-in-Publication Data

An angle of vision : women writers on their poor and working-class
    roots / edited by Lorraine M. López.
        p. cm. — (Class: culture)
      ISBN 978-0-472-07078-7 (cloth : alk. paper) — ISBN 978-0-472-
05078-9 (pbk. : alk. paper)
        1. Women authors, American—Biography.   2. Working class authors—
United States—Biography.   3. Minority authors—United States—
Biography.   4. Working class in literature.   I. López, Lorraine,
1956–
PS151.A54   2010
810.9'9287—dc22   2009024923

All proceeds from the sale of this book are being donated to the Child Welfare
League of America.

For my daughter and my inspiration, Marie

Acknowledgments

Producing a book is hardly the solitary process that captures our romantic imagination, and a collected volume renders the image of the writer toiling alone in a garret particularly absurd and irrelevant. Apart from the gifted and generous contributing authors, many hands have dug into this work. In fact, this book would not exist without the vision of LeAnn Fields, senior editor of the University of Michigan Press, who attended an Associated Writing Programs (AWP) panel I put together on this topic in Atlanta, Georgia, in 2007. I am grateful for her astute instincts about the work and her guidance throughout the project, as well as to AWP for providing the opportunity to initiate this conversation.

This collection also could not have been produced without the dedicated and pragmatic determination of Meredith Gray, my brilliant and ever-rational research assistant. I cannot count the times Meredith has wisely and calmly talked me off the ledge of despair and led me back to the work, renewed in vigor and clear in my thoughts and plans. Her creativity, practicality, and natural affinity for editing made this work enriching, even pleasurable. She is truly in a league with Maxwell Perkins and Gordon Lish, and all of the writers gathered here have benefited tremendously from her insights. I must also acknowledge Vanderbilt University for the funding that enabled me to employ Meredith through the Research Summer Stipend. Ours was an unusual project for the university, and I appreciate this investment in a nontraditional research endeavor.

I am deeply grateful to the Gertrude and Harold S. Vanderbilt Visiting Writers Fund, Women and Gender Studies, the English Department, and the Robert Penn Warren Center at Vanderbilt University, in particular Donna Caplan, Monica Casper, Sara Corbitt, Mona Frederick, Janis May, and Margaret Quigley for all they have done to support the 2008 Spring Symposium: Beyond Our Beginnings, an event that brought some of these authors together for a face-to-face discussion of social class

viii   *Acknowledgments*

and gender at Vanderbilt University. Gracias tambien to Sandra Cisneros and Macondo Workshops for providing the chance for me to meet some of the gifted women writers collected here.

Furthermore, I owe fresh bouquets of thanks to Danielle Alexander, Justin Quarry, Nancy Reisman, and Heather Sellers for their astute help with my contribution to the collection. And as ever, I am grateful to my mentors and friends Judith Ortiz Cofer, Tony Earley, Blas Falconer, and Mark Jarman, for their unflagging support and wisdom, and to the remarkable Adam Grener, scholar, newlywed, and literary detective, who helped us locate a critical piece for this collection. Huge appreciation also goes to my husband, Louis A. Siegel, who does everything in his power so I can realize my dreams.

Finally, grateful acknowledgment is given to *Zzyzzyva: The Journal of West Coast Writers and Artists* for permission to reprint Joy Harjo's "The Flying Man"; Penguin Group and Goldin Agency for permission to reprint "Stubborn Girls and Mean Stories" by Dorothy Allison; and the Susan Bergholz Agency for permission to reprint "Only Daughter" by Sandra Cisneros.

Contents

Introduction: Joining the Conversation

⤚ LORRAINE M. LÓPEZ

Summer 2007—Friday night, my husband's toll-free business line rings and rings. He's out of town, and I avoid answering it, as I am a bad message-taker, deliberately unfit for secretarial work. Besides, I am putting my granddaughter to bed, reading books to her. When the phone begins a third series of rings, I race to his office and lift the receiver to hear my grown daughter's breathless voice. She's calling me from an emergency room. She tells me her husband has been in a car accident, injured, and then arrested for driving with an invalid license (due to missed child support payments for children he's fathered in other relationships). The police, though rude and bullying, have released him for medical treatment, but the arrest stands—he must appear in court soon. My daughter describes the migraine knocking against her skull, her toddler staggering around the waiting room giddy with exhaustion, the long night ahead of them, and she mentions that she has to be at work at McDonald's by four A.M. "What should I do, Mama?" she asks.

Cradling the phone to my ear, I can hear music and laughter spilling from our neighbor's house. On our quiet street of oversized hilly lots, sound carries surprisingly well. The people across the street are moving to an even bigger house. This is a farewell party. At the last minute, I was invited, but declined.

How hard it must be, I tell my daughter. *You deal with so much.* And she does. They live with an aunt of her husband's just outside of Atlanta. The house is packed with other family members who are likewise adrift, without permanent addresses. There's conflict, endless bickering among the many children living there. (Hence, my granddaughter's extended visit with us this summer.) Before moving in with this aunt, they rented an apartment where soon their gas was shut off. They spent the entire winter without hot water before being evicted in early spring. I made payments so the electricity would not also be disconnected. But I feel absurd sending them money directly, when they don't use it to restore the gas or even to buy food, when my son-in-law, who seems determined to prove as many negative stereotypes about his social class as he can manage, drives a new four-by-four truck, rack and pinion steering. Instead, I send clothing for the children, buy grocery-store gift certificates, and pay for unlimited childcare, using my credit card for aftercare and preschool.

There is no way I can convince my daughter of what she should do. No one could tell me anything, when I was in my twenties with two children, working two jobs to pay rent and put food on the table in a roach-infested apartment. No one can tell a woman who is poor and played out how to make better choices, how to take control of her life, and how to make children aware of the consequences of their actions. Notions of control over our own lives, authority to make our own decisions or to imagine future consequences, often evade us when we are yoked to minimum-wage jobs, freighted with children, struggling to head households, or dealing with unemployed husbands or boyfriends. Authority, in fact, is defined as legal or rightful power, the right to command or to act. It is power that results from opinion or esteem, earned through influence of character, position, mental or moral superiority. No one can give another authority. It must be earned, and it must be claimed. The best I can offer my daughter is the example of my life, now that I am a writer and an academic. I must mask the immensity of my guilt, for providing my child such a poor model, and show her—if I can—how to leave this place of poverty, depression, and powerlessness behind.

I have been fortunate in finding others to provide examples for me to follow. Joy Harjo, Sandra Cisneros, Judith Ortiz Cofer, and especially Dorothy Allison showed me how to change my life. Their books provided the roadmap to authority for me. I read of lives beyond my own, and I was transformed by the experience of reading Allison's *Bastard out of Carolina,* Ortiz Cofer's *The Latin Deli,* Harjo's unforgettable poems, and especially Cisneros's *Woman Hollering Creek and Other Stories,* wherein the titular story featured a woman like me, incredibly, as the protagonist. Of course, this is what art does; it changes lives. Literature changed me from object to subject in the long convoluted sentence that is my life. Most important, I read literature by women, women like me who read stories and poems and essays that profoundly altered their lives, so that they were provoked to join the conversation, as Dorothy Allison puts it: "Literature is a conversation—a lively enthralling exchange that continually challenges and widens our imaginations."

A writer is an author in a literal sense, often while also claiming authority over her own life. Even so, leaving poverty and powerlessness behind is no easy feat. Many never have the opportunity to attempt it, and few succeed. Allison observes that "the inescapable impact of being born in a condition of poverty that this society finds shameful, contemptible, and somehow oddly deserved, has had dominion over me to such an extent that I have spent my life trying to overcome or deny it." Changing this condition would have been unimaginable for me, without the wise women writers who provided astute and generous instruction.

This book collects the voices of gifted women writers who like Allison grew up in poor or working-class homes. The personal essays by women propelled by writing to reach beyond their beginnings inscribe the transformation from poverty and its aftereffects (with the compounding effects of family, sexuality, race, religion, and especially gender) as a source of adversity and inspiration. The resonances among these essays—as writers exchange and amplify ideas, build upon shared insights, introduce new concepts, clarify and expand upon one another's points— prove that, indeed, "literature is a conversation"—as if I had gathered these extraordinary women at a particular time and in a particular place for the purpose of conducting a long-overdue discussion on class, gender, and writing.

In fact, four of the contributors to this collection appeared on an Associated Writing Programs (AWP) conference panel that I organized on this topic, an event that directly led to this book. The speakers at that presentation in Atlanta in 2007, like these contributors all accomplished and successful women writers, invariably describe feelings of guilt and unworthiness, stories of familial betrayal and abandonment, fear of imposture and detection. Contributor Mary Childers writes about the tricky business entailed in achieving "dual-class citizenship"; Joy Castro observes that "jumping class comes at a price, and the price is not belonging." At the same time that some colleagues and acquaintances tend to devalue or dismiss our lived histories, family and longtime friends can feel affronted or hurt by our writing about class, interpreting our observations as accusations or criticism. No wonder our loved ones dread this conversation. Contributor Amelia Maria de la Luz Montes shares her mother's characteristic admonition, "*No digas*," echoing the caveat issued by Heather Sellers's mother, "Do not tell anyone anything ever," a warning that actually triggers the author's desire to write and tell everything. What these writers talk about when they talk about class often causes profound unease and misunderstanding on both sides of the class divide.

But these are women—like the braggart's daughter, with help from Rumpelstiltskin—capable of weaving shaggy clumps of straw into shiny nuggets of gold. The alienation they experience emerges as an opportunity for identity formation and for introspection. The Russian formalists, according to novelist Charles Baxter, believed that outsider status provided an ideal perspective for producing literature—granting them the objectivity to attain a state of defamiliarization that renders the familiar strange and the strange familiar. In her essay, Sellers describes how she acquired the ability to "escape while standing right there, how to be in two places at once. Right and wrong, hurts and doesn't, love and hate, loyalty and pain. It's that bi-location trick that every artist has to learn, somehow." This dual vantage point reveals the contingent nature of class difference and allows these writers to reexamine their lives with objectivity and compassion for others.

One clear objective for this collection was to extend inspiration and direction to other women trapped—as I was years ago and my daughter is now—in the crosshairs between desperation and hopelessness. There is no doubt that poverty is a feminist issue. Despite our profound desire to wish sexism, like racism, away in the twenty-first century, gender discrepancy still exists in this country. Julia Alvarez reports in *Once Upon a Quinceañera* on the discrepancy in earning between men and women and the resultant impoverishment of significantly more women than men, referring to this phenomenon as symptomatic of "the feminization of poverty." The women in these pages memorialize the incongruities between their life circumstances and those they encounter in the media, in academia, and in contact with friends from more privileged backgrounds. What is astonishing is the pervasiveness of the condition of poverty, following some past childhood and into adulthood and parenthood.

Work is another focus of the collection. Women work and work and work in these pages, and in the world, too. According to Action Aid sources, women perform approximately 66 percent of the world's work, for which they are paid approximately 5 percent of its income. Small wonder then that women writers here return to this subject repeatedly, the way the tongue seeks out a sore spot in the mouth. The wage difference between men and women is often explained away, writes journalist Ellen Goodman, because women "have this nasty habit of giving birth." Female employees are also assumed to have "opted out," by choosing lower-paying jobs that allow flexibility for family care, or are accused of being poor negotiators. Sex discrimination, Goodman points out, is often ignored as the real culprit behind unequal pay. As is the case with racism, denying sexism does not magically cause it to vanish; it just makes it harder to see.

One's ethnicity can compound the problem of getting ahead, for women like me and my daughter. A woman's race completes what contributor Dwonna Goldstone's mother called the "triple whammy of oppression," while encouraging her daughter to educate herself in order to transcend her circumstances. Just as in the African American community, many Latino households are headed by single parents, and most of these are women. Essayist Richard Rodriguez writes of the perceptual "browning of America," due to the influx of Latin American immigrants and the comparatively high birthrate of this demographic group. Much of this "browning," unfortunately, manifests itself in the lower economic strata, a phenomenon that the selection of essays in this book attempts to reflect. For Hispanic women and Latinas, racial and class barriers to economic stability are often compounded by their immigration status, as well as by linguistic and cultural obstacles.

Two of my three sisters are single mothers, Latinas raising children with little support or contact from the men who fathered their offspring. Until I remarried six years ago, I was a sole parent/provider for my two children, whom I raised while working full-time and completing a doctoral program in English. A number of contributors to this collection have been or now are the sole custodial parent or provider for their offspring, and many were raised by single mothers. Caring for children, even under the best possible conditions, demands extraordinary psychic energy, creativity, and attention, requirements that render the writing life challenging in ways unimaginable to others. Women who have grown up in poverty know well the enormous responsibility entailed in rearing children and the harsh consequences of having inadequate resources in this endeavor.

Toni Morrison writes that "the function of freedom is to free someone else," a notion that Joy Castro takes up in her essay in this collection. Like Morrison, the women writers in this book are moved by a profound sense of responsibility to share what they have learned about changing their lives—most importantly that some lives *can* be changed. Reading and writing can provide opportunities for gifted women, even if they are poor and tapped out, to chisel their own destinies, revising their personal narratives and removing impediments in the same way that disciplined writers pare away empty language and digression. In "The Flying Man," Joy Harjo shows how this process begins with a spark, a dream planted like a seed through a desire to do more than shuffle somnolently from birth toward death. It is a yearning to swoop and dive, to soar like the trapeze artist who captures Harjo's imagination.

Sometimes this dream and its imaginings lead to mistaken conclusions, as in the case of Amelia Maria de la Luz Montes, who takes pride in her mother's appearance on *Queen for a Day* (an early incarnation of daytime reality television) until she learns that it exploits the hardships of everyday women, pandering to the sentimentality of audience members. The misapprehension triggers Montes to uncover the roots of her mother's strength despite her struggles, the sharp dichotomy between personal tragedy and public graciousness that forges her connection to the fairy tale notion of royalty.

Dorothy Allison shows how this dream or desire for transcendence can be instigated by anger. Her disgust at writers and book reviewers and their often caricatured portrayals of poor Southerners provoked in her the irresistible urge to write her own stories. In Angela Threatt's lyrical soliloquy, strong emotion defers the dream for decades, as she examines what it means for a young girl raised in the Projects to travel away from home. For Threatt, the dream is born of the dissonance she experiences in the company of those whose privilege entitles them to take easy mobility for granted. Travel, as a symbol for upward mobility, not only suggests a departure from home; it also means a painful separation from family and self.

Several writers lament what they forfeit in striving for transcendence, once the dream takes hold. For many of the authors, loss results from the sense of family betrayal. Lynn Pruett's father's disdain for those he saw as overachievers, a disdain rooted in his own unfulfilled ambition, shaped her thinking to such an extent that her academic and literary successes brought feelings of ambivalence rather than pride. For others, just the admission of poor or working-class status threatens alienation from family. In fact, a few authors I approached for this project declined, confiding that they could not risk writing about this topic without possibly causing pain to those they love, a risk they were unwilling to take.

Teresa Dovalpage writes of the lack of food and regular power outages that marked postrevolutionary Cuba, deprivation that her mother denied, despite the older woman's repeated assessment of life in Havana as no more than "shit and a brush." The author's keen awareness of the country's limited food supplies granted iconic status to the family's ancient Frigidaire, figuring as the sacred keeper of the few, often unappealing, edible items that were available in her youth. Memoirist Bich Minh Nguyen also singles out a household appliance as a telling class marker: the television. This medium is the portal through which the dream of belonging in a new and alien culture enters the author's childhood home. In "*Laverne & Shirley* Days," Nguyen reveals her immigrant family's unabashed ardor for TV, an enthusiasm that mutates into shame when the author enters academia and discovers that "not to have a television, not to need a television, was to know true privilege."

Often parents, who are convinced their offspring deserve what they themselves never attained, foist this dream on their children. For me, the desire to change my life was motivated by a lie my mother told and retold as I was growing up, a lie I felt compelled to try to make true. Dwonna

Goldstone's strong-willed father determined that she would succeed aca-demically and used his power and influence on her behalf to insure this, despite the embarrassment it caused her as a young girl. Sandra Cis-neros's father, a furniture upholsterer, would offer up his gnarled fingers and thick yellowed palms as evidence when insisting his children study hard and use their minds, not their hands, to succeed.

Achieving this dream is far from easy, and several authors delineate the hardships incurred in the struggle to attain their objectives. Access to education in this nation is an ideal and a privilege—these writers show us—rather than a right. Mary Childers reflects on growing up in the Bronx during Lyndon Johnson's ill-named War on Poverty and succeed-ing academically despite having "only half a chance to begin with." She struggles to understand the source of her extraordinary focus and deter-mination, in contrast with her youngest sister's experience, observing "a class divide that can shape family history as much as it does the U.S." This divide is manifest in their chosen professions. Both have beaten the odds: Childers is a writer and a scholar, while her sister, nearly a casualty of early female sexualization in the inner city, now works as a masseuse in an upscale spa.

Novelist Maureen Gibbon lists the various "stink" jobs she took while still in high school—"chicken puller," fruit picker, waitress—in order to pay her own way. The foul odors associated with these part-time jobs per-meated her clothing and also penetrated her psyche, inspiring her cre-ative work and enabling her to connect with the first-generation college students she now teaches. Pulitzer Prize–nominated journalist Judy Owens recounts the desperate measures she took when "bumming work" as a teenager and her attempt to protect her work-study job by threaten-ing an officious-looking library patron with a Coke bottle, to avoid fulfilling her father's dire prediction that she would "starve out" of col-lege.

Obviously, not all the jobs undertaken lead directly and conveniently to the fulfillment of dreams. Poet Lisa D. Chavez writes of the lingering, limiting effects of class that persist even after she attains professional sta-tus. When divorce results in the near-loss of her home, Chavez resolves her financial problems as the working-class adults of her childhood did: she takes a second job—only as a phone-sex dominatrix. The experience dismantles comfortable assumptions, while jeopardizing her hard-won professional status and bringing Chavez an understanding and appreciation of her mother's methods of managing her resources.

When their objectives are nearly fulfilled, and these women have published their writing and assumed professional positions in academia, journalism, or the arts, class struggles do not miraculously disappear. The incongruities of class that stimulate the desire to move beyond one's beginnings often shadow her and mark her otherness—to herself and others. Karen Salyer McElmurray discusses ongoing class conflicts at her university, where her experiences growing up in Appalachia and her emphasis on transcendence are trivialized or dismissed. Heather Sellers describes not fitting in at a professional get-together and the jarring dissonance she perceives between her present and past selves. Judith Ortiz Cofer meditates on the class-based, cultural, and generational divide that separates her from the young people she teaches.

In the collection's final essay, Joy Castro reads her uncomfortable outsider status as a call to action: "an angle of vision and the will for change" that can jumpstart a conversation among gifted and empowered women who write. Motivated by the experience of growing up in want, Castro suggests ways for sharing resources, ideas, and actions, such as opening once-exclusive literary events to the public and offering "free creative writing workshops through the public library and at the domestic violence shelter."

Extending to others their hard-won privileges and benefits is a desire shared by all contributors to this work. They have generously agreed to donate their customary publication fees to the Child Welfare League of America, an association of nearly eight hundred nonprofit agencies that assists more than three million neglected and abused children each year. The "angle of vision and will for change" are traits that run deep and strong among these dynamic writers, as they churn dark memories into wisdom and humanitarianism while pursuing new desires and destinies.

Seeing a book to publication is a more time-consuming process than most readers imagine. In the best of circumstances, this can take up to two years, and this project has advanced rather swiftly. Authors can be a superstitious lot, and book production is sometimes associated with luck—good and bad. Despite being punctuated by personal tribulation and loss, this project attaches to providence overall for most of the contributors, in recognition of their many accomplishments. And I believe I have had the greatest good fortune from the work. In the first place, I have had the opportunity of meeting, in one way or another, the women writers collected here. Second, my daughter, mentioned at the outset of this introduction, has left her husband and returned home with her children to live with me and my husband last spring. She has embarked on coursework to finish her college degree with the goal of becoming, like my mother and me, a teacher.

But back in that summer, over a year ago, another burst of hilarity explodes from the neighbor's house. My daughter asks again, *Mama, what should I do?* There's no time to answer this in the moment, so I suggest that she call in sick tomorrow. I know she will be in the waiting room well after midnight, and I hate to imagine her rousing herself in the sharp-cold predawn to open the fast-food restaurant. But she says no. They need the money. Her voice is firm and quiet, a stark contrast to the giddiness in the background. I can't help thinking, There's a party going on here in the wealthiest nation in the world, people are celebrating good fortune all over this country. I was invited, as an afterthought, and she has not been asked at all. When we hang up, I return to my granddaughter and the books, some of the same I read to my daughter as a child, not understanding then as I do now how this act provides a means to glance in the window at other choices, other lives, other sorrows, and other triumphs. It stimulates the habit of seeing beyond oneself and imagining the self in different circumstances. Often it offers a glimpse of the celebration itself, the party to which ultimately—if we are lucky enough to learn how this is done—we must write our own invitations.

Stubborn Girls and Mean Stories

➤ DOROTHY ALLISON

The central fact of my life is that I was born in 1949 in Greenville, South Carolina, the bastard daughter of a white woman from a desperately poor family, a girl who had left the seventh grade the year before, worked as a waitress, and was just a month past fifteen when she birthed me. The fact, the inescapable impact of being born in a condition of poverty that this society finds shameful, contemptible, and somehow oddly deserved, has had dominion over me to such an extent that I have spent my life trying to overcome or deny it. My family's lives were not on television, not in books, not even comic books. There was a myth of the poor in this country, but it did not include us, no matter how I tried to squeeze us in. There was this concept of the "good" poor, and that fantasy had little to do with the everyday lives my family had survived. The good poor were hardworking, ragged but clean, and intrinsically honorable. We were the bad poor: We were men who drank and couldn't keep a job; women, invariably pregnant before marriage, who quickly became worn, fat, and old from working too many hours and bearing too many children; and children with runny noses, watery eyes, and the wrong attitudes. My cousins quit school, stole cars, used drugs, and took dead-end jobs pumping gas or waiting tables. I worked after school in a job provided by Lyndon Johnson's War on Poverty, stole books I could not afford. We were not noble, not grateful, not even hopeful. We knew ourselves despised. What was there to work for, to save money for, to fight for or struggle against? We had generations before us to teach us that nothing ever changed, and that those who did try to escape failed.

Everything I write comes out of that very ordinary American history. There is no story in which my family is not background, even as I have moved very far from both Greenville, South Carolina, and the poverty to which I was born. I remain my mother's bastard girl, a woman who treasures her handmade family, my own adopted bastard child and the lover/partner who has nurtured and provoked me for more than fifteen years. We become what we did not intend, and still the one thing I know for sure is that only my sense of humor will sustain me.

Stories I began as a girl seem different to me when I read them now. It is almost as if I did not write them, as if that writer were another person—which of course, she is. Twenty and twenty-five years ago when I first began to publish stories, I was a different person—not just younger but more girlish than it is easy for me to admit today. I grew up writing these stories. I made peace with my family. I forgave myself and some of the people I had held in such contempt—most of all those I loved. That forgiveness took place in large part through the writing of these stories, in a process of making peace with the violence of my childhood, in owning up to it and finding a way to talk about it that did not make me more ashamed of myself or those I loved.

When I was considering the question of a new edition of stories, I worried that the conversation in which they had originated was specific to its time. There is a way in which that is exactly so—though much less so and in different ways than I had imagined. I thought they would have grown boring to me, but they have not. Rereading them, I find myself once more sitting forward and grinding my teeth, or putting the book down and pacing a bit, or sometimes just laughing out loud. Yes, it is true that I wrote many stories out of my own need, satisfying myself rather than some editor or university professor. I did not at first expect to publish anywhere except in the small literary magazine where I worked as a volunteer editor, which is not a bad way to begin.

Before I published any of my own stories, I read a great many stories by people just as passionate about writing as I was, and I learned something from everyone I read—sometimes most important what I should not try to write. I began in the tradition of Muriel Rukeyser, aching to break the world open with what I had to say on the page. There were specific feelings I wanted the stories to create, realizations I wanted people to experience. Sometimes it was grief I wanted to provoke, sometimes anger, almost always a spur to action, to change. I wanted the world to be different in my lifetime, and I truly believed that stories were one way to help that happen. I did not begin with craft, I began with strong feelings and worked toward craft. I wanted to be good and I wanted to be effective, and these are not always the same thing. Sometimes I was trying to write a poem, but the thing would not pare down enough to anything less than narrative. Sometimes I was so angry, I wrote to stop my own rage. Mostly I was angry, and drunk on words, the sound of words more than the way they looked on the page. It is quite literally the case that I wrote out loud, reading the stories out loud over and over until they were closer to what I wanted.

"If I die tomorrow, I want to have gotten this down."

That is how many of these stories started. Once in a while, I had read someone else's story and put it down in a rage, beginning my own to refute the one that had so confounded me. Going back into these stories, I remember those moments even when I no longer remember the actual stories I was refuting. Erksine Caldwell stories, I called them in an early journal—stories in which poor Southern characters were framed as if they were brain-damaged, or morally insufficient, or just damn stupid.

"We are not stupid. We do pretty well with what we have." I'd set out to put that on the page—but often I would go south. By that I mean I would not wind up where I intended. I started "Meanest Woman Ever Left Tennessee" to work out in my own mind what it must have been like to have been my grandmother—and her mother, my great-grandma about whom I knew almost nothing, except that her children hated her and that she had lived a long time. How'd that work? I wondered, and made up a fictional Mattie Lee, a pretend Shirley. I gave the children names that actually figured in my grandmother's conversations—names of cousins, second cousins, and lost uncles. I worked it out as if it were a movie, or the kind of story people in my family simply would not tell. Contrary to the myth of Southern families passing stories along on the porch, people in my family kept secrets and only hinted at what might have happened. Some days I think the way to make a storyteller is to refuse to tell her what happened—as my mama and aunts did with me. I had to make up my great-grandmother, and I did it in a story that was originally to be about her daughter—a story I started when I was still in college, and my mother told me my grandmother had died—but three months after the funeral was past, and long past any hope I might have had of going to Greenville, attending the funeral, or learning anything about how she died.

"In a ditch," my Uncle Jack told me a decade later. "Had a stroke halfway between our house and your Uncle Bo's. Just lay down and died."

"Oh." I just stood there.

"Oh." I was living in Tallahassee then, in a feminist collective household, and fiercely determined to learn more about my grandmother, my aunts, even legendary Great-grandma Shirley. But my uncle's brutal comment was all I gathered in that visit, and almost as soon as I asked about it, one of my aunts denied that was how it happened.

"She didn't die down there. She died in the hospital two whole days later. She just fell in that ditch and lay there awhile before we went out and found her."

Maybe that was the story I should have written, but it was not.

By the time I got back to my big complicated household, I was working on the story of what Grandma Mattie Lee might have been like as a girl. What if? And I was in it, watching Shirley beat on the steps with that broom handle. Would I have made Mattie Lee so heroic if my own mother had not hidden her death from me, if my uncle had not spoken so brutally? Maybe. Still, what I wrote felt right on the page, and from this distance that seems the primary fact. I did a lot of things because it felt right on the page, or sounded right when read out loud in an empty room. I did not finish that story in Tallahassee. I did not finish that story till Brooklyn, fully fifteen years after my grandmother's death. Even then, I think I finished it because I fell in love with that teenage girl, her mouth full of white and her eyes full of fire. It worked well enough that it was another of the stories my mama would never talk to me about. "Now that's mean," my mama said about one of the stories I sent her. She smiled and gave a little shudder when she said it. That is what I intended, I told her. I want it mean. I did not say that I also wanted the story to be about love and compassion. For that sometimes I had to dig deeper, into the muscle of character. Still, I think you can tell that I loved my impossible grandmother with my whole heart, her black brows and wide face, her bulldog glare and frank inclination to tell me things my mother never intended me to learn. I knew she worked her children the way her mother had worked her, putting them out to pick strawberries for neighboring farmers and pocketing the money to buy snuff. I knew she was quick to slap and full of desperation, but I knew also that in the context of how she had been raised and what she had survived, she was almost gentle, almost sweet-tempered. But not quite. I had sweet-tempered cousins and I saw them get ground down. I had gentle aunts and it seemed they almost disappeared out of their own lives. Is it any wonder that when I set out to write stories, I made up women like my grandmother, like my great-grandmother? Troublesome, angry, complicated women with secretive, unpredictable natures—that is who you will find in my stories—and little girls who were not me. What are these stories about? Shame and outrage, pride and stubbornness, and the vital necessity of a sense of humor. I wrote to release indignation and refuse humiliation, to admit fault and to glorify the people I loved who were never celebrated. I wrote to celebrate. I wrote to take a little revenge, and sometimes to make clear that revenge was not what I was doing. Always, I tried not to use the flat metallic language of politics and preaching, but sometimes I knew no other way to frame what I had to say.

I wrote to give back to others who had given to me—sometimes reflexively. I would write particular stories in response to those I read. I began to write about incest only after reading Toni Morrison's novel *The Bluest Eye*. That book felt like a slap on the back from my mother's hand, as if a trusted, powerful voice were telling me, You know something about incest—something you fear, but had best start figuring out. I began to figure things out in story.

I wrote "Mama" to talk about how deeply intertwined love and resentment can be in a family in which violence and sexual abuse are the norm. "River of Names" was an attempt to stop being ashamed of running away from the lives my cousins were living—and, bluntly, it was a slap in the face of all the women I knew who seemed unable to imagine lives different from their own.

Some stories I wrote in apology, but I cannot say the writing was ever simple or straightforward. Even as I tried to apologize on the page I was aiming at an audience who I imagined recoiling at the facts and people I portrayed. I published "Don't Tell Me You Don't Know" before I told my mother I would be unable to have children, though that is the subject of the story. Only much later did I begin to think about what it would have felt like for her to read that story, my heartbroken mother who wanted nothing so much as the grandchildren I could not give her.

Some stories were about trying to figure things out, to understand what had happened and why. "Mama," "Gospel Song," "Lupus," "A Lesbian Appetite," and "I'm Working on My Charm"—all those began with a mystery. Sometimes the mystery was simply how to tell the story at all. How do you write about lust with a sense of humor? Shame? Lesbian desire?

Some of my stories are easily ascribed to rage. "Monkey-bites," "River of Names," "Her Thighs," "Muscles of the Mind," "Demon Lover," "Steal Away," "Violence Against Women Begins at Home"—all of those began with me walking back and forth in front of my desk in the dark of night. Sometimes it was a person that had filled me with outrage, but sometimes it was someone else's story. I had to figure it out. I did it on the page. Reading my stories again, I go back to the time in which they were written. The early women's movement was a genuinely remarkable moment in history, perhaps most of all because we were all so sure that we were going to change the world. Talking to twenty-year-olds these days, I find it difficult to get them to understand what it was like being part of the early liberation movements that so impacted this country in the sixties and seventies. We were fighting for our lives, I say, and I mean it literally. The life I was meant to have is what I was fighting. I did not want to be a waitress my whole life, to be poor or to come to accept being treated with contempt. I did not want to be ashamed of my family, my sexuality, or myself. I did not want to despair or commit suicide out of hopelessness. One generation back, I can name people who did just that—who despaired and died. They were no fiction. When I talk to young people, I find myself telling very specific stories. I tell them about my first decent job, the one with the Social Security Administration, where I was put on probation and almost fired for wearing pantsuits to the office—tasteful, respectable outfits with high-buttoned white blouses, paired with low heels and nylons, even in that Tallahassee humidity. A shiny-haired eighteen-year-old boy at Stanford laughs and says, "What were they thinking?" What indeed? I tell how when at twenty-three with my respectable government job, I tried to get a credit card, I was asked to have my stepfather sign the application. We were never quite adults, I explain, we women. You have no idea how different was the world we set out to change. That was the world in which I began to write these stories. That was the context. Reading them over, I fall back in time and remember the writing of them. I remember working long hours, hurrying home, and napping briefly in order to have the ability to spend more long hours at my desk in the night. I never went after a grant, never believed I could get one. I took it as a given that a woman like me would have to do it the hard way, steal time away from my day job, work without an editor or ready reader, and never have any confidence that what I was writing would be anything that anyone would want to read. But I never imagined not writing.

What I did not imagine was publishing. I read my stories often—at benefits and open readings, and always afterward people would come up and ask me, didn't I have a book yet? I was startled every time. No, I had to say. I had been writing stories, not thinking about a book.

It is possible many of my stories would never have come about if I had not lost my temper. I read a review of a book I loved—*My Mama's Dead Squirrel* by Mab Segrest, a witty, revealing collection about humor—full of stories about her family. The review was not critical, it was nasty. It made easy jokes about Southerners and their "funny" families. In a rage, I called that woman who had asked me if I had a book. "I've got a book," I told her. "I've got a book that will make that reviewer's teeth hurt." It took me more than two years to finish the stories and let that book go. By then I had moved from New York to San Francisco, and was living month to month on what I could put together teaching and writing freelance for whoever would hire me. My temper had run its course, and my first impulse was long past. When I was correcting the galleys, I kept thinking back to that review, anticipating the criticism that would surely be directed at my stubborn girls and mean stories, regretting my temper but not the book itself. I gave the manuscript to a lover I had begun to take very seriously. All these years later she is still here, the mother of my son and the woman with whom I plan to share the rest of my life. Her review was the first. "It's not bad," she said. "You are the real thing." After that, I decided to take everyone else's opinion in stride.

Why write stories? To join the conversation. Literature is a conversation—a lively enthralling exchange that continually challenges and widens our own imaginations. A skinny guy from the Bronx told things I never imagined about growing up a Puerto Rican who had never seen the island. A tall woman from the Midwest talked about apple farms and hiding up among the half-ripe fruit so as not to have to think about dead and lost children. God, yes, I murmured. Yes. In return, I tried to re-imagine the world as my great-grandmother saw it, feeling in my low back the generational impact of giving birth to eleven children in fifteen years. A little later I retold the crime I committed against a woman who loved me with her whole heart, but who, for all that love, never knew who I really was.

Did she really say those things? No, but she might have.

Does it feel like that? Absolutely.

I try for truth, and language. Sometimes if the language works, I let the details slide. But I am a writer, and I know my own weaknesses. In the end, the stories have to have their own truth and craft.

Now for a word on "trash." I originally claimed the label "trash" in self-defense. The phrase had been applied to me and to my family in crude and hateful ways. I took it on deliberately, as I had "dyke"—though I have to acknowledge that what I heard as a child was more often the phrase "white trash." As an adult I saw all too clearly the look that would cross the face of any black woman in the room when that particular term was spoken. It was like a splash of cold water, and I saw the other side of the hatefulness in the words. It took me right back to being a girl and hearing the uncles I so admired spew racist bile and callous homophobic insults. Some phrases cannot be reclaimed. I gave that one up and took up the simpler honorific. By my twenties, that was what I heard most often anyway. Even rednecks get sensitized to insults, abandon some and cultivate others. I have not been called white trash in two decades, but only a couple years ago, I heard myself referred to as "that trash" in a motel corridor in the central valley in California.

In 1988, I titled my short story collection *Trash* to confront the term and to claim it honorific. In 2002, it still suits me, even though I live over here in California among people who are almost post-conscious. In Sonoma County it makes more sense to call myself a Zen redneck, or just a dyke mama. What it comes down to is that I use "trash" to raise the issue of who the term glorifies as well as who it disdains. There are not simple or direct answers on any of these questions, and it is far harder to be sure your audience understands the textured layers of what you are doing—especially if you are in Northern California rather than Louisiana, and in 2002 rather than in 1988. And of course these days I feel like there is a nation of us—displaced Southerners and children of the working class. We listen to Steve Earle, Mary J. Blige, and k. d. lang. We devour paperback novels and tell evil, mean stories, value stubbornness above patience and a sense of humor more than a college education. We claim our heritage with a full appreciation of how often it has been disdained.

And let me promise you, you do not want to make us angry.

Queen for a Day

✌ AMELIA MARIA DE LA LUZ MONTES

My mother is about to appear on the show *Queen for a Day*—I'm sure of it. The screen footage is grainy black and white. Sometimes the images lighten and disappear—an accidental chiaroscuro effect. There are four women on the stage sitting at a table. I leave my chair and kneel in front of the TV to get a close-up view. Three of the women are heavy-set, their arms stiff on the table's surface, hands uniformly clasped together. The fourth woman, slim and small, hides her hands under the table. The modest sweetheart necklines, high collars, and prominent dart stitching on their blouses mark them as differently classed from the four shapely women who are standing behind them in glittery halter tops and tiny dark skirts. The four sitting women do not smile. They look very serious and out of place next to the animated women behind them who are smiling and positioning their graceful arms toward the table. Their pose encourages my gaze to curve around them and end up at the table of these four stern-looking women.

Suddenly the camera pans across the stage to a man in a dark suit. He quickly raises both arms and points to the audience. The camera moves past the stage to a large theater. The host, Jack Bailey, yells, "Would *you* like to be Queen for a Day?" I freeze the frame and notice that the audience is mostly female. They look very much like the women sitting at the table on stage: serious and modestly dressed. I'm straining my eyes, trying to recognize my mother in the crowd. I don't see anyone with my mother's thick eyebrows, arched nose, full lips. I see women dressed like my mother and like the ones on stage: nondescript A-line dresses, button-down blouses, three-quarter sleeves. A few wear white gloves. This is a crowd of women who look like they've been plucked off the street on their way to work. Most have short hairstyles with back or side sweeps of curls, or hair flipped up at the ends. Most are Anglo, or they look Anglo to me: light hair, white faces. I do not see anyone who has my cousin Ricardo's kinky black hair and brown skin or Tía Chala's dark freckled face and reddish hair. Even with a black-and-white screen I can see that the audience is mainly white. However, after watching one show, it's clear to me that audience members are not upper- or middle-class. These are working-class women who tell working-class stories. They may not look like my family, but we're working-class, like them.

This show is one of the earliest versions of what will become twenty-first-century reality television. Based in Los Angeles, the *Queen for a Day* audience and contestants were local. No one was flown in. Instead, any woman in Los Angeles had a chance to become "Queen for a Day," if she had the day off and a ride to the Moulin Rouge Theatre in Hollywood. Once women became audience members, they were invited to write down their sob stories and what they would desire if chosen queen—all on individual three-by-five index cards. They did this before being treated to a nice buffet meal. While they ate, a group of judges backstage read their cards and chose the contestants for each segment of the show that was to tape that day. Audience participation was crucial not only before but during the show. The audience became the judge by applauding the most tragic story. During the applause, viewers at home could see the "Applause Meter" measuring the sound. The chosen "Queen" would win by having the loudest applause noted on the meter.

Single mothers, widows, victims of fires, floods, disease—they're all here in front of me, ready to tell everyone their stories. They tell the announcer they're from La Cañada, Whittier, Pasadena, Bakersfield. Years later, Jerry Springer takes this to a whole new level, and after that, an explosion of other shows emerge: *Extreme Makeover, The Biggest Loser,* sob stories on talk shows with hosts Tyra Banks and Oprah Winfrey.

I carefully place three photographs of my mother on the little shelf next to the television. Someone wrote on the back of each photograph, "Emma 1958." In one photograph, she stands outside the apartment building holding me in her arms. She wears an apron over a tent dress or "shift" as she used to call it. In the other two, she's standing next to a bus stop on a downtown street. She looks shapelier here in a pencil skirt and tucked-in blouse she told me she had sewn herself. In all three, she has short-cropped black hair.

In 1958, my mother has been in the United States for a little over ten years. Since arriving from Mexico with her mother and brother, she has been working in drugstore-type jobs, selling cosmetics and camera film. The women she works with are a mix of Mexican, Salvadoran, and also Jewish immigrants from New York who teach her English sprinkled with a little Yiddish. To this day she speaks English with a heavy accent that at times I call "Latin American New York." When I was little I met her friends from the drugstore. One of them was Mary. I first saw her at our house. She had recently changed her name from María to Mary, and my mother kept making the mistake of calling her María and getting scolded for it. Mary wore flowery print dresses that were belted at the waist. Her hair was teased out on the sides and dyed blond, yet her brown roots were noticeable, like a halo around her forehead. She was loud and talked fast while expertly balancing a cigarette on her skinny lower lip. She frequently gave my mother instructions on what to do, where to buy clothes, find grocery bargains. I never saw her with family, only now and again with a different man. The men seemed to be the same type—heavy smokers like her, loud and bossy. Later, when I was older, my mother told me in hushed tones that Mary had died.

"Mary was an alcoholic," she whispered as she did with any kind of scandalous story. "Everybody knew."

Maybe this is why my mother often lied about her past. Maybe she didn't like thinking there were whispers about her, about us. She also had tragic stories that, for years, I did not know about. She was adept at creating a fictional story about her marriage, her home life. The lies: that she had married only once, that her family descended from upper-class Spaniards, that she had laughed more than cried in her life. The truth: Her first marriage was to a man who was married to three other women. He had met her at the drugstore cosmetic counter and wooed her every Thursday and Friday afternoon. He even escorted his mother to meet hers. There was a formal marriage proposal and wedding at La Placita in downtown Los Angeles with a white dress and *chambelanes y madrinas—*

mainly friends who worked at her drugstore, his sisters, and my mother's brother. Small but sweet.

The wedding night, however, was an assault and a rape, and this continued for a number of weeks. He raped her, hit her and then disappeared for days at a time. At one point my mother went to the priest to ask if this was really what marriage was about, only to be told that she must be doing something wrong. She needed to return to her husband and be a better wife. After another two weeks of beatings, my uncle rescued her and took her back to the priest to ask about an annulment. The priest needed proof she was not pregnant. The test indicated she *was* pregnant, and the priest refused to dissolve the marriage. The day after the priest refused, my mother called her husband's mother to tell her all that had occurred.

"*Ai, mujer,*" his mother replied. "This man is married to three other women and already has three children."

"*Que?*" (Here, I imagine my mom on the phone, tears welling up in her eyes. What horrific news. All she had wanted was to get married and start a family.)

"I thought you could change him," his mother had said.

A year later, my mother was still married in the eyes of the church (her brother had helped her obtain a divorce in civil court), but in reality she was a divorced single mother working in a drugstore.

I was twenty-five years old when my mother first told me these details. She needed me to type answers to questions on Catholic annulment request forms. She had done nothing about requesting another annulment after finding out she had married a bigamist. Instead, when she met my biological father five years later, she bypassed the church and married him in a nondescript wedding chapel in Tecate, Mexico. The next week they repeated their vows in a Los Angeles downtown court office near the Placita church. It wasn't until fifteen years after my biological father died that she again attempted to annul the first marriage in order to formally marry José, the third man in her life. She was determined to marry him in the Catholic Church. And this time she had me to type the forms and make our case.

During the process, I had to stop and cry at various moments while I typed this horrific story of wife battering and betrayal. But at times I found some levity.

"So you never married my biological father in the church, Mom?"

"No, I couldn't."

"*Bueno,*" I answered with a chuckle. "Then in the church's eyes, I'm really the bastard child!"

"*Ai, hija! No digas!*"

No digas is my mother's favorite line. She is always adamant in teaching her daughters to follow her example.

"On the worst day of your life," she says, "you put on your makeup, your best dress, and you walk out the door with a smile on your face."

No digas—don't tell anyone the truth, what's really happening. You want to put your "best face" out in the public. Always tell people you are having a good day. I think about the many times I could intuitively sense that behind that smile and those happy words, something was not right with my mother. The truth has a way of slipping itself through cracks in the narrative.

I unfreeze the frame and fast-forward to the next *Queen for a Day* installment. She does not appear on the screen here either. I feel disappointment but remind myself there are other shows to see. If she's not here, she may appear in another. Over and over again, I see Jack Bailey turn to the audience and with a loud, gruff voice say, "Would *you* like to be Queen for a Day?"

"Yes!" the audience shouts back.

I fast-forward, hoping she'll be on the next episode.

My mother first told me she had appeared on the 1950s TV show when I was in college. I was attending Loyola Marymount University as a scholarship student. There, you either came from wealth or you came from poverty. I was there on a full scholarship, a full-on poverty case because my biological father had killed himself my junior year in high school and there was hardly any other income. The year before he died, he had suffered a stroke and spent months trying to recover from his paralysis. At first he was optimistic, but soon he gave up. For my mother, his suicide was the ultimate in public embarrassment. She went to great lengths to try to change what was written on the death certificate, but to no avail. The priest, her friends at work, her best friend Veronica kept pressing her to go to a therapist. She finally did, but only once. Her one and only experience was baffling to her.

"Why ask me about my childhood when my husband has died? What does that have to do with it? No. I have my rosary and my prayers. That's all I need."

In suicide cases, families can be deprived of life insurance or other benefits, and my mother's only job at the time was as a part-time teacher's aide in a nearby public high school. During my college years, she kept her teacher's aide job while also working in department stores. My sister Rosa (from my mother's first marriage) helped as much as she could. She was, like my mom had been, a divorced single mother. She had managed to go to a junior college, receive a degree in respiratory therapy, and find employment in a nearby hospital. Rosa stayed close to home. I was far away in a very different world of privileged college students living in dorms that overlooked the Pacific Ocean and the Marina Del Rey Yacht Club.

At Loyola, I learned quickly, after a few faux pas, that lying, like my mother had modeled, was not such a bad idea. One day I asked a classmate who was majoring in television communications where I could find footage of *Queen for a Day* to see if I could locate my mother. I seriously believed my mother's brief television appearance could make me look pretty good.

The classmate, a young woman who traveled to Paris in the summers to study French, looked aghast. "Your mother was on *Queen for a Day?*"

I smiled proudly. "Yes, she was."

"Wow. How pathetic."

My face immediately went hot. I felt like Dick Gregory when he wrote, "I never learned hate at home, or shame. I had to go to school for that."

I didn't bring it up again to anyone until I was an assistant professor many years later. A friend I trusted, who was in television writing and producing, suggested I contact the Museum of Television and Radio or the UCLA film archives. I followed his suggestion, but nothing ever came of it. Both organizations informed me that the show was not public domain, meaning I couldn't just come to the archive or museum and see the footage. The manager of research services at the Museum of Television and Radio was the only person who actually sent me an e-mail: Raymond

Morgan Jr., the son of the show's original producer, had the copyright for *Queen for a Day,* and he was not allowing footage for public use. I dropped the search.

Then last year, my mother mentioned the show again, remarking how Jack Bailey had a little thin mustache and a loud voice. He was so self-assured, she said. He also stood very close to her when he asked his questions.

"He was flirting with you," I said. "*Pendejo.*"

"No," she smiled. "He was like Don Francisco, *el del Sabado Gigante* show on Univision."

"Perfect," I said. "Another example of an announcer and show that loves trotting out people's personal tragic stories. It's all so melodramatic."

Mom looked at me carefully. "I like hearing the stories."

This time I felt a reversal of shame—like I was calling my mother "pathetic" the way that classmate used the word against me. Jumping class lines does that. You leave your working-class home to go to college, to get an M.A., a Ph.D., which is a good thing, but you also lose.

I e-mailed my producer friend again and told him of my sketchy attempts at tracking down the show.

To my surprise, a reply e-mail quickly arrived: "Wow—found *Queen for a Day.* It's available on Amazon."

"Wow" is right, I thought, and immediately keyed in the Web site on my computer. A vintage picture of the show came up on the screen, and the ad read: *The 50's were the Golden Era of television's game and quiz shows. Five days a week, the voice of Jack Bailey, Master of Ceremonies, carried across the national television via NBC, ABC and the Mutual Broadcasting System. Ten million viewers settled in to see another Cinderella's wish come true. . . . Between radio and TV, the show had a run of nearly 20 years. These are the only seven surviving episodes of this landmark program.*

Now I'm here in front of the television. I'm worried that my mother will not appear. Even though I have read that it only contains seven complete episodes and fragments of "rare rescued footage," I still want to believe that in the next show or the next, I will be watching my mom on the screen. I continue to freeze-frame various sections to peruse the audience or to study Jack Bailey's behavior and body language. He really does lean in close to each contestant—especially the young women. At one point he tells a contestant how nice she smells. I also pay attention to the commercials and gifts the contestants receive: a Hoover vacuum cleaner, a Westinghouse refrigerator or washer/dryer.

A tall lanky man in a black suit appears on the very right corner of the stage. He holds a cigarette in his hand, takes a puff, then directs the camera to the table in front of him. Boxes of cigarette packs are displayed.

"Today, every contestant will receive a six pack of Old Gold cigarettes. Remember—Old Gold is the smoothest cigarette. Instant pleasure from the first puff to the last," and he takes another drag of his cigarette, exhales and smiles. It all looks very practiced.

Halfway through the entire DVD, I am miserable. "Mom! Where are you?" I say out loud as the next four female contestants are escorted to the stage.

All I want is one program with my mother in it so I can see how close Jack Bailey stood next to her, so I can hear what she sounded like, so I can see and hear her story. Could she have told the truth about her first marriage? No way. If she did, everything she taught me about keeping life's difficulties private would be null and void.

As I fiddle with the TV monitor, I keep thinking that if she were on the show a few months after my birth, she'd still be in her twenties— young enough to tell the truth innocently—what she'd been through, what she desired if chosen queen. Did she realize ten million people were watching? Maybe if I'm lucky, I'll see her footage and understand that my mother was quite a different person from who I know now. People change. Maybe she was as desperate to tell her story as some of these other women seem to be in order to get something significant in return. Who knows? Maybe at that age, she would have gone to see a therapist. I keep thinking about age and events that shape and change a person's attitude, personality, outlook. Maybe this is why I want to see my mother. I want to know all of her during every stage of her life. How did she become who she is now? Either this DVD will let me know, or somehow I can jog my mother's memory enough so that she remembers what she said.

Not only do I want to see her face, hear the sound of her voice, but I am bracing myself to see if she will appear as dark and dire as most of the women appear. Show after show, the candidates tell their sorry stories and ask for some kind of material object to make their life or the lives of their loved ones or friends better. I sit and listen to women who have suffered innumerable losses: the death of a husband or the death of a mother or father. A woman retells how her children died in a fire. She had saved one, but the firemen did not let her go back in to save the others. One woman's husband left her, and she asks for money to get an education so she can get a job. Another woman works in a factory, candling eggs on the outskirts of Los Angeles. She asks for more comfortable seats for her and her fellow workers and better lighting so they can more clearly see the inside of the eggs. Occasionally there are younger contestants—a fifteen-year-old is living with her mother. She is pregnant and in need of clothing for the baby. During that segment, the young girl hardly looks at the camera. By the end of two hours, I am depressed. I stop the show and look up reviews of the show on the computer. There are many. I notice that even Wikipedia has an entry for the show, describing it as "an inverted Horatio Alger story. Instead of the individual making good, the lure of *Queen for a Day* is a woman hitting rock bottom (or close enough to it—the tear-jerking factor seems to be the appeal here) in order to be crowned Queen for one day in her life. The harsher the circumstances that lead a contestant to the stage, the likelier the studio audience will be to ring the applause meter's highest level."

I drag myself through the last hour, including the "rare footage," which does not contain any sign of my mother. There's a part of me at this point that feels relief.

I turn off the television and dial my mother's cell phone number. No answer. My mother has gone on a driving trip with my sister and brother-in-law. They are in Las Vegas for two days. Las Vegas! Never in my childhood do I remember my mother having spent time in Las Vegas. My father was the one who gambled, and there had been many fights in the house about gambling. My mother complained that she didn't have enough money to buy us socks and shoes because he was spending it at Santa Anita Park betting on the horses. This was true. I blame the disappearance of my roller-skating doll on gambling. Every December I would unwrap used Christmas paper taped over the same box. I'd carefully open the box, and there would be a two-foot-tall doll with roller skates strapped to her little feet. After unbuttoning her dress and inserting batteries inside her upper back, I flipped the little switch a few inches below her neck. She roller-skated across the living room, down the hallway, on the cement pavement outside. By the evening, when I tired of playing with her, she would suddenly disappear. My mother wanted to ensure that the following Christmas, I'd have a doll. And I did, whether or not my father spent the money. It was the same doll every year. I just couldn't have her for good. She needed to stay fresh and new.

Perhaps my mother caused him to feel guilt regarding gambling. Maybe this is why he included me in his vice—to show that he was still a good father by taking me to the races or teaching me other gambling games. Either that or I was simply the "son" he never had—a son he could introduce to gambling. He taught me how to play poker and seven-card stud, and he also took me to the horse races. We visited Hollywood Park in Inglewood as often as we attended Mass. I remember standing on the hard and cold outdoor seats in order to see the track below because the cigar- and cigarette-smoking men all around me were either much too tall or much too wide for a six-year-old to see beyond. What I remember most is that it would take forever for the horses to enter the gate. I didn't mind the parade of horses in the beginning ("There's my number seven," I'd tell my dad excitedly), but then there was the wait of situating them within the gate, getting everything just right for a two- to three-minute race around the track. After two races, I was bored. Often I'd watch the crowd. There were men who looked angry and mean, others concerned, one I saw crying in a corner one day after I came out of the public bathroom. He was wearing a torn shirt and looked crumpled up against the wall. My dad taught me at a young age that gambling was a very boring business that could also be dangerous. And since I became involved with it at such a young age, I never wanted to do it as an adult.

Now in her eighties, my mother is somewhere, I imagine, staring at brightly colored cherries, apples, and oranges in a row and hearing bells and jangling machine sounds. I see the curling tendrils of cigarette smoke around her. I dial her number again.

"Hello?"

"Mom?"

are you okay?"

, Mom, I'm fine." My imagining her at a slot machine was no
can hear the pings and electronic melodies quite clearly in the
ound. "Are you winning some money?"

She is laughing. "No, *mijita*. I'm running out of pennies. I need to
stop."

I feel frustrated. I want to talk with her about *Queen for a Day,* but she's
gambling. Gambling!

"I'll call you later, Mom."

I can tell she's glad I said that because she quickly replies: "Yes, *mijita*.
Later." Usually when she's at home, she chides me for not calling her
more often, for not having anything to ask her.

I'm left with these television shows, these fragments of a moment in
history when I was only two or three months old. I watch *Queen for a Day*
one more time even though at this point the programs anger me. Maybe
I'm confused about my mother being on a show like this, which doesn't
seem quite analogous to her carefully staged public persona. And the
staged public persona—well—often I feel that was prized much more
than having real conversations in our family. Maybe this is why I have a
hard time in my own relationships getting through layers of "pretend" to
get to the core of truth. Maybe this is why people always say I'm so
"happy" and "together" because I certainly have followed the rule of creating a facade. Don't let them know what you're feeling today. Maybe
sometimes I have a difficult time being proud of who I am, where I came
from. My partner tells me I've come a long way from being a Mexican immigrant's daughter to a university professor. That long way has been
marked by crossing various kinds of border fences: the language fence,
the class fence, the privilege fence. Many times I feel far away from my
mother. Maybe this is why I want to see her on this screen—not because
of what the show is, but because of what I might see that I don't yet know
about her.

A month later I am sitting with my mother. It's spring break, and I've
come to interview her for a memoir I'm writing. I show her the pictures
I have of when she is young in the pencil skirt and the tucked-in blouse.
She cries when she sees them and tells me she can't believe she is the
woman in the picture.

"Where have the years gone?" She sighs.

I also take out the *Queen for a Day* DVD and begin playing it.

She smiles and laughs through the shows. She takes my hand and says, "I went with your grandmother Mariquita and your *tía* Concha. Your other grandmother, Juanita, was taking care of you. You were only about two months old."

"I know the show was very popular," I say.

I'm noticing the differences between the pictures I've placed on her lap and the way she looks now. She looks much smaller than the woman in the pictures. Frail. Her smile is the same, but there are creases around her lips, under her eyes, and liver spots on her neck. Her hair is dyed blond like Mary's used to be. I don't like it, but I don't press that issue now. We've let go of a number of differences. She now respects me for being lesbian and embraces my partner. I respect her choice of hair color.

"So why did you decide to go to *Queen for a Day*?"

"We went because they gave you a very nice free meal. A few weeks before we went, I sewed up some nice clothes for me and your grandmother and aunt to wear, and we went. They had a delicious buffet, and then while all of us ate, they gave us a card to write down what we would want if we were chosen queen."

"And?"

"I wrote down that I wanted a record player and English-language instructional records so your grandmother Juanita could learn English."

"Well that's not such a sob story. So they called you up to the stage, and what did you tell Jack Bailey?"

My mom looks very intent. "Well. He really came close to me and asked me my nationality. I told him I was French."

"*What?* Why did you say you were French?"

She laughs. "Well, I've told you I didn't speak very good English at that time, and people would try to guess where I came from, and more than once, people would ask if I was French. After so many times, I would just say 'yes.'"

"Oh, Mom, why didn't you tell the truth?"

She smiles. "*Mija,* we were having a good time, and the food was so good."

"Mom!" I'm exasperated. "Some of those stories are so sad."

"Yes," she says in a matter-of-fact tone. "And some of those stories you know were made up. I'm sure of it. But in our group, the woman who won couldn't have been lying. She had a wooden leg. When we saw her wooden leg, we knew she was going to win."

"What did she ask for?"

"A new leg."

I turn to the television. The "applause meter" hits its highest number. A somber-looking woman in a tent dress is being ushered over to Jack Bailey, who envelops her in a bulky velvet robe. The crown he places on her head slips to one side. She looks like a very angry queen. The camera pans to the audience. Women are clapping, standing, smiling. The queen sits on her throne. I wonder if she is still alive. Does she have a daughter, and has she seen this footage?

Somewhere in Between

ANGELA THREATT

Weekends, you bound out of the crib you sleep in until you are eight, because there is no room for another bed in your parents' bedroom, to join Gam, your father's mother, in the morning as soon as you smell the coffee brewing. She cooks mackerel cakes or fried fish, along with other, more traditional breakfast foods, such as oatmeal, toast, and eggs. What you enjoy most is just being in the kitchen with her while she hums and pinches your cheeks, calling you "Snoffy-Snoffy." Your mother's homemade cakes and pies, fried chicken, and cooked greens are everyday meals. Your grandfather, a World War II veteran paralyzed from the waist down in a civilian accident, frequently receives large quantities of oysters from a friend. From this man, her father-in-law, your mother discovers that she too enjoys oysters. Growing up on the Virginia coast, you never go without a full Southern breakfast and dinner, and it is a long time before you realize that oysters, crab, and shrimp are considered luxury foods.

For snacks, there are potato chips, cake, and sometimes, late at night for your father, your mother fries homemade onion rings. At night, you and Gam have ice cream while watching television. In reality, you are a picky and infrequent eater, which strangers can never tell by the way you fill out your clothes, your chubby cheeks and hands. You had been born a little early, not premature, but underweight. Since you could not be brought home until you gained weight, they stuffed you with milk. When you are a young child, your mother tries to feed you solid food, which you push away, demanding "joosh," or milk. The doctor reassures your mother that even though her child won't eat, you seem to be quite healthy. And you are. You grow fat on liquids and sit at the table for hours, refusing the mushy Southern-style vegetables, not old enough to know that you prefer your vegetables crisp and will only eat meat infrequently, but you lack the knowledge to request or the means to access these options. You also grow fat because you can only play inside, or within the white picket fence of the house your grandparents rent. It is not a large house, but comfortable. There are vents on the floor, a large one in the hallway that everyone steps over. You all feel cramped.

The home that you live in is not owned by your parents or your grandparents. It is small and clean. You have a large extended family, and you are never alone, never without heating or lights. On holidays, many people gather here, in the living room. Your mother and grandmother wash clothes in the bathtub and hang them on the line in the backyard. You are taught, from the beginning, about the history of your people, that it is a proud thing to be born on Martin Luther King Jr.'s birthday. You grow up knowing that, with a collective history of families being torn apart, family itself comprises riches. Your mother reads stories to you at night. You demand more even after her voice has given out, so she teaches you to read at four. Seated in a high chair at a restaurant with your parents, you astonish a waitress by reading the menu like a book. "She can read?" the waitress asks your mother. Though, now, you do not recall this incident, your mother tells you the story in detail—how she and your father order frog legs and eat them with gusto.

As integration progresses and middle-class blacks move out, the neighborhood changes. Your parents and grandparents protect you by keeping you within the gate, monitoring who comes in and when you go out. Your family is not among those moving out; those people have pianos in their foyers. Some of the people with pianos stay. Your family does not have a piano, nor are you comfortable with the new class of people appearing on the streets. Your grandmother clucks her tongue and holds your hand tightly, pain visible on her face as the two of you walk past a young woman mumbling to herself, hair askew, clothing in disarray. Halfway down the block Gam whispers, as if to herself, "That's Mamie's child. Mamie's child." Your mother walks you to the bus stop, and she is the only mother there. The girls on the sidewalk hate you because you are clean, your hair neatly combed, and your clothes look new. It doesn't matter that your mother has hand-sewn them and washed them in the bathtub. You think of your parents' bed as large, luxurious, but when you are grown, your mother tells you that the sheets were so old they were dry-rotting, the mattress taped over with electrical tape so the springs wouldn't "poke us in the ass." Until you are eight, you read and skate as much as you can on the sidewalk between the steps and the gate.

You get eight dollars from family members on your eighth birthday and lose it during a shopping trip, though you have clutched it tightly the whole time you are out. You've found nothing worthy of eight whole dollars, nothing worthy of the collective love of so many people. Losing it, you've never felt so bereft, so hurt. You know the money cannot be replaced, and you've wasted it, been ungrateful, held on too tightly, but not tightly enough. Your mother reassures you.

When you are twenty-eight, wearing one of two rings Gam has left you after she died, you lose the gold band in Dupont Circle, trying to find a friend from out of town who is visiting you. After being lost in the city, you arrive home to your studio apartment in Hyattsville wearing one ring, not two. Returning to Dupont, frantic, you walk the circle repeatedly. When you realize you won't find it, you feel homeless, lost in the world, without grounding, as if every brick in the walls that shielded you from rain, every limb on the trees you climbed, and every time Gam clasped your hand tightly on the sidewalks you walked together had been embedded in one gold circle that you have lost. There is no place to return to that is safe. You walk and walk, until every crack in the sidewalk sprouting weeds, every gutter you peer into begins to blur. You've lost Gam not once, but twice. You've failed again. There is nothing material you can hold onto, not flesh, not money, not gold. Again, this time over the phone, your mother reassures you. That night, you begin teaching yourself something new—the habit of checking your ring finger every few seconds, a habit that has lasted ten years so far. You cannot imagine a time when it was not this way.

You move to Gramma B.'s house, the home of your maternal grandparents, after your mother leaves your father. It has three bedrooms on one floor. It feels like home. There are copious woods out back, and you walk through them to get to the elementary school you transfer to after your parents divorce. Life is good for those few years before you move to the

Projects. You are not poor but not rich. Years later you will realize that there is a name for what you are. You are working-class. You've always wondered what that was. It will make sense, because your people always worked. Gramma B. would awaken before dawn. She raised chickens in that backyard, and buried sweet potatoes in winter, things she learned back home in Georgia. Your grandfather is a sergeant, an enlisted man made good. Officers have two-story houses. These days you watch Gramma B. can preserves in the kitchen and help dig in the garden. On weekends, all your cousins camp out on the floor. You have a ball. You love your family, and life is good.

Your aunts and uncles tell stories about how Gramma B. made do with what she had, and they never thought of themselves as poor. They talk reverently about how they always had good breakfasts, big country breakfasts. They kept biscuits in their pockets that other kids coveted. When money was low, she made a one-layer cake instead of three and iced it with chocolate icing she'd make on the stove. They say it was better than the fancier cakes she'd make when money wasn't tight. Even after she's gone, they will still talk about that icing. Gramma B. herself says how she visited thrift shops and took hand-me-downs from the women she worked for, washed them and restitched them, remaking the clothes so that they looked brand-new. "I enjoyed dressing my babies," she tells you, when you are twenty-something, thirty-something, and realizing that her words are your air, that you are learning grace. She's the one grandmother you have left. You have Gam's ring and Gramma B.'s flesh; you knit them together through words. You tell Gramma B. you will write her story.

When you are twelve, after you have lived with both parents and Gam in a rented house that no longer exists, and then with your mother at Gramma B.'s, in a house your grandparents owned, your mother decides she wants her own place. You are excited about your own room until you find out it means a little less for Christmas and the floors are concrete. The squat, pastel houses, once military housing, are not quite ugly, but the lack of grass and the strange way the neighbors act make them so. The people are different from the hard-working, full-of-laughter people you are accustomed to. Some move as if they have no place to go. None of them smile. Some of them are quick to fight. Others look on guard, as if they will have to duck from bombs at any minute.

When you return to college after four years of finding your voice, you will read Gloria Wade Gayle's *Pushed Back to Strength,* wherein she writes about how black people in the Projects used to have pride. The Projects used to mean community. You will recall both your family's discomfort with "trifling," "lazy," "poor-mannered" people and their criticism of "rich folks"—middle- and upper-middle-class black students at Hampton University who arrive on campus already driving Benzes and BMWs, whose attitudes of entitlement prompt your aunts to comment on their rudeness.

You will learn that there is a name for who and what you are, the pride mixed with uncertainty; the mannered behavior and careful presentation you've witnessed and learned, in contrast with both the raucous, poorly dressed children and the chatty, well-heeled children dressed in the rags of the rich, Grateful Dead tee-shirts. A term to describe the one-story ranch-style house paid for with a sergeant's salary and your grandmother's piecework—housecleaning, ironing—the yard outside as neat and clean as you, red brick, pine and oak trees full of glossy green leaves, flowers of every color adorning the yard, your granddaddy's Cadillac, shined to perfection.

At night, when dinner has been eaten, the dishes washed, homework, playtime, and gardening are done, tea has been sipped on the porch and lightning bugs have been chased, you all go inside, and what is left for the world to see are these images of order, of modest abundance: the nightlight shining vigilantly over your Gramma B.'s carefully groomed flowers, vegetables, and melons, the red brick house with its welcome mat, porch, and walkway swept clean, the leaves of the sturdy trees you climb brushing gently against the roof, your grandfather's Cadillac resting in the driveway.

You remember your discomfort at the age of twenty-one at a pool party given by a middle-class black friend's parents. The older people proudly watch their children interacting, eventually asking who your parents are. Where you're going to college or if you've graduated and what you are doing now. It's complicated trying to figure out all of the unspoken subtext while absorbing the fact that they have an in-ground pool.

You realize some of these people your age are probably going to marry one another and their parents will be happy. You can tell this about them, but they don't know a thing about you or your parents. How do you explain you couldn't decide what to major in and they want to know who you are and who you will become? They talk about Jack and Jill and Hampton University's lab school just enough to remind you that you know nothing about these things. You went to public school, and your mother was too busy making a living to socialize or volunteer. Eventually, you become mentally exhausted. You go sit in the car. You remember being invited in high school to attend a potential black student weekend orientation at William and Mary and having a black woman, the dean of girls, attempt to disqualify you from going. Was it because of your blue hair? Where you lived? Or both? Years later you think you have made peace with class, when you refer to a Greek "legacy" as a "legend." Your friend, a Hampton University grad, corrects you gently, and you are only slightly embarrassed.

Powerlessness is insidious. Back in high school you don't know you feel it, a lack of power, because you don't know what power is, but you think this—power is for men and rich people. You learn depression inside out. And you hate history. It's all about men and war. The only wars you know take place between men and women, on the playground, and inside yourself. None of which has anything to do with history. Advanced placement history makes no sense to you, but you manage to earn a "B" anyway. You get out of bed just in time to catch the bus most days. You get kicked out of AP English and drop AP biology. You coast along in college prep with the same middle-class white and black kids you've come to know. They never visit your house and you never visit theirs, but you dance on the cafeteria tables during a band party at school with the white kids, get invited to a party off campus by some of the black middle-class kids, sing "Louie, Louie" on the bus with the white band kids. You fit in with just about everyone, but go home alone.

You've lost the baby fat and stay thin by jogging, doing six A.M. aerobics, and eating very little. Your mother stops cooking because you won't eat her down-home food. A white male coach tells you your body is "perfect" and you should stay at this weight forever. You don't do any homework, but play your flute for hours, stay in first chair, except for when your rival puts you in second. You make All-City every year, but only once do you make Regional. You are good, very good, but you are not clearly one thing or the other: you make All-City but not Regional, you live in the Projects but take college prep classes, and always, always you are somewhere in between.

You don't know anything about SAT preparation courses, but you show up in time to take the PSAT one day. You do okay on it, though you know you can do better. You start getting letters from colleges, save them, but don't read them carefully. You receive offers of partial scholarships to Carnegie Mellon and Virginia Commonwealth University, along with invitations to visit others. At the time you think, what good is a partial scholarship? What if you run out of money in some other state? Later you will wonder if it ever really hit you that you had been offered free money that you could have supplemented with loans. You don't know who to ask, who to talk to. No concept of money, sure you'd go to college, but does it have to be an expensive one? Your mother advises you to stay local, and that fits with your fears, about money, about yourself, about leaving her alone. God knows you don't want to worry her, working two jobs as she is, getting you both out of the Projects, where you landed after Gramma's. She's doing just what she has promised, taking care of you both, by herself. You want to go to New York; the brochure that has arrived from Sarah Lawrence sounds just right, but you know nothing about that world, and the cost is astronomical. You want to try Virginia Commonwealth University, just an hour away, in Richmond, major in music, have private lessons. You and your mother set out to visit the campus one Saturday, but the radiator hisses, warningly. After your mother examines the engine, you turn around and go home.

If you had really been brave when the radiator hissed, you would have spent your birthday money on the Greyhound. But you are not brave. You think maybe it is a sign. You go to the same local college that your mother is attending. It eventually becomes a university. You and your mother will graduate the same semester—nine years later. But until then, your mother works all day and attends class at night. You borrow her car some days, catch the bus others, or carpool with people from your high school, also working- and lower-middle-class students who want to save money. Many of them major in practical things, like business and nursing, as you later learn many first-generation college students do. You are not practical. You believe college is for expanding the mind, and try everything from ROTC to dance to drama. Still a minority within a minority, always "different" in some way, you can't even do first-generation college right. Your mother majors in accounting, the same field she works in. You have been a "good girl," and have not borne a child, so you are not motivated by the need to feed anyone but yourself. You can't decide on a major and drop out during your third year. You live in an apartment with your mother, a nicer one than you had in the Projects. You can't decide: Are you poor or privileged?

You realize you are still in the marginal space when you find that two friends from high school are sharing an apartment downstairs, doing what college students do. Their parents live in houses, like your grandparents do, one a rented house, the other paid for. Still, you never know who you are, where you fit. All you learn about class, you learn from black people. The first time you eat lobster is at a middle-class friend's house. You watch carefully as they crack the shell and follow suit, dipping the meat in butter, and wondering why lobster is supposed to be so good. Lobster is to crab what salmon is to mackerel—less obtrusive, mild. You prefer eating crabs on newspaper spread across the picnic table in Gramma B.'s backyard, but you learn to eat the lobster. And you enjoy your friend's house, her little sister and both parents at the table. At the same time. Her father cracking jokes. No grandmothers or cousins living in the house. The girls have their own rooms. A nuclear family. The house is roomy to you, but they will move to a larger one when her father receives a promotion. All you know are ranch-style homes and cottages. A house with two floors is what "rich people" live in.

When you finally graduate from college, you tell a friend that you will be happy to make $10,000 a year. The friend is shocked. "Don't you know you're worth more than that?" You have no concept of money, of how what you've learned can translate to the marketplace. You can only imagine yourself as a secretary, or continuing school until you can imagine yourself as something else, somebody worth being paid more than minimum wage. As hard as it was to visualize yourself a college graduate, even after being encouraged all your life, you've never had to deal with being offered more than minimum wage at your work-study jobs. So you don't know how to feel entitled, how to transmit that feeling to others and trade upon it like currency. You get a job as an administrative assistant. Then you go for a master of fine arts, the least practical degree imaginable.

You still think art, somehow, will save you. But even after you find your voice, after you have overcome the fear of leaving home, of not being able to support yourself on your own, of cars breaking down and tuition going unpaid, after you have finished college at VCU and been accepted into the MFA program at the University of Maryland, in the first week of classes, a fellow student, another black woman, remarks that you aren't far from home. Instead of answering her, you shrug your shoulders and stand in shocked silence. Shocked at how much you know about her in that moment, and how little she knows about you. Shocked at knowing instantaneously that she must have taken many flights, maybe even out of the country, and many drives, maybe even cross-country, and that she is probably not worried about the money running out, that the people at home are not worrying about her either, that they have probably done this very same thing—traveled widely in pursuit of a goal. If the radiator hisses, they may curse it, but it won't hinder them, nor will they take it as a sign. There are rental cars to be let. You stand in shocked silence, feeling like you have traveled light years rather than 180 miles and having no way to say this, in spite of having been accepted into a program based upon your facility with the written word.

Sometimes taking a trip is as simple as roller skating for the first time all the way down the sidewalk, no one holding your hand. Sometimes it is traveling cross-country. Sometimes it is a journey of 180 miles; other times it is finding something new in your own backyard or your own mind. Though you're sure you'll love California and England and long to visit these places, you're still afraid to get on that plane by yourself. The distance to Washington, D.C., New York, the Carolinas, Florida, and even Georgia is now only a matter of miles. You've traveled the East Coast by train, plane, bus, and automobile; you've left the mainland once, to visit Puerto Rico, and gone as far west as Colorado. But you still panic when you imagine traveling to a new place alone, and you realize now

that the fear is about more than money or safety. It is about a sense of belonging in the world.

At thirty-three, in Colorado, you witness the extraordinary beauty of
the mountains, the red clay similar to Georgia, and discover why people
from the West, like the driver who takes you to the Denver airport, call
the mountains of Virginia hills. At thirty-one, in Puerto Rico, you see the
countryside, and marvel at how it feels like the Georgia countryside, only
with pastel houses, how the palm-dotted beaches remind you of Florida.
At nineteen, two years after high school, you finally make it to Richmond, a seventy-five-mile drive, for a private lesson with the flute
teacher. She listens, tells you that your technique is excellent, but your
tone merely good, that it would be so much better if you would just open
your throat while playing. You start to play again, and as your fingers fly
and your head begins to spin from the deeper intake of air, you hear a
sound from your instrument that you have never heard before, one that
is deep, full, and resonant. It seems to come from your soul.

The Flying Man

⤜ JOY HARJO

As I was being born, I fought my mother to escape, all the way out to the breathing world, until I was pulled abruptly by the doctor who was later credited with saving both my mother and me. I dangled there from his hands, a reluctant acrobat caught in flight. I took note there was a rush with the release, with flying free, and like an addict I flew whenever I could, from crib bars to jungle gyms and once the roof of the garage. Later, it was anything dangerous, like smoking cigarettes in the bathroom of the church, or jumping off a cliff into the lake after drinking illegal beer. And then the plain stupid: I leaped from the house of the proverbial cruel stepfather to the arms of a young dancer I met at Indian school who could not love me. And now we were stuffed into an apartment over a pizza restaurant, living from paycheck to paycheck. At seventeen, I was a mother with a nursing child and a hyperactive three-year-old stepdaughter.

When I looked out the window to where the sun, moon, and stars flew by, the only view was a rundown street bypassed by the freeway and progress. Anything that took root had to break through the asphalt and concrete and climb the walls of decay. Anything that flew over this city of stolen land and oil had to have wings.

I could see the roof of my mother-in-law's apartment. She blamed me for the fix her son was in, as if it hadn't happened before. He was supposed to return from Indian school with a postgraduate degree and support her, his half-sister, and the daughter he'd kidnapped from her teenage mother in Oregon. Instead, he returned with yet another pregnant teenage wife who would once again shift the fortunes of her son. I was the other woman, the reason for his lack of success, for her suffering. I had the one man bound to her by blood and guilt, a most volatile bond.

Every man she had been with had given her a child then abandoned her, including her son, who had left her with his daughter while he went to school in the Southwest. I was in the way and she took every opportunity to remind me.

She was now without a man, but she made sure she wouldn't be without everything she and the children had ever owned. Every item of clothing that her children had ever worn, every toy they had ever played with, every piece of paper with their names on it, she packed into boxes she piled high into a maze that filled up her apartment to the ceiling. She threw nothing away. She would not throw away her son to a strange, foolish girl.

Of course I wasn't ecstatic about the situation, either. None of this had figured into my map for a life, though I must admit the map was never clearly drawn. My path meandered according to the whim of failed adults and chance. It headed wanly to the life of a painter, like my aunt Lois, who traveled from the Creek Nation all over the country without the encumbrance of children and a husband and had the money to buy paint, canvas, and a car. Living as an artist was as close to my now limited universe as the planet Mars. Despite all my attempts at flight I couldn't afford art supplies, not even a junked car.

Each day was predictable. We got up, ate cold pizza for breakfast, left over from my husband's shift at the restaurant the night before. I washed the children, cleaned, and he went to work, and I worried about money and what we would do when he lost his job. And he would lose it, as he had lost all the others. The only question was, when? The last time he walked out on a job we had only an industrial-sized box of pancake mix, a gift from my mother, for meals to supplement beans, commodity cheese, and a squirrel once in a while. My mother was disgusted with the mess I had found myself in and did everything she could to keep from coming to the side of town I was now living in. She had grown up in worse and had cleaned and cooked her way to decency. My life was now a mockery of her struggle.

Every night he came in from work in a furious cloud. He had yet another story of how someone had tried to pull one over on him. Most recently he had barely managed to keep from punching out the skinny white boss who was riding him even though the new waitress was the one screwing up the orders and apparently the boss, too. We had nearly starved until he got this job, and I hadn't been able to work yet because I was still recovering from birth. The baby was nearing eight weeks old, and, as I watched my husband open another beer and pace the room, I decided I had better start looking for work. I would wash dishes, dance on tables, or fly to the moon if I had to, rather than starve the children or myself again.

Some days his mother would come over and we would pool our re-sources for food. We were bound together for raw survival and her mood shifted according to the nature of our predicament. On the nice days we would hit the yard sales together. Then I was her ally as we searched through junk for dishes and clothes. If she were feeling especially hos-pitable she would buy me something to wear for under a dollar.

She felt sorry for me and even that was difficult for me to swallow, but understandable considering I had first shown up in that small town of the tribal capital, where they were all living then, my blooming stomach leading the way. My then-to-be husband attempted to hide me from his mother at his grandmother's house, but it is impossible to hide a preg-nant woman or anybody in a close Indian community in which everyone knows everyone else's business, or thinks they do. Word got out, espe-cially after I was seen sitting in the town square with the old lady who spent the crisp mornings with her friends under the eaves of the old bandstand. They were the heart of the nation and made note of the cur-rent state of affairs as they watched people enter and leave the bank and the various establishments and agencies around the square. They were also still checking each other out for romantic liaisons. At least they didn't have to worry about getting pregnant at that age. They didn't say much and I didn't understand much of their Cherokee. To be included in this daily meeting under the oak trees gave me a fresh peace that was rare everywhere else.

Once, when the grandmother got her monthly check, we ate lunch at the diner across the street. I watched her unclasp her black patent leather bag and empty the basket of crackers into it to take home. I was horrified and tried to duck down, but my growing belly made it impossible. I bumped and spilled my glass of water, which called even more attention to us. She, however, had grace as she carefully left change for a tip, and we walked back to her house.

Soon thereafter I was summoned to my soon-to-be mother-in-law's house. I was nervous. I had been warned by anyone who could take me aside that she was jealous, overprotective, and mean. They were right. What they didn't say was how attractive she was, how she was still in perfect form despite the rough years, her dark hair thick and lightly curled with energy. It was her dark eyes that told the other story, took in the edges of things, the tatters, and left the good behind. My lively new daughter ran up to us as soon as she saw her father. My new sister-in-law quietly drew pictures of horses at the table.

We moved in with them to her tiny one-bedroom house that afternoon, because, as she told her son, "You can't stay there and live off your grandmother." Which was true. But she also wanted to think she had some control of the gossip. Of course, there's no controlling gossip, but if I were in her house she would know my whereabouts, could be the authority. She was also pragmatic. I could watch the children. And so it went day after day. I adjusted. I had no choice. My center of gravity plopped there, weighted with frustration and a baby who was growing pound by pound. There was no way I could fly.

I hated the days she was moody and critical. I could smell them coming from far off, like the ozone in a storm front. She might start with: "Why aren't you with your mother?" meaning, why doesn't your mother take care of you? She would reproach me as I washed dishes after eating food bought with her hard-earned money. Or she would say, "Your mother is rich. Why can't she send us money?" I would be humiliated and swallow hard. I didn't like being at the mercy of someone else's kindness. I did everything I could to make myself useful around the house. "My mother isn't rich," I would answer, and knew that she assumed my mother was rich because she was a lighter-skinned Cherokee who passed for white and lived in Tulsa. I promised myself as soon as the baby was born we would find our own place.

I never knew what to expect. Strange things would happen around the house at dark. One night, one of her enemies came to her in the shape of a bird. It sat in a tree outside the living room window. I'll always remember the sound, like the peculiar howl of the dog in my family that always foretold a death. It sent shivers through all of us. I picked up my newly born son and took my girl into my arms, while she sent out her son with a gun. She told him to get rid of it, that she knew who it was. I hummed to the children louder and louder so we wouldn't know any-thing, so we wouldn't think about evil in the world. We heard the shot into the tree and the haunting singing abruptly stopped. It was shortly af-ter that that we moved to Tulsa. My mother-in-law followed with her daughter and moved in next door.

One morning as I was toweling off the children from their baths, she pushed her way roughly into the house, puffing, then blowing smoke from a cigarette into my face. This was a new one. She didn't smoke cig-arettes and she had been nice lately; in fact, we had just taken a drive. She had a car. We didn't. My husband surprised me with the swiftness of his leap between us. He had never taken up for me before when she slid into her enemy mode. "Mom, get out of here, now!" he warned her. She stepped back, surprised at the vehemence of his reaction as he slapped the cigarette from her hand and determinedly pushed her out the door, slamming it behind her. The smoke followed her like a puppy. "That cig-arette was doctored with curses," he told me. "She's witching you."

Then it began to make sense. One morning as we struggled to put a bag of stuff from a yard sale into the trunk of her car, she showed me the book of spells written in Cherokee that she had acquired during her last trip home. The book was so old the pages were turning to powder. I did-n't touch it. I wanted no part of it. She had stolen it from a witch she saw regularly to combat the many enemies she had in the world: the terrible men, the minimum wage jobs, the unwanted daughter-in-law.

I didn't get sick or die that day or in the weeks that followed, but nei-ther did our fortunes change to happiness and luck. I began to believe that I dreamed the smoking curse, that it had happened far away from my babies, my house. What I didn't dream was that each day after she blew the smoke in my face she began to stoop. Just a little at first, imper-ceptibly even. Then it became noticeable, how the weight of the smoke bore down on her as it sat on her back, kicking its legs as it rode.

We all have a story. They are a means to an introduction, shining markers on the map to destiny. The night my husband-to-be and I met it was an accident. We ran into each other as I flew down the sidewalk to a dance. He was on his way to party with the over-twenty-ones. There were a few of them at the school in the postgraduate program. Later, we sat out on the porch of the girls' dorm and talked about our plans to be artists, about our families. "My father is Creek," I told him, and built him up as a descendant of warriors, when he was running around somewhere south of Okmulgee with a woman or two on his arm. My husband-to-be's parents were both Cherokee, his father mixed with German. His mother was full-blood and had been adopted by another full-blood family in Tahlequah. This wasn't unusual in that many of our peoples had died of tuberculosis and other diseases that took root from loss. When her son was small, she had left him with her adoptive parents when she left for the city to find work. We discovered that our mothers were probably distantly related.

His first memory, he told me that night as we talked under a night sky rich with flying stars, was of a boy with burned skin being brought to his grandfather for a healing. The skin was flayed over the boy's face in waves. He watched as his grandfather sang and prayed, then took water in his mouth, spitting on the burn. He did this many times. The boy and the boy's father returned two weeks later with some bags of groceries and a wood carving in gratitude for the healing. There was no sign of the burn on the boy's body, no mark at all.

This was the truth of the world. "My story is like a falling star," I said as we watched a small universe blaze and fall from the sky. It was there and then it wasn't there. This state of affairs could go on nearly forever, until the law of stasis won out and the next world replaced this one. I knew that night I was headed in a new direction, stopped literally in flight. Everything turned.

I measured the falling world by the baby's small accomplishments. He could hold his head up, he smiled, he laughed. Each increment was a promise of change. Not long after the witching incident, his mother and I were allies again as we were short on food and resources. It was spring. My mother-in-law, the children, and I went walking at dusk toward the rich neighborhood that bordered our part of town. Most of the flowers lived there and were blooming. My stepdaughter was also blooming, outgrowing clothes and shoes that were difficult to afford.

We stepped into an alley, attracted by a pile of used furniture and barely worn clothes thrown in a bin for trash pickup. We sifted through, holding things up, chattering with our good fortune, until a child from the huge house spotted us from his immaculate yard and yelled to his parents that Indians were going through their trash. We ran, holding our new stuff and the children, until we reached our neighborhood. We laughed after we had made it, and felt rich enough with our new treasures to buy ice cream. I still harbored a vague sense of shame at being discovered digging through someone else's trash, but was angry, too, that the residents would rather it be thrown away than given to someone who could use it.

Another sign of spring were the posters announcing the circus coming to town. We got discount passes from the grocery store, and I took the kids and my sister-in-law to the Sunday matinee. It was my first venture out in over a year. I felt expansive, as if my orbit had changed to accommodate the light of a new path. The arena was packed with families that afternoon, the city's kids swirling with snacks, circus toys, and excitement. We sat next to a concrete aisle for easier access to the bathrooms. The girls asked about everything as we waited for the show. They wanted to know what-time-the-show-started-exactly-and-how-long-would-it-be-before-the-show-started-where-were-the-tigers-could-they-have-balloons-if-they-couldn't-have-a-balloon-could-they-ride-the-elephant-and-why-couldn't-we-sit-closer-so-we-could-see-better-and-could-they-go-to-the-bathroom-even-though-they-had-just-been-a-few-minutes-ago? As I answered them, I watched people intensely, imagined their lives and how I would paint them, rejuvenated by the smell of popcorn, the change in scenery.

Out of the churning crowds came a slim man in tights and a cape. As he headed up from the ring, he grew larger and larger as people parted to let him by, an incongruous figure in the middle of the flatly ordinary. He stopped next to me and surprised me by speaking to me. At first I thought he needed directions or had mistaken me for someone else, but he casually introduced himself as one of the brothers of the featured trapeze act, the Flying-Something-or-Other Brothers. I felt suddenly awkward and mumbled a response. I didn't know what I had done to garner such attention. And I had forgotten how to speak to anyone but small children and a husband who was so desperate for youth and fun that he had taken to riding around and drinking beer with his high school friends. This strange man from Italy was the first person who had talked to me in months, the only one who had asked me a direct question about my own life. I responded by talking about my husband. I told this caped performer who had suddenly befriended me that my husband had been a dancer who was compared by critics to Rudolf Nureyev when we performed together a little more than a year before. He had many offers to join dance companies in the East, but had turned them down. I nervously talked up his attributes, but didn't really know where I was going with any of it. Then I agreed to meet him after the performance.

When I look back, I can imagine how I must have appeared that afternoon—a vulnerable young woman dressed neatly but poorly, fixed at point zero under the big top, accompanied by an infant, by children waving their cotton candy clouds, urgently asking for the bathroom after they had just returned from the bathroom. I was in terrible need of flight.

That afternoon the children and I watched the Flying Brothers swing gracefully from one small platform to another, suspended by muscle and nerve, as if by magic. I began to consider what it would be like to fly, like this man from Italy who traveled the world flying into space beyond fear, risking his life while the crowd watched in awe. It was then I became convinced that this was a job my agile husband could learn, as quickly and easily as he learned to toss and twist pizzas. We could travel together into a world much larger than the one that was squeezing us flat, far, far away from his mother. We could fly.

I am surprised now at my naïveté when I tell this story, though when I was in it I didn't feel naive. By the last harrumphs of the circus band, I was utterly convinced and felt extremely practical about my new plan. I knew the days of the job at the pizzeria were almost over, and a job on the trapeze in the circus was something I became absolutely convinced my husband could do.

I don't remember how we got from the circus to the pizzeria where my husband was working the afternoon shift. I do remember the way the sun came in through the colored dark glass in the restaurant as the manager retrieved my husband from the kitchen, and how excited I was about the possibility of the opportunity for a job, something that might engage him, use his dancer skills, and keep everyone in food and clothes. I introduced the acrobat to my husband. They were civil to each other as I explained my notion. As a ripple of tension coursed through all of us, I realized I had made a serious mistake in my assumption of a job possibility. It was my own dream of flying.

After I left the pizza parlor that afternoon, the flying man insisted on accompanying me to my apartment and waited as I put the children down for their naps. I was confused about his intentions but played the perfect hostess, offered him coffee, water, and food, which he declined. Then he praised my beauty and abruptly asked me to leave with him immediately for Corsica. Everything stopped. I considered the sudden shift of events and a story that would shine garishly when displayed next to all the others in my small, rude life. The exhilaration of the force of possibility pinned me there, for a moment, in the slant of late afternoon sun. This was what I had been waiting for, but it wouldn't fit, and nothing I could do would make it fit into a map that was apparently there, but not there. I told him I couldn't go anywhere, not even Corsica, I had babies. I asked him to leave.

The circus left town that afternoon. My husband did lose his job a few weeks later, as I had predicted. We had to move to another part of town after he found work in another pizza restaurant, and his mother followed us. Things got worse, but I eventually flew far from that place, those times, and the story of the flying man.

Our Mother's Lie

⤝ LORRAINE M. LÓPEZ

We were poor, but we lied about it. My mother, a woman of legendary bluntness, was the biggest liar of us all on one particular point. She'd say we were *not* poor. She'd say we could be anything we want to be. She'd say, "Girls, after your brother Kenny serves his two consecutive terms, you can be presidents, too, one right after another." She'd say, "Why, Kenny could be a brain surgeon with those long fingers of his. There's nothing holding him, or any of you back." And she would also say, "By the way, can I borrow the money Grandma sent for your birthday to get bread for tomorrow?"

She would tell us, "I will love you no matter what you do. Why, if Kenny were to become an ax murderer, I'd love him the same as I do now and visit him every single day in prison." (We four sisters often complained among ourselves about our only brother, the middle child and our mother's favorite. "Well, *Kenny.* Of course, *he* can be an ax murderer, no problem, but what happens when we forget to wash the dishes? Where's all that forgiveness then?")

And what if we became cocktail waitresses? Would she still love us if we started slinging margaritas at the Dug-Out near Dodger Stadium? The way she said it—*Cock.* Tail. Waitress.—was an indictment in itself. Though she probably would have gotten over it, neither I nor any of my three sisters has ever worked as a waitress of any kind. I am sure that among us, we have broken almost all of the Ten Commandments, while my mother's rule against serving mixed drinks has remained inviolate. I did work once in food service as a pizza chef in a small Italian restaurant in North Hollywood. But when the owner asked me to bring salads to a party of diners on a busy night, I refused, blurting, "It's against my faith."

My mother still had the immigrant's approach to life in the United

States, though her family had migrated during the Spanish Inquisition to central New Mexico. Sephardic Jews, her ancestors settled in what is now the United States before Jamestown. Though our ancestors went to all the trouble to escape persecution in Spain for Judaism, perversely, one of the first things they did in the New World was convert to Catholicism. Perhaps they felt they were inoculating themselves against future pogroms. They certainly threw themselves into Christianity with vigor, becoming vehement Catholics. My mother was the only member of her family not to attend Mass every day and to lead a life that did not revolve around the schedule posted in the church bulletin.

She was more patriotic than religious. My mother likely believed her family had been American before there were Americans, and who could blame her? Whenever "The Star-Spangled Banner" played, she would place her hand over her heart and sing with gusto. She was a passionate baseball fan with deep allegiance to the L.A. Dodgers. Though diabetes prevented her from enjoying sweets, she'd often send us to the corner grocery to buy crushed or day-old apple pies, and she'd take vicarious pleasure in watching us eat slices for dessert. And in completing the trinity of national devotion with her usual thoroughness, she not only endorsed motherhood; she practiced it. She *was* Mom. The television mothers with aprons tied around their trim waists, wearing pearls and high heels while they dusted, those women weren't *real.* They weren't *Mom.* Mom was heavy, tall, and strong. Her voice could rattle windowpanes. I *never* saw her dust.

My father's family relocated to New Mexico during the civil wars in Mexico in the 1800s. He and four of his brothers served in the U.S. Army during World War II. After the war, when jobs were scarce even for returning servicemen, my father and mother moved to Los Angeles, where my father was hired by the city. A loyal Democrat who took his voting privileges seriously, my father was also active in his labor union and a steadfast civil service employee during the forty years he worked for the Los Angeles Department of Water and Power. Furthermore, I submit that his name should be entered in *The Guinness Book of World Records* for the most jury duty served by one man. Until advanced age forced him into retirement, he was a regular at the courthouse, nearly as familiar with the bailiffs as he was with his coworkers. In voir dire, he was much sought after by both the prosecution and the defense for his favorite answer to ethical inquiries: "Well, that depends, doesn't it?" No reason to question his support of this country, including its Dream that promises success to anyone willing to strive for it, regardless of circumstances of birth.

Yet, my parents never owned a home. We moved from rental property to rental property, incessantly anxious about disturbing downstairs neighbors and displeasing landlords. My parents rented a one-bedroom apartment and then a one-bedroom bungalow before moving to a place where all five of us children finally slept together in a proper bedroom. That is, until my oldest sister and I cleared out a cobwebby office in the attic and moved into it—a room of our own—when we were in our teens.

For years, we inhabited the upper floor of a dilapidated duplex smack in the backyard of the Hollywood Freeway. The rush of cars roared like waves ceaselessly cresting and tumbling, day and night. Our parents, who sacrificed mightily to invest in our education, had no idea then that living close to a persistent source of carbon monoxide and particulate matter from auto emissions would delimit the flow of oxygen to our brains, potentially lowering our IQs by about ten points. They never knew this exposure put us all at risk for asthma, which afflicted my brother; respiratory infections; anemia; and even leukemia and heart disease. But they might have guessed something was up if they'd looked beyond the craftsman-style homes in our pre-gentrified Echo Park neighborhood and the few tidy lawns maintained by the retirees who lived on both sides of us, home-owning holdouts rapidly being outnumbered by immigrant renters.

Dividing us from the freeway was a narrow weed-choked strip, an overgrown alley inhabited by the homeless, whose charred cookware and dusty clothing we would encounter, when taking the shortcut to school, like artifacts from a lost civilization. Our own house was so decrepit and gloomy that my schoolmates teased me that it was haunted. I begged my mother to move us into the neat complex of Creamsicle orange stucco apartments, also alongside the freeway, but a few blocks away. She said we could only afford to live there if we ate beans every night. How I hated beans. They tasted like tiny parcels of mud. But I gulped hard and vowed to eat beans every single night. Only now, when I look back, do I understand that the newly constructed complex I lusted after was the low-income housing project. And we could not afford to move into it.

We all wore secondhand clothes. I proudly wore bright floral muumuus handed down by our across-the-street neighbor, Susan Fujimori, whose family relocated to Los Angeles from Hawaii. Susan was taller and heavier than I was. Her blouses and dresses were roomy, "floaty," I would say, spinning to twirl the resplendent hibiscus-patterned folds. In family photos, the bespectacled one wearing loud tropic prints with bobby sox and Keds, looking like a maniacal secretary on her way to a luau, that would be me. After I was enrolled in the parochial school where my mother taught, I had to wear a uniform: white cotton blouse, dark blue sweater, and navy skirt of heavy wool plaid. My skirt, inches shorter than my older sister's, was coveted by her for the purpose of better displaying her shapely legs. She'd persuade me to lend it to her when I did not need it.

One afternoon, while wearing my skirt, she fell from a bicycle, somehow ripping gashes in it without injuring herself too much. I was supposed to be glad she was unhurt, but I was heartbroken over my skirt. Of course, my parents could not afford to replace it. Instead my mother, an especially inept seamstress, tried to mend it with brown thread. Nearly the entire school year, I wore a skirt that looked as if a drunken, color-blind surgeon had performed an appendectomy on me without bothering to remove my clothes. "The Frankenstein skirt," a cruel friend of my sister's called it. No wonder I'd race home to kick it off and dive into my cool, breezy Hawaiian garb, the unscarred, flowing yards of eye-smarting color as light and airy as butterfly wings.

I was lucky that my wardrobe migrated from Hawaii with Susan, an only child who had worn it gently. Until I had a job, I rarely wore new clothes, and every new item of clothing—even underwear—was shared by my older sister. Except for my brother, we all shared, and when we could get away with it, we didn't. My brother, sisters, and I scrapped over coins we found behind couch cushions, we flattened aluminum cans for recycling and returned deposit bottles for change, we drank cases and cases of room-temperature Fresca even though it was given away because the artificial sweetener caused cancer in lab mice, and if we didn't want to surrender it for groceries, we spent that birthday money. Fast.

My oldest and youngest sisters are social workers. My second-youngest sister works in banking, and Kenny, the would-be presidential neurosurgeon, teaches elementary school. I, second born, am a college professor and an author, a Latina—one of only 3.1 percent of Hispanics earning doctoral degrees in the U.S. the year I graduated. I am among the 1.5 percent of full-time Latina/o faculty members at the prestigious Southern university where I teach. For every hundred of my colleagues, only one and a half of me exist, and sometimes I search faculty assemblies, idly hoping to catch sight of a half-sized Latina. Recently, I learned that a fellow junior faculty member, an astronomer who is in a peer mentoring group with me, is half Iranian and half Mexican, so together we embody the full percentage of tenure-track professors of Latino descent at our institution. My relief upon learning this was absurd in its enormity.

We could be whatever we wanted, my mother said. But attempting this would not be easy. She left that part out, though we should have gleaned this from the example of her life. When my youngest sister entered kindergarten, my mother herself enrolled in school. She pursued a degree in education and made enough progress to be hired as a teacher at the Catholic school we attended. She never completed her course work and often pointed out, "A degree does not a teacher make," to which I'd say, "And you haven't let the weird syntax hold you back either." She became an elementary school vice principal before heart disease curtailed her career. My mother didn't live to see us be whatever we wanted, though I expect she would have been proud of all of us, especially of me. *I* should be proud.

And yet, not too long ago, I sipped coffee at Starbucks with a graduate student, explaining how perspective works in short fiction and why it is important for him to control this, when he interrupted me. "Now, *where* were your books published?"

Earlier in the semester, this student inquired in class about my residency status, wanting to know when I "crossed over," and on another occasion, he baffled me by asking if I had been offended by the portrayal of a South American character in the short story collection we were reading. These are not unusual questions from my students or my colleagues. Some of my colleagues don't know the difference between Latin American and Latino literature. They are brilliant, but busy; they only have time for matters important to them. I am used to this. In this context, though, these questions added up uncomfortably, the subtext issuing clearly from the inquiry. This student wanted to know one thing: *Why should I listen to you?*

I told him my publisher's name. A small nonprofit press. One book is a short story collection, the other a young adult novel. He raised an eyebrow, nodding. I swung the discussion back to point of view, and he interrupted again. "The next book," he said, "who's publishing that?"

Later I learned that after our meeting he sent an e-mail to the director of the MFA program to ask when my colleague, a white male writer whose books are published by a major press, will be teaching the fiction workshop. The student claimed that he'd entered the program in order to work with *him*.

When I complained about this to my friend, an Appalachian writer who also teaches in an MFA program in the South, she speculated that students see me as the Latina maid. I agreed. "*La criada*," I said, "fit only for cleaning up messes." My friend told me she deals with this type of disdain regularly where she teaches, and she's convinced her male and middle-class colleagues do not confront questions of authority the way we do as working- and lower-class women, the way I do as a Latina in academia.

"They don't think I have the cultural currency my colleagues have," I said.

"I hate that term," she said, "cultural currency. It just grates on me."

"Sorry. It's an oxymoron, isn't it?"

And it is a cliché. I made a mental note to abolish the phrase from my lexicon, hoping I've not used it with any of my colleagues. One effect of a lower-class background has been that I am never sure what to say, how to behave. I spend a lot of time watching others, being silent and circumspect, concentrating my attention on not slipping up and not being detected for what I am, not betraying where I am from. I think I am good at this, but sometimes I make mistakes, like the time I balanced a wine glass on a coaster at a faculty get-together, and a senior faculty member laughed outright. "You don't need a coaster with stemware," he said. My face felt on fire, and I don't remember anything else from that evening.

Only now, years later, do I understand that my senior colleague's behavior, not mine, betrayed limitations in upbringing—a lack of class—

but in that hot, humiliating moment, my uncertainty offered me only one option: to slink away hoping that he'd had enough to drink that he would forget our encounter, forget I had even attended the party.

Diversity, we are discovering—in our dogged pursuit of affirmative action at our university—hinges on more than race and culture. Class and gender are powerful, persistent influences in determining and defining human experience. For me, lower-class status is akin to a pernicious genetic trait, a chromosomal aberration that can be managed like bad posture with exercise and a back brace or covered up like blemished skin with foundation cream and controlled by careful diet, only to resurface again and again when the spirit sags and defenses are low.

As we grew up, my family's economic condition improved somewhat. My mother's career flourished. She made a significant contribution to the household beyond paying parochial school tuition, and my father labored steadily for the Department of Water and Power. Still, they never bought a house, but by the time I moved out, they were able to afford a microwave oven and clothes dryer, so the laundry no longer flapped on a line collecting soot from the exhaust pipes of cars whizzing past. My younger sisters and brother didn't have to work at part-time jobs while in high school if they wanted to eat in the school cafeteria now and again or to go to movies with friends.

On our own and separately, my sister and I thrived in the proud poverty of the young and newly independent. Our mother had always insisted that we would go to college, but wisely never said one word about paying for it. We moved in with our boyfriends, applied for financial aid, and took work-study jobs to attend the local state university. My sister, a gifted student who never had to apply herself much to make the high school honor roll, was undone by the mediocre grades she earned in college classes she rarely attended. She was more interested in parties and friends than school anyway, so she soon dropped out. My ego was more adaptable to the idea that my intellect needed improvement. Not being socially inclined, I had nowhere better to be than in class or at my work-study job in the library. And my favorite pastimes—obsessive reading, idly thinking things over, and writing fiction, my own elaborate lies, wherein *I* determined what happened and to whom—served me surprisingly well in the college years.

But after a few years of enthusiastic though impoverished independence for my sister and me, and relative stability for our family, that aberrant tendency to be poor and discouraged reasserted itself. My mother suffered a heart attack and then a stroke. She was hospitalized for a long time before she passed away. Despite their insurance, the cost of her medical care—co-pays, deductibles, the expensive treatment and prescriptions deemed "experimental" and, therefore, uncovered by the HMO—nearly destroyed my father. Here, the cliché "crushing debt" is apt, even illustrative. Picture a small brown man in a hard hat and olive green coveralls, flattened and adhering to the heel of a giant's foot. If they had owned a house, they surely would have lost it then. My older sister married a guitarist, a functional alcoholic who predictably became less functional and more alcoholic, while I lived with a succession of boyfriends before dropping out of college in my senior year and settling to marry and bear children with the worst of these, a violent and disturbed person, who—as if to make matters worse—lost his job just before our second child was born.

We rented an apartment where the oat-colored shag carpeting had gaping holes worn clear through to the cement flooring. Roaches—flying and crawling—infested the place. My young children and I spent nearly a decade in that apartment. The complex was not designated as government-subsidized low-income housing, but in some ways it was worse than the Projects, which would at least have been more affordable. Fistfights, squad car sirens, and occasionally gunshots punctuated noisy late nights of music and drunken laughter pouring from the neighboring units. The unfenced pool was laced with algae, littered with fast food wrappers and the occasional disposable diaper; it was murky as bilge water. Gravel-voiced young mothers puffed on cigarettes and confided in me their aspirations to become manicurists, cosmetologists, pet groomers, anything to get off assistance or "leave that bastard for good," as we waited for the mail to arrive.

During most of that time I was a bookstore supervisor, then manager. As supervisor, I worked evening shifts, hiring out my days as a babysitter for other mothers. These women could not afford to notice gaping holes in the carpeting, the roaches, the comings and goings of raucous, foul-mouthed neighbors, or the fetid pool. They were like me, women whose options and opportunities fell away with successive childbirths, with each year of menial work at low wages, with every anniversary commemorating abusive or unfulfilling relationships they did not have the resources to escape.

Once I provided daycare for a six-week-old and a four-year-old—children of a young woman who had just left her husband. She worked for minimum wage at a factory in Van Nuys, and she complained that she handed over most of her paycheck to me each week, though I charged 15 percent less than the going rate. One afternoon, she simply did not return for her children as expected. As the minutes ticked past, I watched the window anxiously. My husband, who'd finally found a job, would be home soon, and then I had to leave for my evening shift at the bookstore. Though his moods were unpredictable, he would not be pleased to have two more children in his care on that night. My hands shook as I prepared a casserole for supper, the six-week-old strapped to my chest while the other children watched *The Muppet Show* in the living room.

Finally, the phone rang, and I lunged for it. It was the mother who should have picked up her children over an hour ago. "I can't do this," she said. "I just can't."

"But you have to pick up your children," I told her. "My husband will be home any minute. I have to go to work."

"I can't do this." The phone clicked and the dial-tone buzzed in my ear.

Just before my husband returned home, the woman's sister arrived to collect the two children. My heart thudding with relief, I stuffed toys and clothing in the children's diaper bag. The woman explained that her sister had quit her job and returned to her husband. "It's a big mistake," she said. "He'll murder her one day."

Mistake or not, I understood that young mother's dilemma all too well. When I am anxious or scared, I read and read and read. I'd absorbed the statistics, knew them better than prayers. From magazine and newspaper articles, I learned that a woman's standard of living falls anywhere from 27 to 45 percent in the first year after divorce, while a man's rises by an average of 10 percent. I was not surprised to find out that one-fourth of all divorced women in America live at or below the poverty line. But I was dismayed to discover that children raised in single-parent families perform worse academically than children from two-parent families, and children from divorced families are more likely to get in trouble with school authorities or the police. Children of divorce, I'd read, are more likely to have low self-esteem and feel depressed. In adolescence, they are at risk for early sexual activity and experimentation with drugs. In the long run, chances are they will experience difficulty forming intimate relationships and establishing independence from their own families.

And I knew that women who leave abusive relationships place themselves and their children in imminent and grave danger. A few years earlier, a coworker of mine, a newlywed, had been murdered and dismembered by her husband when she tried to get away from him. He'd buried most of her body parts in the desert and claimed she had left him, but he was caught when a neighbor's children discovered his bride's severed head in a disposal bin behind their apartment. *Her head in the trash.* At the time, I didn't let myself think about this long enough to deconstruct it. Though I'd been fickle and flighty girlfriend material, my knowledge and this memory manacled me to my marriage, shackling all of us to that shitty apartment as if it were in a maximum-security cell block.

During this time, I formulated a rather handy definition for insanity: lying without knowing it. By this rubric, my husband was certifiable in his surety that we made a "perfect family," that everything he did was for a reason, and that when he exploded it was only because of something I had said or done to set him off. Whereas when I denied the parking ticket I'd gotten, I *knew* I was lying. But I was a touch insane, too. Though I was not writing then, I continued to dissemble and fabricate. I told myself that my husband was ill. I would not leave him if he had cancer or heart disease, so why should I desert him for a sickness that happened to afflict his mind instead of his body? And like any addict or a gambler, I constructed elaborate rationalizations. A placid afternoon, a joke shared between my husband and me, an embrace, a compliment bestowed, and it was as if I'd pulled the arm of a slot machine and a row of bright cherries flashed before me, the cascade of coins obliterating all memory of the fortune squandered in the days leading up to this. When weeks passed without incident, I was convinced we had just pushed through a bad patch. That's all it was, those hard times behind us for good.

After my client's sister fetched her children, I never saw that young mother again. But her sister's words stayed with me, metastasizing and morphing as I thought about them again and again. "He'll murder her one day" became "He'll murder *me* one day" and then "He's murdering me every day," before transforming to "This, *this* is killing me." On the afternoon when my husband throttled me for damage done to our car when it was struck by another driver who was turning illegally, the thought shifted once more: What a terrible way to die. And before I lost consciousness, my larynx nearly crushed, I had one more thought: But it's a worse way to live.

When my husband and I finally separated, the bleak prophecies of the statistics were quickly fulfilled for me and my children. Their grades fell. My daughter acted out, and my son became apathetic, listless. We moved to another infested apartment, we bought cheap furniture that soon sagged and splintered, and we ate macaroni-and-cheese mixes, hot dogs, peanut-butter sandwiches, and pots and pots of beans with homemade tortillas.

Things were worse, but also better, much better. There was peace in our home—no rage, no fear—and we could have friends over. The small apartment was often filled with friends, relatives, playmates—people we loved and trusted—but who had been banished from our lives by my former husband's aversion to outsiders. I returned to school, earned a teaching certificate, and was hired to teach at a nearby middle school, where like my mother, I enrolled my twelve-year-old daughter and then, a few years later, my son. At home in the evenings and on weekends, I wrote poems, stories, even plays. I hired a babysitter two nights a week so I could begin course work toward a master's degree in English, and I met another man, someone who seemed to appreciate me and my children, though they were wary of him.

This man, a fellow graduate student, understood and encouraged my desire to write. He took me for the first time to poetry readings, wine bistros, and jazz bars. By the time he proposed, I had an inkling that he hailed from a privileged background. When my children and I flew to South Carolina to meet his family, I discovered they lived in a gated community, on a golf course. We had to be cleared by a security officer in a booth in order to drive around the lake to his family's home. Birch trees, loblolly, and pine scrolled past the car windows, and a lacy mist rose from emerald water.

The stately edifices we finally approached had nautical names. Hidden behind these, my fiancé's family home was grander than any dwelling I had ever entered. It was as if I had stepped into the glossy pages of a magazine devoted to interior design. My fiancé gave the tour. He led us through the hunter-green-and-burgundy study, the sandstone living room, the sea-foam bathroom, the sauna-and-hot-tub bathroom, and the Laura Ashley bedrooms with canopied beds. My children went mute with awe. Throughout the visit, they clung to me, trailing me wherever I moved, as though they feared they would lose their bearings in that great house if they lost sight of me.

Late at night, I whispered to my fiancé that I had no idea his family lived like this. "You are so wealthy," I said. "How do you live like this?" This was not an accusation, but an expression of wonderment. I wanted to know *how* his family had managed it.

He paused, as if thinking this over, and when he spoke, his voice was confident, even forceful. "My father works very hard."

I remember squinting in the dark, thinking, *His father works very hard.* I pictured my father in his work boots and khaki coveralls as he'd head out to fix a water main. I flashed on images of his blackened fingernails, permanently bruised by the heavy tools he handled; his many scars; his swayed back, contorted by a pinched nerve; the permanent sunburn that leathered the back of his neck. And while there are no doubt challenges entailed in inheriting an auto-parts distributorship, I could not see the dapper man who'd mixed us martinis all evening crawling out of a sewer while wearing a twenty-pound tool belt.

The phrase stayed with me, looping in my brain, as I watched my fiancé cash the monthly checks his parents sent so he could attend graduate school without having to work. *His father works very hard.* I thought it when he scolded me for neglecting to congratulate a poet after a reading we'd attended, as if I'd committed a social gaffe akin to yakking over the poetry, instead of just rushing home when it was over to save on the hourly babysitting rate. *His father works very hard,* I reminded myself after he gave away my Corell-ware dishes. "Those tacky things," he said when I asked what had happened to them. Then he explained that he'd replaced them with imported china—cups, saucers, and plates as fragile as potato chips in the hands of my adolescent children. And when he raged over nicked dishes and cracked cups, his misplaced Swiss Army knife, a graduate student award that went to a single mother raising five children instead of to him, when rage returned to our home and I broke off the relationship, again I thought about his father, how hard he'd worked, and my father, my mother, and me—how hard *we* have worked, how little we have earned, and how we have never been able to afford such a thing as this rage.

We could be whatever we wanted to be: My mother was right, and she was wrong. We would have to change what we wanted, adapt this to what we could attain, and even then it wouldn't be easy. She must have suspected that, but didn't let on, and really, she didn't know the half of it. I think she believed we could just pop out of the state university, diplomas tucked under our arms, and catch the first Greyhound to the White House, with a brief transfer stop at Princeton or Yale for medical degrees. We were her children, after all, anointed with her love and infused with her ambition, fed on her fierce intelligent dreams. A tall heavyset woman with a loud, deep voice, *she* had authority. As I strode the halls of the Catholic school where she taught so that we could attend tuition free, I would hear her voice thundering from her classroom.

"Mom," we would say after school, "do you have to be so loud?"

"Why?" she'd ask. "Are you ashamed of me?"

We *were,* but we said, "Do you have to be so blunt?"

"I call it as I see it," she'd say. "A spade is a spade."

And we'd cringe. "Do have to use clichés all the time?"

Mom is *so* unsubtle, my oldest sister and I often agreed between ourselves. We could be whatever we wanted, but we didn't want to be big, loud, unglamorous women; God, we didn't want to be *her.* We would never go as far as serving cocktails in nightclubs, but we would remake ourselves as whispery Latinas, dainty and flirtatious, and in this, the hard way, it would take us decades, it would take us marriages to abusers and alcoholics, it would take us through divorces and single motherhood, it would take us to shitty apartments where the phone service and electricity would be cut off when we couldn't pay the bills, it would bring us to ask our children—without meeting their eyes—if we could borrow *their* birthday money. But eventually we would be delivered back into classrooms, classrooms where we were older than everyone else, including the professor. It would take us every scrap of our youth, in fact most of our lives, to eke what truth we could from our mother's lie.

Laverne & Shirley *Days*

✦ BICH MINH NGUYEN

During my family's first years in the United States, settling in Michigan after fleeing Vietnam in the spring of 1975, my father worked as a machine operator in a feather factory. He would come home coated in a fine layer of down that would tickle my sister and me when he grabbed us up and tossed us in the air. We loved the squishy comforters he brought home, and the puffy down coat he wore in the winter. I think we must have imagined him working in a magical place of slow-motion feathers swirling in the air like a snow globe. We didn't know what it meant to work in a factory, to punch a time card and spend breaks smoking outside, wishing the shift were over.

I was eight months old when we left Vietnam, and those years before I started kindergarten, before the world of classmates shifted my perspective on identity, seem to float in my memory—a tawny haze of pre-consciousness. All I knew was that my sister, grandmother, father, and uncles and I lived together in a drafty house on Baldwin Street in Grand Rapids, Michigan. The winter brought the astonishment of snow; the summer brought roses and fruit from the farmers market. During this time my father seemed to have a delightful feathery job, my happy uncles listened to lots of music, my grandmother fed us copiously, my sister and I played every day—and we all watched a great deal of television.

A TV was one of the primary things my family, like most immigrants, perhaps like most Americans, wished to acquire. Our first black-and-white set, with knobs that made a loud clicking noise when you turned them, and antennae that sprouted up in formations my uncles kept fiddling with and, sometimes, for reasons unknown, wrapped in aluminum foil, gave us glimpses of American life and language. My sister and I gleaned English as much from *Sesame Street* as from *Charlie's Angels* and *Days of Our Lives;* my father and uncles favored action shows like *Hawaii Five-O, Starsky and Hutch,* and *The Bionic Woman.* That television became the beacon of our household. It was our oracle. We gathered in front of it with our bowls of soup and rice, awed by all of the information given to us.

Back in the late 1970s, television shows didn't turn away from issues of class in the way they seem to now. *Good Times,* for example, centered on an African American family living in the Cabrini-Green housing project in Chicago. The show had a laugh track but I remember thinking, even at a young age, that the mother of the family—her face, her gait—seemed tinged with sadness. I felt the same about the sitcom *One Day at a Time* and its protagonist, a single mom struggling to raise two teenage girls. The lead actor in *Welcome Back, Kotter* always looked depressed and slump-shouldered, as though he really didn't want to be back. Even *Sesame Street* had an urban, working-class vibe to its neighborhood. And then there was *Laverne & Shirley,* one of my favorite shows because the two stars were practically sisters, sharing an apartment and working together at the same Milwaukee brewery. It all seemed so wonderfully grown-up. My sister and I, no doubt like countless other girls in America, would link arms and try to mimic Laverne and Shirley's chant from the opening theme, then race down the sidewalk.

Yet the show's opening sequence also lingers on a moment of sadness: Laverne sticks one of her factory gloves on a bottle of beer, then waves good-bye as it rolls on down the conveyor belt; a moment later we see a glimpse of both women looking wistful, lost in thought while the bottles keep whirring around them. I didn't have any way to understand or explain this television melancholy, but I think of it now as my first rudimentary reckoning with socioeconomic class, images I would return to in later years when I realized that most people thought of factory work as menial and unskilled. My stepmother, who married my father when I was four, introduced me to the phrases "blue collar" and "manual labor." She was an ESL teacher, had grown up with a father who worked in fields and factories, and she loved a good strike. When she said "blue collar" it was without bitterness, simply acknowledging America's class stratification in ways that I was far from grasping.

Whenever I go into people's houses I always notice their television, or the lack of one. Is it out in the open, hidden in a cabinet or closed-off room, or truly absent? I notice books, too, of course. But how people display books and how they display televisions often mean different things.

I grew up in the Midwest, among working- and middle-class families, with a few upper-middle-class kids thrown in during high school. All of my friends' families and all of their houses had televisions, usually more than one. TVs anchored the living room or family room as firmly as the big puffy sofas that sat in front of them. I don't think it even occurred to me to think otherwise about the role of televisions—they were an assumed presence, as much a fixture of a house as a front door. The display and presence of a TV took precedence over that of books.

It wasn't until college that I met people who claimed they never watched TV or didn't even own one. Television was the devil, I heard people announce. It rotted the mind. It was a "boob tube." Trash. Mindless entertainment for the masses. If a television had to exist—merely for the news, or perhaps PBS—at least tuck it away in a cabinet, shuttered behind doors so that the screen, its very blankness a sign of the viewer's blank mind, remains invisible to guests. While I can't remember the first television cabinet I saw, the feeling of it stays with me: something akin to shame. The hiddenness threw my own wide-open television ways into sharp contrast.

My father and uncles, like their friends, like pretty much every Vietnamese or Asian person I've known, have always strived to get the biggest television they could afford. Stereo systems were important too, and thanks to my uncles I had cassette tapes and CDs back in the 1980s, long before any of my friends. But a television, big and bold, with superior picture and sound quality—that was the ticket. After my father married my stepmother and we all moved to a house in a better school district, my uncles replaced our old black-and-white TV set with a gorgeous behemoth encased solidly in oak. We acquired cable, a new and strange system that involved a long wire stretching from the TV to a brown cable box with a dial that could zip left and right, up to nonexistent stations numbered in the forties. We ordered HBO. When MTV started, in 1981, we were there.

Television is an absorptive medium; to watch it is to take it in, consume it, engaging both sound and sight. Maybe that's why so many people look slack-jawed in front of a TV or in a movie theater—they're trying to breathe as much in as possible. For many immigrants, and for my family, television was a mode of assimilation. The bigger the TV, the stronger the desire to assimilate, acculturate to American behavior, dress, manners. In the 1980s TV was the most dependable way to gain such information, so it's no wonder everyone in my family gathered around it as often as possible. It took center stage in the living room, all chairs pointed toward the screen. I knew the network schedules by heart, and just like that, the words and wishes and dreams of the girls on *Facts of Life* or the boys on *Diff'rent Strokes* became my own. Many evenings, I read books and watched television at the same time. I mimicked commercials in the morning, sometimes narrating my own actions as I ate a particular brand of cereal. (*Hey Mikey! He likes it!*) I thought I could become, through television and in my imagination, as American as I wanted to be.

Before TiVo and streaming video, television truly was central to the American conversation. I remember my family planning our hours around movie nights, *The Cosby Show* on Thursdays, and various network mini-series. We tuned in to learn something, to feel like we were taking part in the conversation. A turned-off television signaled both sadness—the silence of the medium—and potential. Who knew what might be waiting when the screen lit up?

So the idea that not everyone needed or even liked television marked another shift in perspective for me. It seemed not a coincidence that my friends whose families shunned television also had prominent bookshelves laden with literary fiction, classics, and nonfiction tomes. Such a sight is almost never found in a Vietnamese American household. When I was growing up, books came from the library and were kept in the bedroom. While reading became to me as essential as television and food, my father, uncles, grandmother, and stepmother didn't seem to care about it much. They did flip through *Newsweek* and *National Geographic*, and bought Vietnamese-language magazines from the Saigon Market. But actual books didn't matter to them the way they mattered to me. I didn't understand this, or even really think about it, until college, when it occurred to me that probably few first-generation adult immigrants could spend much time buying and reading books. They were simply too much a luxury, and non-English books weren't easy to find. A television, on the other hand, was communal. Familial, and easy to understand. My grandmother, who spoke very little English, had no trouble discerning the dialogue and intricate plots on *Days of Our Lives.* And we could all watch a show together, entering into the same knowledge about how American life might be lived.

Yet when I encountered the marvel of TV cabinets pushed back in houses filled with books, houses that had been built on a bedrock of generations and jobs, I felt, instantly, intuitively, the smallness of my many years of sitcoms and dramas and soap operas. I finally understood that those who didn't need a TV—its offer of admittance to the immigrant, its offer of equality no matter how imagined—truly didn't need it. They were already above or beyond it. Not to have a television, not to need a television, was to know real privilege.

My Asian American friends and I sometimes joke about our parents' desire for big televisions, elaborate stereo equipment, fancy cameras and computers. Cousin to these are Louis Vuitton handbags, expensive department-store cosmetics, and any kind of high-karat gold jewelry, preferably involving jade and diamonds. *It's so Asian,* we can laugh, identifying the stereotypical markers of Lancôme, Courvoisier, karaoke machines, surround-sound speakers. In truth, all of these objects, their rising prevalence, do make a kind of sense. They are evidence of money, status, and achievement, in that order, one leading to and creating the next. They provide a way to disguise the taint of the foreigner, immigrant, refugee. The disguise *is* status, meant to be an equivalent of not just equality but class. (After all, when people say someone is "classy" or has "class," they don't really mean high class.) And so my family participated in this paradigm, needing cable and HBO in the same way we had to have the first microwave in the neighborhood, the first video game system on the block. My siblings and I were urged to go to college and not for the sake of education but for the sake of future white-collar jobs.

And then I participated in another paradigm, planning it from the first moment I beheld those houses filled with the hush of books rather than the noise of television. In college I hid my TV-watching ways from all but my family and best friends, pretending not to be interested in the 1990s fixations with *Beverly Hills 90210* and *Melrose Place*. But I knew. I watched. Around me, books gathered in my apartment, overflowed shelves. Slowly, over time, their presence quieted the television, pushed it farther back.

Today, my father and stepmother have a fifty-two-inch set in their house. It's too old and too small, they lament. Already out of date. Nothing plasma or high-definition about it. They scour the Sunday advertisements for good deals, afraid to commit lest a whole new technology appear on the market the next day. Meanwhile, their house's ailing appliances—stove, refrigerator, furnace—will have to wait. My own television is a no-frills twenty-seven-incher, neither flat nor fancy, and it fits neatly into a media cabinet. Often when I'm opening or shutting it I feel a twinge of wonder, a kind of *how did I get here* moment that, I think, must be familiar to all first-and-a-half- and second-generation immigrants. And my relationship with television, what it represents, remains uneasy. Maybe that's why when I watch it now I gravitate toward reruns like *The Golden Girls* for their mix of nostalgia and camp, and channels like TV-Land. A part of me wants the old-fashioned promise of television, the days when a mere antenna meant free access, when a digital machine couldn't command the flow of a show. There were long days, pre-consciousness days, when I didn't know the meaning of "blue collar" and "white collar," when the snow outside seemed a fanciful reflection of the feathers falling from my father's jacket, whirling into a cloud on the screen we tried to get just right. All of this happened so long ago, it seems, back when shows were filmed before a "live studio audience," when every episode seemed a circle, when every channel and every hour seemed to hold great repositories of information, as dependable as two young women rushing arm in arm down the sidewalk after a full day of work.

Another Frigidaire Sketch

⤜ TERESA DOVALPAGE

My Maytag refrigerator is a modest appliance, white and medium-sized. Its contents are equally unimpressive: a gallon of milk, a package of steaks, a few vegetables. On top of it there is always a can of cat food because one of my cats won't eat anywhere else. Frequently, when I talk to someone in Cuba, I feel a great desire to send the refrigerator, cat food and everything, to the island. Particularly on Saturdays.

Saturday mornings, my mother and I have a fifteen-minute conversation. She still lives in Havana and I phone her every week.

"*¿Quién es?*" She shrieks into the receiver as if startled by an earthquake.

"It's Teresita!" I shriek back.

That's the unchanging prelude. I have come to enjoy such talks, though my mother and I didn't get along when we lived together in Cuba. Now we exchange family gossip and I keep her updated about my writing projects, classes, and dissertation progress. She offers a few editorial comments about all that. She also complains about the food (or lack thereof), the heat, the humidity, and everything under the Cuban sun.

"I am going to write an essay about growing up in poverty," I informed her last Saturday.

"Who said you grew up in poverty?" she asked. "Here you go, making things up as usual. Another Frigidaire sketch, *eh?*"

"What does the Frigidaire have to—"

She snorted. "*Carajo!* You love to make the family look bad. That's what you do in all your books. Why don't you write about something else, eh? You are such a liar, *chica!* We aren't nearly as bad as you portray us. And we *weren't* poor, hear?"

Her question "Why don't you write about something else, eh?" stayed in my mind and kept ringing there for days. I'll go back to it later. Now, it's true that in my novels *Posesas de La Habana* (Haunted Women of Havana), *Muerte de un murciano* (Death of a Man from Murcia), and *A Girl like Che Guevara* I have depicted dysfunctional families ruled by matriarchs that look suspiciously similar to my mother and grandma. But all the books have the disclaimer "This is a work of fiction, blah, blah, blah," so I don't understand why she gets so excited.

As for the Frigidaire incident, it occurred in a drama workshop I took at Southwestern College, in San Diego. The instructor asked me for something "with a Cuban flavor," so I did a sketch about the tiresome process of defrosting our refrigerator in Havana. That Frigidaire was originally a sturdy, white metal appliance, but it suffered several transformations. After its surface got too dirty and scratched, my father painted it dark brown. The new coat masked the filth but made the refrigerator look like an Egyptian sarcophagus. When my mother made a scene and called him a tacky, inept *cabrón*, my father repainted it green. And green it has stayed for over three decades.

Defrosting the green monster was a long, slow operation. All the food had to be taken out and the refrigerator disconnected and left opened for the ice to melt. Water poured down. It was wiped with a kitchen towel until the last ice cube vanished. The ice had to be chipped away, unless we waited enough time and it melted on its own. Unfortunately, the longer we left food outside, the faster it spoiled. And ruined food was something we just couldn't afford.

In my sketch I pretended to defrost an imaginary Frigidaire. I ended up exhausted and disheveled, while the ice kept the consistency of a well-built igloo. Frustrated, I set the stubborn thing on fire and escaped. A few kids in the audience, who had grown up in the times of Google, didn't get it. "What were you really trying to do?" they asked me afterward. They had never seen a refrigerator that was not frost-free.

Later I sent a video of the sketch to my mother, who wanted to see proof of my artistic skills. She wasn't impressed either. "But you never defrosted the refrigerator yourself!" she barked. That was true. A spoiled only child, I seldom did a house chore. But the refrigerator was still defrosted, no?

Back to last Saturday and the poverty issue. My mother, the eternal contrarian, took it personally and rebuffed me. "We own our apartment," she said. "You got an education. And if you looked like a skeleton, it was because you didn't want to eat, not due to lack of food."

During my Cuban years I was labeled skinny and called Gata Flaca, Scrawny Cat, although I wasn't undernourished or even underweight. My problem was that I didn't have a big *culo,* the prominent rear end that is Cuba's foremost mark of beauty. I was *una desculada,* an assless girl, and so were the other females in my family. As a teenager I felt so ashamed of my modest proportions that I longed to get silicone butt implants. Though it wasn't an authorized procedure, some doctors did it clandestinely for seven hundred pesos. But I was never able to get in touch with one.

Anyway, I try to see things the way my mother does. Yes, she owns her apartment. In fact, everybody in Cuba owns their home. But the government owns everybody's home, too. When my family wanted to move out of our old house in 1971, we couldn't just sell it and buy another. The revolutionary laws forbid such transactions. We traded the old house for a smaller, more modern apartment only after requesting a special permit that took three months to arrive.

Before 1995 ordinary Cubans couldn't rent, sell, or buy houses on the island. Now they can rent rooms to foreign tourists, but only after applying for a license and paying a monthly three-hundred-dollar fee, regardless of how many clients they get. If my mom leaves Cuba and stays abroad one day after her exit permit expires, she may come back to find her home occupied by a family of ten. So, to say that we *owned* that Centro Habana apartment is an overstatement.

However, she concluded, "Things aren't too bad here, after all." Apparently she forgot that only a week before she stated that Havana had become *mierda y cepillo*—shit and a brush—because of the constant scarcities and blackouts. "The city isn't what it used to be," she said. "We only have electricity ten hours a day. One can't find meat or chicken or a tilapia burger, even if one offers to pay with dollars. *Mierda y cepillo* it is." *Mierda y cepillo* is her favorite term of derision, though I can't figure out what the brush stands for.

My big-mouthed mother reminded me of a family friend named Zoila who came to the United States with a visitor's visa a few months ago. After two weeks in the southwest area of Miami known as La Sagüesera, whining about everything from the heavy traffic to the bland taste of the chicken, Zoila returned to Cuba. She swore that she was going to kiss Fidel's beard as soon as she touched Cuban soil.

My mother didn't last over a month either when I invited her to visit me last year. She claimed that Albuquerque was the rear end of the world, and as full of "shit and a brush" as Havana itself. She found the American ice cream sugarless, the people snotty, and the malls kitschy. The house walls were too thin, she maintained, and looked as if they were made of saliva and cardboard paper. Here she couldn't enter a neighbor's kitchen and ask nonchalantly what was being cooked for dinner. The land of abundance, La Yuma, as we called the United States in Cuba, had let her down. But at least she didn't go back to the island with the intention of kissing the old man's now gray beard.

Now, I recall my first La Yuma impressions. Unlike my mother, I wasn't disappointed. I was in shock. And not because of the chock-full clothing stores and supermarkets—I had seen all that abundance in movies, after all. What dazzled me was food, *la comida*. And its effect on people. Used to the small, rationed portions served in Cuban restaurants, where it was forbidden for many years to take leftovers home, I couldn't believe my own eyes the first time I went to a Red Lobster restaurant in San Diego. *Coño,* all the *langosta* we wanted to eat, and *legal* lobster, too! In Cuba, lobster is now reserved for tourist consumption. The few times we bought one on the black market, my grandma cooked it at the same time she did black beans, so the *langosta* smell wouldn't betray us.

But here at the Red Lobster everybody was eating their *langosta*, salmon, or crab cakes without any concern or fear of breaking the law. I wondered if these people knew how lucky they were. Then I started looking at them. Closely. Indeed, being able to eat all you want is a good thing. But you *can* have too much of a good thing. I noticed the enormous behinds, *langosta*-like, actually, of some Red Lobster patrons. Of course, at that time I considered it as yet another sign of wealth. It would take me a few years to learn that in La Yuma, big *culos* aren't cool.

But let's go back to Cuba, where the possession of a big ass is an asset, no pun intended. Was my family, run by two assless women, poor or not? Money was never *un problema,* an issue, at home. *El problema* was that many times we had money, but there was nothing to buy with it. A doctor and a pharmacist, my mother had a pretty decent income. She made around three hundred pesos every month. My father, a stonemason, made half of that amount. He contributed sixty pesos to the family budget and smoked or drank the rest. His pockets were full of holes, which he showed us contritely, and money had a penchant for slipping through them.

No matter how many times my grandma mended my father's pants— my mother disdained such domestic tasks as sewing or cooking—the holes opened again on paydays. It was such a lame excuse that even I didn't believe it. Had my dad been the breadwinner we would have been in trouble. But it was my mother who held that title. *Gracias a Dios!*

Now, looking back (and looking from *here*) it does seem that we were quite poor. All the furniture in our apartment was older than I. The dining room set was bought for my grandparents' wedding in 1934. The heavy mahogany table remained true to itself, but the eight chairs suffered a series of mutations. Their seats went from brown leather, to a cheap Cuban version of suede, to red vinyl, to plain wood. The mattresses were re-stuffed every five or six years with a variety of materials. In the good years we used the secondhand foam that my enterprising grandma bought on the black market or traded for cigars. In the worst ones, old rags kept the springs from lacerating our skinny butts at night.

The Frigidaire of my sketch is now fifty-three years old. The motor works like the first day but the metal handle came off long ago. We then resorted to a screwdriver, inserting it in the place where the handle had been and sliding it to the right. The trick worked, except for a few electric shocks. It seemed as if the green monster wanted to warn us about something dangerous that dwelled in its metallic entrails. "*Cuidado!* Be careful when you open this door. You never know what is inside." It wasn't much, most of the time.

The refrigerator is still in my mother's dining room, next to the mutated chairs. I wonder how many old Frigidaires are kept on active duty, like hers. Maybe it is more valuable now than when it was brand-new, having become "an antique."

I remember another culture shock. Like the Red Lobster incident, it had to do with food. When I opened the door of an American refrigerator for the first time, there were a couple of dishes covered with transparent plastic wrap. My husband, looking ashamed, took a perfectly good steak and was ready to throw it into the garbage can. "I'm sorry I have so much *caca* here," he apologized. "I've lived by myself for too long." I convinced him not to dispose of the steak by eating it at once. Cold steaks do taste good, I explained to him.

El pobrecito couldn't understand my refusal to get rid of "old" stuff. He must have thought he had married an anal-retentive, crap-hoarding Cubanita. But several months passed before I started using the garbage disposal without feeling guilty of an abominable sin. How could one take unspoiled food, particularly protein, and throw it away? *Ay!*

In Havana we wouldn't throw away anything that was remotely edible. The contents of our Frigidaire were sacred, and the most important items at home. Furniture and clothes may be the visible signs of wealth, but it is in the stomach, *la pancita,* where the truth lies, my grandma used to say.

Cubans haven't always been thrifty as we are today. During the fifties, when my grandparents bought the Frigidaire, it was often full of the tasty goods that my generation only heard of. Cuba got its share of the post-war prosperity, and it came in the form of Libby peaches, Spam, and soft-serve ice cream. A Sears and several ten-cent Woolworth stores were opened in Havana where American products enjoyed immense popularity. My grandma, a zealous animal lover, would take leftovers every night to a nearby colony of semi-wild dogs that were kept well-fed by compassionate neighbors.

However, by the time I was born, in 1966, the postwar affluence was gone. I don't even remember seeing a peach in my twenty-nine Cuban years. The Frigidaire usually contained a quart of milk, a pot of beans and steamed rice, a tilapia burger, and two plastic jars with water. My grandma boiled tomatoes and brown sugar to make a concoction known as "cherry jam." She kept it in the refrigerator to defend it from the ants that colonized our kitchen. "Cherry jam" was our most common dessert.

Days began with a glass of *café con leche:* coffee, milk, and three spoonfuls of sugar. On weekends we also had a buttered toast. Before the nineties it was possible to buy fresh milk at the grocery store without the ration card. Sometimes we also got a pound of butter on the black market, so breakfast wasn't too much of a problem. But lunch and supper were.

All through the seventies and the early eighties, Cubans depended on ration-card products. Six pounds of rice, five pounds of sugar, and a few ounces of meat per person were our monthly quota. It was illegal to buy beef and pork on the black market. But enterprising farmers hid their fattest pigs from government inspectors and sold them before Christmas. At any other time of the year, pork was extremely elusive. Chickens, raised in backyards and balconies, were easier to find.

I had lunch at school. Our usual menu included soup—insipid black beans or watery red beans—rice and protein. The latter meant a chicken thigh, a tilapia burger, or canned beef stew for special occasions. But it was generally a boiled egg. At night, in the brief periods of prosperity, our family of five would share four small, thin-cut steaks or a fried chicken once a week. Most often, supper consisted of eggs, black beans, and rice. The Frigidaire never hosted more than two "protein dishes" at the same time.

Havana suffered frequent blackouts, *apagones,* while the sugarcane harvest took place, from November to April. We wouldn't open the Frigidaire when the electricity was cut off so as to "keep the cold inside." A rotten steak was a tragedy. Throwing food away, a luxury we couldn't afford. I learned early to conserve energy. "Turn off the lights!" yelled my mother when she spotted one on before eight P.M. Radio and TV ads reinforced the notion. There was a cartoon character called "The Click Patrol" that sent a not-too-subtle message to both adults and kids: If you don't turn off all the lights before going to bed, the next day you will be greeted by *el apagón.*

These days, I think of the many times I went after my husband in our San Diego home, turning off lights, lamps, televisions, radios, and computers. He complained that his eyesight wasn't that good anymore and that he needed enough light to read. What was "enough" for him, a five-hundred-watt bulb, was extravagant in my opinion. I had the vague, ridiculous fear that "The Click Patrol" had followed me to La Yuma and would catch me if I didn't behave.

In the late eighties things started to improve in Cuba. The ingredients for lunch and dinner came from stores that belonged to the Mercado Paralelo. No coupons were needed to buy there, though merchandise had higher prices than in regular, ration-carded shops. Farmers were allowed to sell part of their crops in the Mercado Libre Campesino. Before that, they had to sell everything to the state. But then they used agents called *intermediarios* (middlemen) to transport and trade their products in the cities. Chicken and pigs reached legal status. Cows remained sacred, though, and so did lobster.

The former Sears building was transformed into a modern supermarket, Supermercado Centro. Bulgarian cheeses, German hams and sausages, and national-production sodas and cakes filled the shelves. Our Frigidaire had fleeting days of glory. When it was packed, eggs were left outside "because if they get bad, we can always buy more." We were getting close to communism, my teachers said.

Supermercado Centro opened at noon, but the *coleros,* people who sold waiting-line places, arrived before midnight. They charged one hundred pesos for the first places in the queue. Since we didn't want to pay the fee, standing in line became a family venture. My grandfather went to Supermercado Centro around ten P.M. the night before. My father replaced him at two A.M. At seven-thirty, when he headed to work, my grandma took over. My mother arrived at noon. She was the one who made the purchases. "Chicken, *sí*. Cheese, *no*," she would say in her imperious manner, and that settled the matter.

Treasurer and budget queen, my mother made all the important decisions in quite an autocratic manner. We called her *la mandamás,* the boss. My grandma (my mother's mother) was the second-in-command. My father and maternal grandfather weren't even consulted most of the time, and they weren't used to protesting, either.

"Men," *la mandamás* told me once, "need to be carefully guided in life. It's not their fault. Left to their own devices, they end up lost, broke, or dead."

"Amen," my grandma said.

It was one of the few issues they agreed on.

Hector Zumbado, a Cuban humorist and writer, called the late eighties our golden years. Blackouts vanished. Not only was food more available, but products from the socialist countries appeared in the parallel-market stores. There were Electron TV sets—black-and-white and unreliable, but a necessary replacement for the RCA Victor consoles. There were Selena radios. And electric typewriters made in Germany. For months I pestered my mother about getting one. *La mandamás* finally gave in. She bought an Underwood twenty years my senior and told me to be happy with it. "American stuff works better and lasts longer," she said. But we *could* have afforded a new one. We didn't buy it because *la mandamás* was *muy* stingy.

On the other hand, there were weeks when Supermercado Centro was empty except for bags of Russian crackers and jars of sour Hungarian preserves. The Mercado Libre Campesino didn't have a long life. Three years after it was opened, Fidel Castro accused the farmers and their middlemen of becoming "Cuba's new bourgeoisie" and of charging exorbitant prices for the aforementioned pigs and chickens. The Mercado Libre Campesino was closed and we went back to square one.

Until the "special period" came. Then we moved to square zero. The "special period" was the crisis that heralded our nineties, when Cuba lost the financial help it used to receive from the socialist bloc. Fresh milk, eggs, cheese, and butter disappeared. Meat became a tasteless mixture known as a soy burger. Dogs and cats vanished as clandestine vendors of suspiciously cheap *fritas de carne*, meat fritters, appeared. I never dared to buy them, no matter how low-priced they were or how hungry I felt.

We might have finally reached communism, people said.

Our world was turned upside down, *patas arriba*, when the crisis started. And it wasn't just because of the scarcities or the blackouts. After all, we were already used to them. But what we were taught to consider "bad influences"—tourism from the capitalist countries, advertisements, and private enterprises—began to flourish with the government's blessing. Posters portraying curvaceous, scantily dressed mulattas under palm trees appealed to foreigners with ads written in English, French, and Italian. Spanish corporations like Meliá opened or remodeled hotels in Havana and Varadero, hotels where Cuban citizens were forbidden to stay. *Las shoppings*, Cuban stores where only U.S. dollars were accepted, carried butter Guarina and cans of condensed milk, the very merchandise that had emigrated from regular peso stores. Their labels read "Made in Cuba." In English, yes.

Many a "special period" night I went to bed with just a glass of sugary water in my *pancita.* An epidemic of polyneuritis, caused by lack of vitamins, swept the island. Big behinds melted. Programmed blackouts were announced in the newspaper and lasted for several hours. Unprogrammed ones took place any time and lasted a whole day. Our Frigidaire became a useless, empty metal shell.

At that time I was finishing a B.A. in American literature. It is difficult to read *The Great Gatsby* and write essays about the roaring twenties by candlelight in the middle of an *apagón,* but somehow I managed to graduate. One day, when I complained about being hungry, my beloved professor Licia Servia, who was a hard-nosed communist with a sweet personality, scolded me. "Teresita, in Cuba we are not hungry," she said. "That's what the Yankees want to hear. We are only *in need of food.* We have to be stoic, like the Spartans."

But I don't have a Spartan bone in my body. At the heart of the "special period" I met a wonderful man, an American who seemed as if he could use, as my mother would say, some guidance in his life. He was a psychologist forty years my senior and a true Southern gentleman. I married him, and that was how I arrived in the United States in 1996, to be dazzled by the brightness of city lights and shocked by lobster consumption. By the time I came to this country, I had finished the B.A. and an M.A. in Spanish literature. My education was the only baggage I took when I left Cuba.

It's easy to get used to a better situation—a car instead of a crowded bus, steaks instead of tilapia, real cherry jam instead of the tomato-and-sugar blend. A frost-free refrigerator instead of a Frigidaire! Yet adjusting to a new life has presented challenges and surprises. I had to learn how to drive at thirty years of age. I had to learn to use credit cards, which aren't the benevolent, plastic Santa Clauses I thought at first. I had to learn how to operate DVD players, dishwashers, microwaves, and peculiar can openers.

I am happy to say that I transcended my needy circumstances. In the United States, and with the help of my husband, I went back to the university, and I am now finishing a Ph.D. in literature. I have also written and published three books. But *all* my novels, up to now, have only dealt with life in Cuba and with the struggles, efforts, happiness, and love in our "special period" times. So maybe my mother had a point when she asked me, "Why don't you write about something else, eh?" Why am I not able to write about my new country using the same critical eye I keep so alert for all things Cuban?

The fact is that I find it difficult, and somewhat hypocritical, for me to write about *problemas* here. There are two main reasons for that. One is rather self-centered—on a personal level, I haven't experienced these problems myself. I can talk about eating a soy burger as the only protein dish in the whole day because I still feel the dusty taste of soy in my mouth when I think about my last "special period" days. But it is hard for me to pontificate about, let's say, obesity and the waste of resources here—though I am aware of their existence—since they aren't part of my American experience.

The second reason is that I never took up my pen in Cuba to write one word against a regime that I consider intrinsically oppressive and cruel. I didn't do it for three powerful motives: fear, fear, and fear. I don't mean writing articles or books, as independent journalists have done risking long prison terms. *No, señor.* I didn't even dare to take a piece of chalk and scribble "Abajo Fidel" on a grocery store wall. How then could I go around labeling things here *mierda y cepillo?*

I am grateful for the opportunity to open my mouth if and when I feel the need to do it, and put in my three cents about issues here, but it will take time. More time, perhaps, than what it took me to use a garbage disposal without regrets, or to buy a decent reading lamp for myself. I can only talk and write about what I know, or I risk sounding and feeling as fake as if I had placed silicone implants inside my posterior. And now, against my mother's best judgment, I will sit down at the computer and start working on another Frigidaire sketch.

Home Economics

— DWONNA GOLDSTONE

"I'm going to be rich and pay someone to cook for me."

This was my nonchalant, but naive response to two angry black parents who could not understand why I would continually bring home Cs in junior high home economics. I hated home economics more than I hated these ugly confrontations with my parents, which is probably why I settled for the Cs the teachers gave me (though I'm fairly certain that I did not actually earn those Cs—I don't think I did well enough to even pass the class). I had straight As in the classes that I thought really mattered—math, science, English, social studies, and PE—but my parents did not care because they thought I should be getting As in everything. For three years, I had been placed in home economics, not because I had a penchant for cooking, but because I was a girl. The school system in Moline, Illinois, had decided that girls should take home economics while the boys took shop. They did, however, allow us to switch classes for two weeks every February so that the "boys could learn to sew on a button in case their wives were not home."

We spent our two weeks in shop learning how to make a lamp. I suppose it was so that we would have ample light by which to sew on our husband's buttons. In February, I brought this project home to show my parents how I had successfully constructed a lamp and a shade. My parents warned me not to plug in this lamp because they didn't want me to burn down the house with my faulty wiring. Afterward, I would put my carefully crafted lamp in the toy box behind the burnt-orange love seat in the family room, and there it collected dust and cobwebs until August, when my father directed us to throw out all the things that he deemed worthless just before the start of a new school year.

As I continued to do poorly at cooking and sewing, my parents and I continued to fight about my grade. When it came time to choose a course of study for high school, the white counselors at Wilson Junior High School thought it prudent and wise to place me in an industrial-track program rather than a college-track program of study. When I showed my parents my class schedule for the following year at dinner that evening, my father—a rather imposing black man who at thirty-four probably looked too young to have four children, including two teenagers—balled up the small piece of paper and announced that he was tired of fooling with these white folks and that they were "not going to get away with this one." He then informed me that I needed to "wear some decent clothes" because he would be coming to school at ten A.M. the next morning. "They're messing with the wrong black man's child," he told my mother. My father had come to discover that when there was a problem with white folks, it was much more efficient to bypass the lower-level people and go straight to the person at the top. He also did not believe in calling to make an appointment. "This way, they can't prepare their lies," I once overhead him tell my mother.

My parents were sticklers about my siblings' and my education because of their own backgrounds. My father had grown up in Newport News, Virginia, the second of four brothers, all raised by a poor, single mother in a housing project next to the James River. Their father "missing in action" for years, my dad and his brothers stole coal in order to keep the family warm during the winter months. When we were children and seemed to be ungrateful about our blessings, my father would tell my brothers, sister, and me stories about how poor his family was, including tales about having to stuff newspapers into his worn-down Chuck Taylors to cover the holes in the bottom of the soles. I never believed these stories, especially since they were usually followed by a long-winded monologue that involved him and his brothers walking five miles uphill to *and* from school in a foot of snow. I learned later from my uncle Daniel that, though my father probably did not walk to school in a foot of snow, the stories of his poverty were hardly exaggerations and that the Goldstone family was indeed very poor. Often, at the end of the month when the monies from the welfare check had been spent on necessities, they survived on "jam sandwiches"—two pieces of bread jammed together. The product of a "separate but not equal" school system and well aware of the role race played in his impoverished upbringing, my father vowed that if he ever did get out of that James River housing project, he would protect his children from the pain and humiliation of racism, something he said his father never did for him.

My mother, however, had a much different upbringing. Her father, a native of Trinidad, had graduated from Meharry Medical College in Nashville, Tennessee, in the 1930s and later became the "colored doctor" in Smithfield, Virginia, a small town that lay across the James River. My grandmother—who had grown up very poor herself in Davenport, Iowa—was his nurse. Though I'm certain my grandparents and my mother felt the sting of racism in Smithfield, they lived a relatively good life, and my grandparents made sure that my mother, an only child, got everything she needed and most of what she wanted. They sent her to a private school in Smithfield, provided her with piano and singing lessons, and sent her away every summer to visit relatives. I'm sure it must have come as a complete shock when my seventeen-year-old mother informed my grandmother that she had married my father, a man who was most definitely from the "wrong side of the railroad tracks."

After they eloped, my angry grandmother whisked my mother to Maryland, where she had secured a nursing job at Bowie State College a year after my grandfather's sudden death. Meanwhile, my father earned his GED and then joined the U.S. Army, and my mother saved his meager checks from Uncle Sam so that they would have some money when she joined him after her high school graduation. After three years of the army and fearful that he was going to be sent to Vietnam, my father left the service and my family settled in Moline. In their early twenties and with two children, my parents decided to go to college, believing that was the only way to pull themselves out of poverty. They began at Blackhawk Community College, and when working, going to school, and raising children became too much for both of them, my father dropped out to let my mother finish her degree at Augustana College. After she earned her B.A. and landed a job teaching special education at Rock Island High School, my father went back to Augustana, earned his degree in business administration, and took a job as an entry-level claims adjuster for Allstate Insurance Company.

Shortly after ten A.M. the day after I was given my industrial-track high school schedule, a skinny white boy handed my algebra teacher a note that requested my presence in the principal's office. As I wandered nervously toward the office, I counted my steps to distract me from what awaited me at the end of the hall. Although the school yearbook had dubbed me "Miss Gossip" that year, I was really quite shy, always searching for my voice in a relatively hostile, predominantly white junior high school environment. I knew I was not in trouble, but I was afraid that my father was going to say or do something that would make me feel more shame about my black skin and my parents' financial situation. I had been born and raised in Moline, a factory town on the Mississippi River and home of the John Deere tractor, and though it is only about two hundred miles from Chicago, not many African Americans lived there, and the few who did struggled like my parents to keep their households running.

Because only ten of the nine hundred students at Wilson were black, the joke was that if I wanted to see another black person, I could either look in a mirror or go downstairs to see a family member. I had spent the years from 1980 to 1983 trying to pretend I was no different from the white girls at Wilson Junior High, but I was not like them—my hair was nappy and sometimes greasy, my lips were thick, my milk-chocolate skin had freckles, my front teeth were crooked, and my rear end was disproportionately large. My mother had tried to instill in me a sense of racial pride, but I rarely felt it, especially when surrounded by white girls and their soft and silky hair that they flipped as they walked down the school's hallway, their Polo shirts and Gloria Vanderbilt jeans that fit them so well, and their thin bodies that seemed to attract the white boys' attention.

After I walked into the main office, the forty-something secretary extended her pale, wrinkled hand to take my note, then she pointed toward the principal's office. My father, a claims adjuster for Fireman's Fund Insurance Company, stood impatiently in the doorway with his arms crossed. At five feet eleven inches tall, my father probably seemed rather intimidating in his navy blue suit, white-collared shirt, red tie, and black spit-polished wingtip shoes. Although he always made sure to wear "decent" clothes whenever he left the house, he always dressed especially well when he had to meet with the people at school. My father's skin was darker than mine, perhaps because his face was splattered with freckles. His eyes were quite big, his short black Afro nicely coifed, his black mustache neat and trimmed. There was no smile on his face—my father rarely smiled. I imagine that the stress of raising four children must have been difficult, but that having to deal with racism must have really worn him down.

As I approached the doorway, the principal beckoned for me to enter his office, and then he directed me to sit down at the chair near the window. The principal was a tall, portly man in his early fifties, and he was dressed in a navy blue suit too, though *his* suit was not as nice as my father's. He seemed self-assured in his mannerisms, but I knew enough to realize that this was a fight he was not going to win. Dressed in my favorite purple capri pants and off-white ruffled blouse, I blindly shuffled past my father, who continued standing in the doorway, his arms still crossed, his facial expression unchanged. Neither my father nor the principal said a word, and the silence both frightened and worried me since I did not know what to expect. Both men took note of my movements as they waited for me to take my seat. As I sat down, tears formed in my eyes, but I knew that crying would simply anger my father, not make him sympathize with me. "Never let the white folks see you cry," my father had warned me previously. He believed that crying was a sign of weakness, and he especially hated when I cried because I could not have something that the white girls at school had.

"We are here," my father said, finally breaking the silence, "to discuss the class schedule the counselor put together for Dwonna yesterday." As the word "yesterday" left my father's lips, I decided right then and there that I would rather be any place but there. I sat in the chair looking out the window, staring at the snow-covered tennis courts. I wanted instead to be curled up in the bed with my cocker spaniel Goldie, listening to Michael Jackson on my clock radio. I hated these moments when my parents went "toe-to-toe" with white people, especially when it concerned me. My father pulled out the wrinkled schedule, and he asked the principal why I was not assigned to college-track classes. The principal, unsure about what to say, grabbed his phone while telling my father that he was going to call in the counselor, since she was the one who had put together the schedule after a consultation with me. My father replied that that was not necessary—he really did not care why she had done what she had done. "The bottom line is this," my father said, his voice getting louder and more firm as he emphasized each word for clarity. "You will put her in college-track classes because she is going to college. I know you put her in those other classes because she is black and you believe that black children don't go to college. But let me just tell you, she's going to college." The principal opened his mouth to say something, but my father cut him off before he could get a word out. "So far, in three years at Wilson, Dwonna has received nothing but As, except in home economics, where she receives Cs. She doesn't need to know how to cook to go to college. You will place her in college-preparatory classes."

And with that, my father was done speaking. After having seen this exchange many times at Butterworth Elementary, I knew my father was not in a mood to negotiate, and he had made it very clear that his purpose that morning was to change my schedule. The principal agreed to set up an appointment with the counselor and me, and then he looked at me and sheepishly asked what college I wanted to attend. "The University of Iowa," I replied softly, very little confidence in my voice. The portly, red-faced principal faked a smile that seemed to suggest that he was interested in my academic goals, but my father's expression remained unchanged. My father then looked at me and informed me that it was time for me to go back to math class. "If you have any other questions," my father directed the principal without actually looking at him, "you have my home and work numbers." I stood up, walked out of the office, and returned to math class. My father headed back to his office, his actions having changed the course of my life.

With her job as a teacher and his as an adjuster, my parents felt they had finally broken into the white-collar world they so desired after more than fifteen years of working at below-minimum-wage jobs. Still, as for many poor, working-class families, money was always tight as my parents tried to raise four children and pay off years of mounting debt from having lived way below the poverty line. Their financial situation worsened three years later, however, when my father lost his job with Allstate following a downturn in the economy, and the union representing Rock Island teachers went on strike for a more favorable contract. Despite these monetary setbacks, my parents continued to believe that their tenuous job situation in the white-collar world was still better than one of the disappearing lucrative manufacturing jobs at Case, International Harvester, John Deere, or Caterpillar—one of the four farm equipment plants in the area.

The stress of raising four children also took an emotional toll on my parents. Perhaps to offset the lack of power he felt in his own day-to-day life, my father made sure that *his* children understood that he was "the HNIC" (the Head Nigger in Charge) in *his* home. My father exacted control over his children, and he did this by bullying and shaming and whipping us with the tattered black leather belt he kept in the kitchen cabinet. My father was also a very proud man, and he did not want people to think we were poor, even though there were nights when the milk we drank came from a powder, our toothpaste came from the Arm & Hammer baking soda box in the kitchen cabinet, and our wall decorations were purchased with the S&H green stamps my parents had saved. Still, my father wanted the white people in Moline to see four little black children who were both well behaved *and* well dressed, even if most of our clothes came from K-Mart or the Salvation Army. For that reason, my father insisted that on Sunday evenings my brothers, sister, and I were to prepare the five sets of clothes we planned to wear for the upcoming school week. We went to the bedroom he shared with my mother to show him the outfits—complete with socks, panties, and bras—we hoped would win his approval. My father required us to do this in order to make certain that we were not wearing the same clothes every week, lest the white people at school think my parents did not have the money to dress us as well as the white parents dressed their children.

This weekly ritual often ended with me cursing my father under my breath as I wondered why God did not bless me with the kind of gentle father I imagined my best friend Julie Brewer had. Each Sunday evening I stood in front of my father, balancing the five sets of clothes on my bony arms, silently praying that he would approve my selection. As he methodically picked through my compilation of clothes, my father—quite cognizant of what we had worn because he was the one who did the laundry every weekend—would systematically remove those items of clothing he said I had worn the previous week. He would then order me back to my room, and as I turned to walk out the door, my father would sternly remind me to return only after double-checking to make sure the clothes I brought to him were ones that had not been worn the previous week. As the word "not" left his lips, shame would overwhelm me because I knew the clothes I had remaining in my drawers were ones that would give the "preppy" white girls at school a reason to laugh at me. These were the clothes that were too small, or they were clothes that bore the marker of having been purchased at K-Mart—flimsily made polyester clothes that came apart after just a few washings.

I resolved to at least do well in my studies to compensate for my inability to compete with what I saw were the white girls' advantages: their beauty and their fine clothes. When I entered ninth grade and my grades really mattered, my mother reminded me often that the white world was sometimes a cruel one. "You are black, a woman, and poor," my mother would tell me. "You have the triple whammy of oppression. The only chance you have is with your brains." Thus, I diligently spent my weeknights studying in order to earn the top grades in my classes. My mother also warned me that many white people would judge all African Americans by my behavior, and so she insisted that we speak the Queen's English so that white people would not judge us as poor black children with "no home training." Therefore, I said very little in class, always making sure that my actions reflected well on *all* Americans of African descent. Though her advice felt like a heavy burden for a poor black teenager coming of age in the 1980s to bear, my mother was going to make sure that her children had the tools to compete with the rich white kids in Moline and wherever I went after I graduated from high school.

Throughout my childhood, I watched my mother continue her education, sometimes at the expense of her children. She spent many weekends and most summers working on her master's, then her specialist's degree, and finally a doctoral degree in education. My father, meanwhile, was responsible for making sure the day-to-day workings of the house ran smoothly. My brothers and I were charged with cooking dinner, loading and unloading the dishwasher, sweeping and mopping the floors, folding the laundry, mowing the lawn, shoveling the snow, and whatever else was necessary to keep the house tidy and neat. There were times when my siblings and I believed that my parents had had children because Abraham Lincoln had freed the slaves, and this was the only way my mother and father could get their house and yard work done for free. As I observed my parents in their non-traditional gender roles, my mother implored me to go to college, get a good job, and not get married so that I would "not have to depend on a man for my livelihood and my happiness." My mother truly believed that dependence on a man could lead to a precarious economic situation that would only be avoided if I stayed clear of marriage.

I have always found her message somewhat ironic, since her marriage has left her fairly dependent on my father. My mother could take care of herself financially—she is the principal at Walcott Elementary and Intermediate School, a school located in a town whose claim to fame is that it is "Iowa's Largest Truck Stop." Yet, after forty-three years of life with my father, my mother is probably more emotionally dependent on him than she might admit, even if he is her best friend and they get along remarkably well for two people who have been together since they were teenagers. Though I truly appreciate my mother's wisdom and her advice, her words have left me unable (perhaps unwilling) to make a long-term commitment to a man. My focus has been on school and work in an effort to be able to take care of my financial well-being, but it has come at the expense of love. It has taken me almost thirty years to embrace a different way of thinking.

The irony is, however, that my mom and dad's insistence that I use education as a means of becoming financially independent has meant missing out on a chance at love and a family. As I read about the debates being waged between second- and third-wave feminists and the very public falling out of Rebecca and Alice Walker, I find myself thinking back to the conversations I have had with my own mother and grandmother. Though both of them believe that they were making sacrifices in their own lives so that my sister and I would have more choices in how we would live ours, their constant reinforcement that marital relationships were to be avoided has left me questioning my past and unsure about my future. At forty, I wonder if I made the right decision to forgo a family in favor of a career as an English professor. My college students often ask me whether or not I want to get married and have children, and my ambivalence probably speaks more about my inability to come to terms with my fears about what it means to want a man, both financially and emotionally. After all, I am supposed to be a "strong black woman" who, to borrow a phrase from Gloria Steinem, "needs a man like a fish needs a bicycle." I do not regret the choices I've made so far, but the truth is that I often wonder what marriage and motherhood would be like. I finally have the financial wherewithal my parents wanted me to have, and now I'm learning something that school couldn't teach me—how to let a man be in my life, how to let me be in his.

Only Daughter

✌ SANDRA CISNEROS

Once, several years ago, when I was just starting out my writing career, I was asked to write my own contributor's note for an anthology I was part of. I wrote: "I am the only daughter in a family of six sons. *That* explains everything."

Well, I've thought about that ever since, and yes, it explains a lot to me, but for the reader's sake I should have written: "I am the only daughter of a *Mexican* family of six sons." Or even: "I am the only daughter of a Mexican father and a Mexican American mother." Or: "I am the only daughter of a working-class family of nine." All of these had everything to do with who I am today.

I was/am the only daughter and *only* a daughter. Being an only daughter in a family of six sons forced me by circumstance to spend a lot of time by myself because my brothers felt it beneath them to play with a girl in public. But that aloneness, that loneliness, was good for a would-be writer—it allowed me time to think and think, to imagine, to read and prepare myself.

Being only a daughter for my father meant my destiny would lead me to become someone's wife. That's what he believed. But when I was in the fifth grade and shared my plans for college with him, I was sure he understood. I remember my father saying, "*Que bueno, mi'ja,* that's good." That meant a lot to me, especially since my brothers thought the idea hilarious. What I didn't realize was that my father thought college was good for girls—good for finding a husband. After four years in college and two more in graduate school, and still no husband, my father shakes his head even now and says I wasted all that education.

In retrospect, I'm lucky my father believed daughters were meant for husbands. It meant it didn't matter if I majored in something silly like

English. After all, I'd find a nice professional eventually, right? This allowed me the liberty to putter about embroidering my little poems and stories without my father interrupting with so much as a "What's that you're writing?"

But the truth is, I wanted him to interrupt. I wanted my father to understand what it was I was scribbling, to introduce me as "My only daughter, the writer." Not as "This is my only daughter. She teaches." *Es maestro*—teacher. Not even *professora*.

In a sense, everything I have ever written has been for him, to win his approval even though I know my father can't read English words, even though my father's only reading includes the brown-ink *Esto* sports magazines from Mexico City and the bloody *¡Alarma!* magazines that feature yet another sighting of La Virgen de Guadalupe on a tortilla or a wife's revenge on her philandering husband by bashing his skull in with a *molcajete* (a kitchen mortar made of volcanic rock). Or the *fotonovelas,* the picture paperbacks with tragedy and trauma erupting from the characters' mouths in bubbles.

My father represents, then, the public majority. A public who is disinterested in reading, and yet one whom I am writing about and for, privately trying to woo.

When we were growing up in Chicago we moved a lot because of my father. He suffered bouts of nostalgia. Then we'd have to let go our flat, store the furniture with Mother's relatives, load the station wagon with baggage and bologna sandwiches and head south. To Mexico City.

We came back, of course, to yet another Chicago flat, another Chicago neighborhood, another Catholic school. Each time, my father would seek out the parish priest in order to get a tuition break, and complain or boast: "I have seven sons."

He meant *siete hijos,* seven children, but he translated it as "sons." "I have seven sons." To anyone who would listen. The Sears, Roebuck employee who sold us the washing machine. The short-order cook where my father ate his ham-and-eggs breakfasts. "I have seven sons." As if he deserved a medal from the state.

My papa. He didn't mean anything by that mistranslation, I'm sure. But somehow I could feel myself being erased. I'd tug my father's sleeve and whisper: "Not seven sons. Six and *one daughter.*"

When my oldest brother graduated from medical school, he fulfilled my father's dream that we study hard and use this—our heads, instead of this—our hands. Even now my father's hands are thick and yellow, stubbed by a history of hammer and nails and twine and coils and springs. "Use this," my father said, tapping his head, "and not this," showing us those hands. He always looked tired when he said it.

Wasn't college an investment? And hadn't I spent all those years in college? And if I didn't marry, what was it all for? Why would anyone go to college and then choose to be poor? Especially someone who had always been poor.

Last year, after ten years of writing professionally, the financial rewards started to trickle in. My second National Endowment for the Arts fellowship. A guest professorship at the University of California, Berkeley. My book, which sold to a major New York publishing house.

At Christmas, I flew home to Chicago. The house was throbbing, same as always, hot tamales and sweet tamales hissing in my mother's pressure cooker, and everybody—my mother, six brothers, wives, babies, aunts, cousins—talking too loud and at the same time, like in a Fellini film, because that's just how we are.

I went upstairs to my father's room. One of my stories had just been translated into Spanish and published in an anthology of Chicano writing, and I wanted to show it to him. Ever since he recovered from a stroke two years ago, my father likes to spend his leisure hours horizontally. And that's how I found him, watching a Pedro Infante movie on Galavisión and eating rice pudding.

There was a glass filmed with milk on the bedside table. There were several vials of pills and balled Kleenex. And on the floor, one black sock and a plastic urinal that I didn't want to look at but looked at anyway. Pedro Infante was about to burst into song, and my father was laughing.

I'm not sure if it was because my story was translated into Spanish, or because it was published in Mexico, or perhaps because the story dealt with Tepeyac, the *colonia* my father was raised in and the house he grew up in, but at any rate, my father punched the mute button on his remote control and read my story.

I sat on the bed next to my father and waited. He read it very slowly. As if he were reading each line over and over. He laughed at all the right places and read lines he liked out loud. He pointed and asked questions: "Is this So-and-so?" "Yes," I said. He kept reading.

When he was finally finished, after what seemed like hours, my father looked up and asked: "Where can we get more copies of this for the relatives?"

Of all the wonderful things that happened to me that year, that was the most wonderful.

Child of the Air House

◂— LYNN PRUETT

My two sisters and I chopped wood for the one working fire-place in our old farmhouse. At night we huddled in front of the burning logs finishing our homework in the dimness. I pretended that we lived like my hero, Abraham Lincoln, had on the frontier. At ten o'clock, we rushed upstairs with breath-clouds billowing from our mouths, bur-rowed under patchy quilts and slept, heads covered until morning—if it did not rain. If it rained, my sisters and I, shivering and blowing steam, retrieved pans from the bathroom closet to catch the water dripping from the ceiling . . . *plink plank plunk* puncturing our dreams.

And yet from the outside, the house looked prosperous. Set back from the road behind an eighty-foot hemlock, amid century-old oaks, the frame house was bigger than the split-levels and ranches under con-struction on Old Mill Road in Kent County, Delaware. We had an acre and a half; the previous owner had owned a horse.

Built in 1840, the house still had wavy glass windows, a brick floor in the kitchen, a banister we were not allowed to slide down, a six-inch brass key in the heavy front door, an attic where squirrels and bees lived, pipes that froze seasonally, wallpaper that dangled above the baby grand, a trapdoor in front of a fireplace you could lift and reach beneath to touch the cold dirt ground, two bathrooms that took turns functioning, and above the kitchen sink, a curved iron pipe, the faucet.

According to my father, anyone successful was (1) related to someone important or influential, (2) had cheated to get their position, or (3) was an overachiever, i.e., had *worked hard*. My dad delivered frequent rants about people who took care of their things, about friends of mine who studied all the time and received unfair help because their parents were teachers. These people were dumb overachievers, to be pitied. According to my father, we Pruetts were the naturally intelligent superiors of everyone we knew. We girls should get good grades without effort. We did.

I always thought my family's poverty was the result of my father's personality.

I began to understand my father somewhat after I read Wayne Flynt's book *Poor But Proud*. My father was a product of his Southern working-class culture, kept low-down by religion and anti-union suspicion. His attitude was built on the scrabble floor of great sins, which mostly involved the accumulation of money. The reward for a life of poverty was literally waiting in heaven where the last would be first, and so to rise was to condemn oneself to an eternal hell reputedly far worse than the living hell of poverty, with its attendant shame and discomfort.

So because we were poor, we were the moral, spiritual, and intellectual superiors to all those around us. Our old farm house sat in the midst of a suburb. All the neighbors' homes had carpet and air conditioning. We alone lived the life of pioneers.

My parents were both college educated. My father graduated from the University of Kentucky. He lived in a boardinghouse during the week and went home sixty miles north on the weekends to Walton, where as a high school senior, he'd been voted Mr. Dixie Heights. A creative, intuitive, disorganized, critical man, he became an engineer because someone told him he wasn't capable of its discipline. At UK, he was involved in the development of air houses and went to the 1956 World's Fair in Belgium to help build one. An air house is a fabric dome held up by compressed air. Though they have been used to cover tennis courts, football stadiums, and small construction sites, the most popular incarnation of the air house is the inflatable funhouse where children jump and tumble at birthday parties and fairs.

My father also went to work as a missionary in Rhodesia, setting up a water treatment plant and bringing irrigation to dry areas. Occasionally he'd disappear into the hills around Mount Kilimanjaro and talk with tribesmen who thought he had special powers and perceived an affinity because of his tightly kinked red hair. Next came a brief stint with the highway department in Michigan, where he claims he was given LSD as a treatment for depression, before he landed a job with ILC industries in Dover, Delaware, making space suits for the moon launches.

Some elements of my childhood read like a fictional invention—like *Chitty Chitty Bang Bang* without actual flight. My dad sewed us an air house in Dover. Using a giant industrial sewing machine, he pieced together a gray nylon dome, adding exactly enough fabric floor to keep it from lifting off the ground. My sisters and I loved the inflatable building. In the fall we'd rake leaves into hills and Dad would spread the air house across them, then fire up his air compressor. The dome slowly filled until it stretched taut and sat like a thrumming flying saucer in the backyard. My sisters and I slid under the edges. Inside we jumped and dove and laughed in pungent crisp free fall, leaping with pure animal gladness into the piles of leaves, safely never hitting the damp ground. It was the best house he ever made for us.

My mother has been described as "a woman from Upper Main Line," having "the demeanor of a New England birdwatcher" and "the elegance and beauty of Jackie Kennedy." In high school, she was voted the Ideal American Girl. She had majored in home economics at the University of Kentucky and taught us manners, to wear white gloves and sit with our knees together, which served me well when I became a scholarship student at Mount Holyoke College and had to attend Friday teas complete with silver service. But, unlike most students at Mount Holyoke, I did not worry over getting into law school or if I was a lesbian or doomed to depression or if a dud from Dartmouth would call me back. I loved college—three meals and a snack every day, hot water in the shower any time at all, heated rooms in the winter.

At first, I was ashamed of my fancy college education and of anything that smacked of success. (Was I a cheat, an overachiever?) I moved to Alabama for graduate school, where few knew that Mount Holyoke College was a Seven Sisters School and some did not even know Delaware was a state. I pretended I was no different from my cousins and their friends as we chased escaped cows through the snowy lowlands in Western Kentucky, the long-haired guys with reefer breath who thought I must be in a sorority at the nearby state college that was beyond their reach. But I was different from my family now, always shifting up and down the social scale, always watching, always in flux.

Much to my surprise, my fiction in graduate school did not receive praise. It induced ire in the red-haired writer at the head of the table. My voice was apparently too high pitched, my vision too low. I cried in workshop, paralyzed by the brutality of the process as it played out in a verbal gang bang. I had done well enough with first drafts until then, had even graduated cum laude for my undergraduate thesis on country music. But writing well required *hard work,* many drafts, revisions, the penance of the less intelligent, the less blessed, the overachievers.

My ambition to become a writer was fierce. My family had high expectations of me, and I felt, too, that I could erase the shame of my upbringing and prove accurate the myth of our superiority by being successful. But to work hard, to "overachieve," was to condemn myself to hell and expose my father's lie. And yet the humiliations I suffered in workshop were unbearable.

According the mindset of my family, I had to become "immoral" to become a writer. I took up the tools of the damned, then honed my new skills. I learned how to write. By choosing a working-class story for my first novel, I bridged the chasm between my background and my education. Writing became, in a way, my salvation.

My first novel, *Ruby River,* is about Hattie Bohannon, a single mother who runs a truck stop. I showed a world I knew, where interesting, smart, lively people, limited for economic reasons, actually lived dramatic and worthy lives. I wanted Hattie's work to figure in the plot because few books I knew placed women's work in the center, and few books treated women of the truck-stop arena as anything but trash. Hattie and her daughters are assumed to be "easy" and "trashy" because they are working-class women. They must literally fight off economic, moral, and sexual assaults to maintain simple personal integrity, that birthright assumed and honored by those of quality.

Once my women were in print, they still faced obstacles to acceptance. *Ruby River* was Atlantic Monthly Press's fall debut fiction selection. It received national publicity, tours, and reviews, but the *New York Times* did not review it because the Southern women writers' "slot" had been designated for Lee Smith and Fannie Flagg that season.

My family's reaction to the novel was varied. Dad announced, without having read a word of it, that there would be recognizable characters in the book, meaning himself. Despite his assurance, the father-figure in the novel, Oakley Bohannon, is not a significant presence. He dies at a VA hospital, is mistakenly cremated, and his remains are lost, or rather appropriated, by a former girlfriend. My dad basked in the book's limelight and still brags when he can. I don't believe he knows how hard the work of writing a novel is. He has composed his own autobiography, a manuscript of 120 pages, and believes writing is easy.

When I received the initial shipment of *Ruby River*, my mother hosted a get-together with her friends. It was a tactful presentation, no unseemly bragging in the presentation of the book. My mother's friends passed the novel around and said, *Wow*. My youngest sister had brought pictures of the eight-inch rock wall she had built for her garden, and thus the conversation swung toward that subject and stayed there all night. Rock wall, well-placed novel. Concrete versus abstract, earth versus air. I was definitely more air.

Maybe because I had imagined myself into Abraham Lincoln's life as a child, maybe because books eased poverty's reality, maybe because I could be true and fine in my mind while dressed in tatters and hand-me-downs, I was drawn to work in a university. In some ways academia is a haven for a smart poor person. Here we revel in our thrift store finds, that pair of crocodile Ferragamos snatched up at the Methodist Store of Opportunity in the mountains of Eastern Kentucky, the red Amalfi heels picked up for a buck in Alberta City, Alabama. Here we supposedly value cultural over material perks.

But even in academia, there are haves and have-nots. I spent a couple decades working as a trailing academic spouse, overqualified, underpaid, hopeful that my true worth would be recognized by the great institution for my publications and top-notch teaching evaluations, that familiar refrain. Having grown up knowing everyone else had more money than I did, that they somehow deserved more than I did, that I was tough enough not to need what lesser beings did, let me accept the crumbs that came my way.

I am a single mother now. The judge in the divorce hearing marveled at how two professionals with apparently equal experience were paid so unevenly by the same institution—both of us were teaching two classes a semester and my ex-spouse earned $100,000 more per year than I did.

As is typical, my household income dropped dramatically and my ex-husband's, by virtue of a new job and a new wife, rose significantly. Our three sons live with me. We moved to a smaller house but the quality of our life improved. Children who used to cower in my ex-husband's presence come and go cheerfully. My friends, too, feel welcome here. There is light and laughter. It is a fun house—painted aqua, almost tropical in décor, but located at the stepchild end of the street. When rescue squads needed more precise addresses, we became Memory Lane to distinguish us from the bigger houses at the upper part of Mentelle Park.

The burden of being a single parent is much heavier than I imagined. I had thought I'd have weekends alone to do my writing while the boys were with their dad. I cobbled together part-time work in order to keep the children in the same neighborhood and same schools. But my ex-husband took a new job and moved 450 miles away, which means no easy child-sharing.

My father, whom my mother divorced, lived in a series of odd places, at one time in a warehouse where he made small air houses, one he sent by train in a very heavy box to my oldest son. Now he lives in an apartment his brother owns in Florida, with a very tall, narrow red door.

My mother reunited this year with her high school boyfriend, an imaginative, successful film producer, and they share a condo in a building on the national historic register. One sister aimed for middle-class normality, a McMansion, an SUV, the life of a soccer chauffeur, paying with plastic and living on the brink of financial collapse. The other, the rock-wall builder, bought an old house of the same era as our childhood home. She is meticulous in its maintenance, almost obsessive in her record-keeping and finances. She lives close to the earth, works for the Department of Natural Resources, and has started an organic vegetable farm. We have each, in our own way, revised our upbringing in our adult lives.

On Memory Lane, trumpet vine, peaches, plums, blackberries, coneflowers, hibiscus and roses grow instead of grass. Two black Jetstar chickens lay brown eggs, and five cats purr in the windows. Though my sons and I do not jump and tumble—except into the pool, yes, there is an aboveground pool—we make music on guitar and mandolin. The boys shoot movies that end up on YouTube, showcasing for the world the disarray inside our house. And yet, despite the chaos and responsibility, I write in my studio bedroom, a small space with glass walls and a fireplace, stories born of air.

Sex and the Inner City

⌁ MARY CHILDERS

Before she strides into the spa waiting room in the posh Manhattan hotel where she works, my sister Tami takes a breath, lowers her shoulders, and vows to remember not to be herself. Over the years she has met quite a few massage therapists who can't keep the best clients because they don't get it: when people fork over two hundred an hour plus tip, they're paying for your buff personality as well as your technique.

While appearing uncalculating, Tami aims for a pleasantly blank demeanor onto which customers can project, according to their needs. Her presence should promise serenity despite the fact that she's giddy as a result of excavating two fifty-dollar bills from a tip envelope. A masseuse must come across as relaxed, even if harried by overbooking or such management shenanigans as reducing hours from twenty to eighteen in order to cut health insurance eligibility.

Measured, predictable emotion is essential. Otherwise, you're exerting too much control over the critical initial minutes. Some people will reflexively smile back at a toothy, effusive greeting, which increases their tension if they're seeking a treatment when they are low. Let them—not the lighting, music, temperature and sheet quality people in the spa business fuss over endlessly—set the mood.

With Tami's dedication, you'd think she'd aspire to management. But to be lured into bossing others, she'd have to be thoroughly convinced that only selling her soul and devoting all her time to work will rescue her from crushing debt. She renounces moving up the ladder because she was too recently a problem employee herself and would probably let staff get away with everything. Stealing from someone else's tip envelope because your support payments didn't arrive? Okay, I'll let it go this time, she might say. "Late because you and your girlfriend were up all night fighting" would strike her as on a par with "late because of a sick kid."

Management entails benefits and more security, but that's not the future she envisions. How could she control and judge people like herself? Although she yearns for a moral and caring life, she's still getting over growing up demoralized. Excessively grateful for a second chance, she doesn't go along with me, one of her five older sisters, when I claim that attending elementary school in the Bronx in the 1970s means she had only half a chance to begin with. In an embrace of efficiency, Tami adopts "no excuses" as a motto for herself. It would take a lifetime to distinguish lack of opportunity from irresponsibility, and she has no time for trifling.

Tami insists that she was destined to become a massage therapist. She loves the oils and aromas, the fleshy life stories that stretch out before her eyes and hands. All the ways that people get naked: the shy and the exhibitionistic; the demanding and the laissez faire. What she witnesses is better than erotic. Every day she plies flesh, she observes something profound and is more gratified than she ever was during her decades as what she calls "a sperm-of-the-minute kind of girl." Expecting nothing reciprocal and anticipating appreciation for the pleasure she confidently delivers, she feels no temptation to add pressure that makes people retreat. Most of her clients are as tranquil with her as they can ever be with another person.

Of course I'm never in the massage room when my beloved youngest sister kneads the muscles of people who shell out a small fortune for her physiological magic. But I've glimpsed who she is with them from her stories and from her entrance into a spa waiting room in the days before staff members were forbidden to slot friends in between bona fide customers. She'd greet me with the satiny friendliness most estheticians and masseuses strive for when they glide into peaches-and-cream waiting areas of chaises, overstuffed chairs, herbal teas, pitchers of water and stacks of *Vanity Fair, Vogue, Bazaar* and *Elle.*

Once we were inside the sensuous twilight of the massage room, Tami warmed my muscles with scented oil, followed my instructions about where and when to dig in deep, and expertly identified problem areas. As if they were sweet nothings, she murmured her acute diagnoses: "Your right hamstring is knotted with adhesions" or "You're hunching over your laptop too much and bunching up your shoulder muscles." Knuckles embedded into my flesh, she rocked and pummeled my legs and back until a searing sensation comprised of pleasure as well as pain traveled up my spine.

But I never relaxed enough to swallow her New Age talk about eliminating toxins from the body. I'd say things like, "It sounds like mumbo jumbo to me." I prodded her to elaborate on how the body is a repository of negative emotions, pompously expecting her superstitions to evaporate when she articulated them to a nonbeliever. Of course, edgy defensiveness crept into her voice. That I understood. For years my importuning questions had hit her as an outsider's challenge to her worthiness and intelligence. I was often clumsy in the ways I touched the pressure points of this massage therapist.

On those occasions when I left my rural college town to visit New York City and Tami spirited me into a spa, none of the paying customers could have guessed I was her sister laying in wait for a freebie. Her sturdy tree trunk legs, broad shoulders and platinum blond hair qualify her to be a stereotypical Nordic massage therapist, as if enthrallment by appearances led to her choice of profession. Sometimes when I look in a mirror, my bony, freckled and bespectacled face, sparsely adorned with a salt and pepper bob, brand me as a bookish black-Irish maiden aunt. It's not because we have different fathers that our accents, vocabulary, demeanor and cultural frames of reference are markedly dissimilar. At the age of thirteen—the same age at which I was scrounging for grades and jobs, determined not to become a lowlife—she was already avoiding school and on her way to becoming a runaway, the wife of a thug who's now in prison for murdering three people, and a coke-snorting party girl. In her early thirties she began collecting community-college credits; in contrast, by twenty-eight I had a Ph.D. in English literature. She divorced her second drug addict before I finished my pathologically cautious thirteen-year test drive with the fine man I eventually married.

Tami was, until recently, the wildly quivering boomerang in contrast to me, the straight arrow. Occasionally we regarded one another across a class divide that can shape family history as much as it does the U.S. Tami abruptly quit a job and I lectured her, once again, about fiscal irresponsibility; at the same time I was sticking it out in a managerial position long after I realized that my integrity and perhaps stability were in jeopardy. I felt guilty that I didn't help her more when she was young, and I was furious about how frequently she squandered my assistance by repeating the same mistakes others in our family had made; she resented that I continued to experience her as requiring help. She labeled me "smart with no heart." Within families and in the political sphere, resentment can become the basis of myths about others that justify disregarding mutual obligations and shared complexity.

After years of reciprocal wariness, Tami and I are now friends who travel socially in distinct strata and help each other both enjoy and reasonably suspect our separate slices of reality. Tami is grateful that she's straggled into the luxury sector of the service industry. We both recognize the irony that she is thriving in a career she chose with a belated sense of calling, whereas I've stolen time to write while careening from job to job: migrant scholar for nine years and one administrative appointment after another that left me in class-based despair. I'm pleased for her, but rueful about the deflating of my own vocational dreams. It has turned out that we are both irrevocably marked by our origins.

For many years I agonized over relatives who weren't trying to get ahead and hoarded cash so that I could bail them out at crucial moments. Although I experienced an involuntary gag reflex at the social mores of the professional classes, I kept trying to adapt. I held what is called "dual-class citizenship" in Alfred Lubrano's *Limbo: Blue-Collar Roots, White-Collar Dreams.* Because of my upbringing and the people I love, there was no way I could echo typical justifications for huge salary differentials. Nor could I reconcile faculty and administrators touting diversity and community while ignoring socioeconomic barriers. Those of us who have smuggled ourselves across class borders should be able to express class conscience at work, but I learned that doing so can lead to an arrested career. Badgered by vocal and divergent constituencies, colleges and universities depend on employees who can verbally repress for success.

One boss who counseled me to socialize more with office mates also advised me not to mention my past when they talked about theirs: "When you talk about growing up poor, people think you're asking them for something." Of course, they were right. I was asking that they realize we did not all come from the same place. But they apparently experienced a request for awareness as a demand for a handout. No doubt reading me that way was punishment for me making them self-conscious about how much they paid the women who cleaned their homes compared to what they spent on annual vacations.

Rather than comply with social coercion and obligatory conviviality, around the age of fifty I chose upward immobility. I quit "a good job" and wrote *Welfare Brat: A Memoir.* Years of veering between shocking and placating colleagues had left me bursting with the desire to unshackle unwelcome, embarrassing, liberating truths about poor families like mine, one in which five out of seven kids dropped out of high school and four fathers dropped out of sight. I wrote with the energy and abandon of a recovering academic.

These days I'm earning a steady, ethical half-time income that allows me to carve out time for the adventures that the book has made possible for me. I've led discussions for various lower-income groups through welfare-to-work projects, library programs for school children and state humanities efforts to engage a cross-section of people in reading. Again and again, audiences ask about my siblings who skipped out of high school but later made it into the middle class; they want proof that one can correct mistakes and overcome the multiple effects of deprivation and frequent childhood anxiety about food, dental care, physical safety and the future.

It is for them as much as for me and my family that I'm writing about Tami's accomplishments as a massage therapist in relationship to how she conducted herself earlier in life. Having finally pushed aside academic taboos against enlisting the "literary" for practical purposes, I can address a theme that especially preoccupies me: the temptations and costs of female sexualization in lower-income environments where few other sources of stimulation are available. If I make it clear that even relatively good girls like I was end up banging our bodies against class barricades and slapping together our own destructive and uninformed choices, Tami can tolerate me evoking her saga because of what it reveals about the hazards of growing up a poor girl in a pornography-saturated culture.

I've cheered as several of my siblings recuperated, at least partially, from the ills that frequently befall high school dropouts. They wound their way into professional and para-professional work while crawling away from neighborhoods disproportionately populated by the frequently stoned and fitfully employed. Inadequate education and limited economic opportunity are important factors in their stories, but sexuality is also a crucial element. For women especially, the trajectory of social and economic class tracks along with the roller coaster of romance.

Like an increasing number of children, my sisters and I grew up caked with sex grime: a residue of sexual awareness built up from living in a dirt-poor family in which boozy coupling was sometimes treated as recreation and in which women experienced masculinity as a malevolent natural force that had to be appeased. Tami grew up under worse conditions than I. The quality of both popular culture and public education had deteriorated by the time she crashed into puberty in the mid-1970s. Opportunities for lower-income men and women shrunk even when the economy boomed. In her formative years, she personally knew few people who earned an honest, adequate living or who maintained cooperative relations with others. Not surprisingly, her warm and generous heart was open to many experiences she would have been better off without.

In *Welfare Brat,* I end the chapter "Sex and the Inner City" describing Tami as a five-year-old stripper, flirtatiously whispering *Daddy* before she climbed, half-naked, into the laps of unfamiliar men who slouched into our smoke-congested Bronx, New York, apartment. She garnered the attention she craved by showcasing her TV-commercial platinum blond hair and the porcelain skin we admired in white children until they entered their teens, at which point we opted for a bronze glaze. It wasn't enough that, when they weren't self-absorbed, her mother, brother and five older sisters doted on her. Tami was compelled to make men smile by dancing, undressing and cuddling, as if she were on a mission to secure what the other women around her mislaid. It was the job of the beautiful baby of the family to make things right by demonstrating that men can be enchanted into sticking around.

Craving an audience and distraction, carrying the weight of the needs of others, Tami prematurely mounted a sexual stage. After witnessing the grief of lovelorn women, with vague alertness she sought to master her own fate by quickening its arrival. The best she could imagine was control in replaying the lives of those around her. Let's face it: many of us are inducted into families in which we try to emerge from brutal basic training with accolades.

In later years I was dismayed by the way Tami denied the sexual intent behind the way she dressed. Tall, lovely young women shouldn't sashay down New York City streets in skin-tight black Lycra pants and then claim they're not deep-down hungry for random male attention. She avoided that debate with me by pretending she didn't hear the whistles and obscene greetings. Those men were the surround sound she could take for granted but not live without. To me they were jackals, and she was a jackass for calling them out of hiding. I wasn't yet ready to see the symptoms of cross-generational transmission in her because I had not yet personally confronted them.

While Tami in her teens would persuade herself that her sexual gaminess was an indication of independence and power, she now knows that she regaled men for multiple shadowy purposes. She was, of course, involved in a clichéd search for a father, having grown up hearing snippets about five of her siblings' fathers but not a peep about the man who was responsible for her not resembling several of her sisters, whom unobservant strangers could immediately peg as related. Her visible difference had to be justified somehow or other. In the inner-city fairy tale that had filled her head and heart, sexy girls land fly daddies.

When she was in her teens, there was no one guiding her, her needs were attended to only intermittently. Even her own family members, people like me, shut their eyes. I have spent considerable time as an adult haunted by our few encounters and bedeviled by guilt that I did not reach out to her more when she was young. Decades later, I still vividly recall the puffy, rumpled face my fifteen-year-old sister presented to me in 1979 on a rare occasion when I scraped together the time and money to ride the Greyhound 430 miles to New York City from Buffalo, New York, where I was a teaching assistant deluding myself about a future as a college professor. I was worried enough to scramble home because I had heard that Tami had moved in with a boyfriend who had just been discharged from prison. She's too young to be living with a guy, I protested to another sister. Calm and matter-of-fact, my sister reminded me of what I witnessed the previous time I had been in New York: our dying mother's physical abuse of Tami. We agreed that this kid was unable to handle Mom slapping and berating her one day and being sweet to her the next. Pathetically enough, perhaps shacking up with this guy made sense. But I had to see for myself.

Tami insisted on meeting me in our mom's apartment rather than her own, so on that Saturday I waited for her for two hours. "She won't be on time for her own funeral," Mom griped. I gagged from the dust that was gathering everywhere since Tami was no longer around to clean up. When I tried to lift the blinds, Mom winced as if I had stabbed her. In a guttural voice earned by years of smoking cigarettes, she cursed at me. "What the fuck are you doing? I don't want the neighbors looking in here." Then she meekly apologized; her string of surgeries had lassoed not only her bladder and part of her colon, but also her good humor.

When the impasse between us rendered us both oxygen-deprived, my mother reluctantly scribbled Tami's address and rattled off directions for weaving my way through the maze of Astoria, Queens. Walking the eleven blocks to Tami's apartment cleared my head. Even if she wasn't home, I could slip her a note that might make her regret standing me up enough that she'd call me at the apartment of a friend I was staying with that night. Once I noticed the pay phone near her building, I crafted a sentence that would motivate but not insult her, something like, "Just in case you don't have the change, here's a couple of dimes." I didn't want to leave her any excuses not to call, but I also didn't want to corner her with a reminder that I had come all the way to New York expressly to see her.

After briefly ringing the bell twice, I leaned on it a minute to entertain myself and expel my frustration that she was not home. Where the hell was she? My luck, she probably just made it to Mom's house, so I confirmed that the phone functioned by calling Mom, who resented the intrusion. "What d'ya expect?" she muttered before hanging up. Mom knew damned well that Tami was behaving just as she did when we were young. I fumed as I tramped back to Tami's apartment, still mentally editing the letter I hoped would spirit her into communication with me.

As I wandered back, I spied a shadow inside the first-floor apartment I now realized was hers. Someone was home, and ignoring me. At that moment, my composure decomposed completely.

When I once again faced the apartment door, I banged with one hand and pressed the bell with the other, while also shouting. If she had no shame with me, maybe she would, at the very least, not want her new neighbors to know that she counted lunatics among her acquaintances. "Hey, it's Mary, I know someone's home. Let me in." For comic relief, I squealed about having to go to the bathroom.

Tami, or whoever was rustling inside the apartment, wasn't even coming to the door. I leaned harder into the bell and then, once again my mother's daughter rather than a highly educated woman, began yelling, "What the fuck's the matter with you?"

Finally the door creaked open and Tami stood there, looking like a costumed fan of *The Rocky Horror Picture Show*, a hip, campy flick with a cult following that endured more than a decade. Her hair, over which she had fussed as a child, repeatedly twirling a brush and aiming a hair dryer like a salon pro, was matted. A chewing gum wrapper prominently stuck out above her right ear. She sported skunk eyes from gobs of smeared black mascara and eyeliner. Definitely it was Maybelline.

Tami hugged me diffidently while mumbling an apology for oversleeping. She asked how long I had been at the door as if she had no recollection of arranging to meet me elsewhere. Her eye contact with me was the equivalent of what I'd expect from an inquiring stranger joining me on line outside of a kiosk or dry cleaning store that was late in opening.

She rolled her eyes at her boyfriend René instead of denying or explaining when I accused her of deciding to ignore me.

We slumped on the bed in the tiny, smoke-filled studio apartment while René tidied up, as if I hadn't already spotted the joints, liquor bottles and cat shit on the floor. At least she was not cleaning up after this creep as she had for Mom, I consoled myself as I scanned the scene, searching for something to say.

René announced a cigarette run, and I put off going to the bathroom in order to have as much time alone with Tami as possible. With characteristic bluntness, I assumed the inalienable right to interrogate her.

She blew suddenly breezy and lively, as if only the opportunity to act could awaken her from slumber. Really, she assured me, she was just out late having some fun the night before. Her words were slurred when she promised she was not going to waste all her time partying and sleeping. Once she was eligible to take the test, she would get her GED.

The cheery effort to tell me everything she knew I wanted to hear stirred her into needing to vomit. I had missed the chance to use the bathroom for a while, but had no intention of going anywhere until I'd made her even more uncomfortable. Rather than venting my dissatisfaction, I vowed to implement what I'd read about tough love for people going through self-inflicted tough times.

Back from the bathroom, Tami crawled into bed, pulling the covers up to below her eyes except when she wanted to recite another joke or tall tale. Even hungover, this self-destructive clown had an uncanny memory of comic lines from television shows. But she was a victim of her own bravado. My heart sank when out of the blue she began boasting to me about having an orgasm by giving René a blow job. I knew immediately that she was not deliberately taunting me with a lie; she was in the process of channeling the druggy, sex-slave role from the screen to her soul.

I began to cry as I gave Tami the lowdown on the damage women do to themselves by faking orgasms. She laughed at my earnestness when I insisted that what she was describing was not physically possible. Only fifteen, she had retreated to a parallel universe where the feminism and primness I represented were threatening. It was clear to Tami that a frigid girl spends a lot of nights alone. To her, being able to mimic an orgasm giving a guy a blow job guaranteed status, and maybe love.

Tami was more open to being influenced by movies like *Deep Throat* than by me. Sitting in the dark in front of that luminous screen that transfixed multitudes of men, she had discovered what many of us need as adolescents: an ideal.

These days, newspapers and magazines intermittently erupt with stories about the pathetic sexual activity of middle-class teenage girls desperate for attention from boys, who are also desperate for attention. This increased activity is not about the sexual satisfaction of girls; it is often about them servicing boys with oral sex in return for being noticed.

More and more girls of all social classes are gagging on the pornography of mass culture.

Before anonymous sex games and dissociated enactments spread to the upper middle classes and became objects of media attention in prep schools, they occurred in the types of under-class neighborhoods in which Tami grew up. Teens like her were the canaries in the coal mine of American girlhood. Although newspapers and magazines often highlighted the triumph of feminism in the 1970s, girls who grew up on welfare in New York City were probably more likely to dress for sex than success and to experience virginity as a badge of immaturity. As she prepares to climb into the lap of middle age, Tami deserves a badge of honor for transmuting the affective labor she performed for males (and for our mother). Now she performs, physically and emotionally, through skills that bolster her identity and pay her bills.

To this day, although I distrust those who focus on the risks of sexuality while downplaying its pleasures, my eyebrows also dart up my forehead when I listen to someone who hypes sexuality as primarily a benign, potentially ecstatic aspect of our lives. Sexuality, in addition to being a biological mainstay, is a dangerous, delightful force. It can tornado through our lives and communities, or it can deliver sweet ease that inspires us to glide cooperatively through the world. We can torture ourselves with yearning, pretzel our aspirations with repression, and soar or glide with momentary contentment that supports us through the inevitable incursions of despair for the world at large or our own small sphere.

We are all animals of an unnatural sort, fortunately and unfortunately. Driven toward sexual release, perhaps primarily because of a reproductive imperative, we also come equipped with power brakes we often automatically floor. Shyness, taboos, physical limitations, gender roles, family ruts and routines and religious values and insidious popular images all conspire to complicate the path of our sexual being. It's not a straightaway with occasional intersections and well-regulated traffic lights. It's a Roman or Massachusetts rotary with multiple poorly marked points of exit and entrance. Collisions and going round and round in circles are unavoidable. Sometimes we feel trapped on that rotary, as if it's another circle in Dante's hell; sometimes it feels like a merry-go-round, with music that gladdens our hearts rather than jangles. There are, undoubtedly, many opportunities to take unexpected turns, or to pull over in frustration or giddiness and end up in a ditch.

In his groundbreaking and controversial analysis of the underclass, the sociologist William Julius Wilson criticizes recreational sexuality; poverty-stricken single motherhood; and fertile, uninvolved fathers. He worries, sometimes judgmentally, in ways people on the left have avoided for fear that they would appear to be policing the sexuality of others or imposing middle-class norms that aren't even being followed by a large majority of middle-class people. "Bring on the judgment!" I have silently cried, utterly sure that the under-class excesses in my own upbringing stunted, to varying degrees, all six of my mother's girls, including me, especially Tami. We grew up pathetically vulnerable to manipulation by the most recklessly licentious aspects of popular culture, with consequences not only for our romantic choices but also for our attitudes toward education and employment.

My youngest sister is my muse; images from her life provoke questions that galvanize my imagination. If you're raised to believe men are no-good but essential, how do you develop standards for heterosexual intimacy? Fearing men while being dependent on them, how do you respond to supervision in the workplace without inflecting contact with gender? If your leisure is swiped by sexual hype, how do you develop curiosity about other aspects of the world? When you practice inauthenticity with people you let inside your body, what happens to your capacity for agency and consent?

Respecting sexual freedom, while also speculating about the consequences of promiscuity, strikes me as an important cultural, political and personal task. The more religiously motivated people on the right try to ham-handedly levy controls, the more other populist, secular voices should speak out. Those of us who are liberal, devoted to a separation of church and state, and comfortable talking about sex better explore that vast terrain of human possibility bordered by the extremes of the conservative American Taliban, the commercially motivated pornographers and the clinical sexperts. If for nothing else, we should do it for the sake of fifteen-year-olds, both male and female, who are filled with yearning while cramped by a limited horizon. Young people who lack the resources to master the cello or to enjoy being nerds or to excel on one of the field hockey greens that dot prep schools around the country strut their stuff on the streets and ingest substances in hallways. Like my sister Tami, they should be seen as harboring talents, and even monumental possibilities.

In My Mother's House

~ LISA D. CHAVEZ

It happened like this: I have a friend, a former graduate student, who'd worked as a dominatrix for much of the time I knew her as a student. She worked for a well-established company specializing in fetish fantasy conversation—phone sex—and they needed someone to do data entry for ten dollars an hour. I was trying to dig my way out of a mountain of debt from the financial crisis that followed a divorce, and so I decided to add this job to my other two, one at the university and the other at a tutoring center.

In the years I'd known my friend, I'd learned a lot. Her MFA thesis was heavily weighted with poems about sex work and we'd discussed the issue many times. I'd learned that it takes many forms: from call girls to porn actresses, from phone sex operators to strippers. For years, I'd had only the vaguest ideas about what sex workers do, and I'd swallowed some of the myths: that all sex workers are forced into it, that all have had some sort of trauma in their lives to cause them to do this. The implication was that sex work was so awful and demeaning that no woman would do it voluntarily unless she was seriously damaged. These myths implied that women in the sex industry basically had no agency, that they couldn't possibly have chosen the work. As my education continued, I learned that like most generalizations, these were not true. My friend was intelligent, articulate, and beautiful, and while she enjoyed writing and teaching, she also enjoyed sex work. And she was very good at all three.

My friend does not look like a dominatrix, but neither did any of the other women who worked for the company, and I quickly discovered there is no one "domme" look. My former student was lovely, busty, and under thirty at the time, and she tended to dress in the chic designer clothes her job afforded her. Most of the other women who worked at the company were quite a bit older than my forty-five years. Several were grandmothers. While I typed in names and schedules and credit card numbers, I listened to the mostly working-class women talking in the office, and sometimes overheard scraps of phone conversations with clients. Except for the content of their conversation, they could have been my mother or my mother's friends.

I saw pictures that had been taken for flyers or for the Web to promote the business, and I liked that the ads were pictures of these real women of various ages with all the beauty and imperfection they possessed. No one looked like a porn star or a centerfold. The ladies were costumed and smiling, and I was told that the pictures were all posed and that photo shoots were like a game of adult dress-up, with lots of laughter and camaraderie but no sex, despite the suggestive poses. The poses were like the business itself: provocative, but without actual sexual contact. The company was in the business of fantasy phone conversation and fetish talk, the reality much less sexy than the images projected. They were women doing a job, and in fact, they rarely saw one another, as most of the work was done from home. It was all very different than I expected, much tamer and much more mundane.

My tenure as a phone sex counselor began because my curiosity was piqued. I wanted to write about sex workers, specifically dommes. But just talking with the other women didn't quite help me understand the dynamic between client and domme. I learned that much of what they did was simply to be nonjudgmental—listening and not judging someone for a foot or spanking fetish or a desire to play at being a puppy. If I wanted to know more about this, I thought I should try it. I have always felt that as a writer I should write about what I know, and it seemed to me I could only ethically write about dommes if I really knew what they did.

And I am a practical woman. I needed the money. I took the job.

When I think of the conversations I've had with my mother in the past I cringe—I can hear my patronizing voice telling her that her life is the way it is because of the choices she has made. When she was younger and longed to be married again, I knew she couldn't "keep a man" because she was too needy, and I told her not to be possessive, not to give herself away. I was proud of my own independence, and in lecturing her, I managed to ignore the parts of me that were not always strong.

We talked about money, and I was smug then, too. My mother complained about money or the lack thereof, bills due or overdue or in collection. She never had enough. Impatiently, I used to calculate how much she made and tell her she needed to save for her bills. She needed not to spend extra on lottery tickets or compulsive shopping (I once found five or six pairs of gloves, still with the store tags on them, in a file cabinet in her house). I told her if she budgeted she could manage.

Now I am amazed and shamed by my own arrogance.

My mother's house, with its cedar-shingle siding, is smaller than many of the other homes in this working-class neighborhood in Fairbanks, Alaska. Smaller than the bland split-levels built in the sixties, big drafty homes not particularly well-suited to the climate. My mother's house is also more eccentric, even in a state where oddness is tolerated. There are the Christmas lights that linger year-round, and the hand-lettered signs: *No parking! No trespassing! Do not feed the dogs!* But most of all there is the yard itself, a double lot encircled by an eight-foot chain link fence, a yard which resembles nothing so much as a low-budget zoo, one of those shabby places with bored animals that used to be found along highways before the arrival of the interstates.

My mother has wolves. Or she used to. The male wolf died, but she still has the wolf-dog pups and their mother, an old husky mix. In the winter especially, my mother's yard is particularly and peculiarly Alaskan: the wolf-dogs howling in the snow, ravens squabbling and squawking over dog food. One winter morning when I was visiting, a moose ambled by on a cross street, completing the picture.

To enter the house is to experience my mother's eccentricities full force. The walls in the front hallway are papered with pictures of animals cut from calendars. Some are from calendars I've sent her, one year a wolf calendar, another year one with pictures of dogs. My mother sleeps on a couch in the living room, sharing the space with magazines and dog toys and sometimes a dog as well. There have never been curtains in this room, but she keeps out light and the curious glances of neighbors with

blankets pinned over the windows. The cheap fuzzy blankets are illus-
trated too—one with a howling wolf and another with lions, zebras, and
oddly, a tiger. My mother loves animals.

The place is also full to the brim. When I visit, I must move piles from
tables, even from the bed, because there is no free space in my mother's
house. It is a trial to clear off the bed and make it, to find small spaces to
set down what I need handy such as my computer, my toiletries. I leave
my clothes in the bag I brought them in. Inside or out, the house is not
in good repair.

This is the only house my mother has ever owned.

This is the house I grew up in. Where we grow up shapes our lives.
Not just the place, as in region, as in Alaska for me, but also as in the values of that house and the way it is run. This little house and my mother's
habits have shaped me, though I spent years denying it, years running
away.

I did not expect to go back, to again dwell in my mother's house, either literally or figuratively. I had made my own life, which was, as I
thought it should be, superior to my mother's in every way.

These are some of the lessons I learned in my mother's house: You must
be strong to survive. No one will ever hand you anything. Fight to get a
good job; work hard to keep it. You can succeed with education, with
good luck, and with strong will—all things my mother didn't think she
had. Most of these lessons were unspoken, but I learned them from my
mother's strength, from the way she shifted jobs from waitress to secretary to pipeline worker, and from the way she continually took classes,
though she never earned a degree.

Those were actions, but the lessons my mother tried to impart in
words were at odds with how she lived. A woman needs a man to take
care of her. She needs to be pretty and feminine so a man will want her.
Only good girls get men, and they need to hold on to them, by being
pretty, by being decorative, so they won't lose what is so hard-won. Other
women can't be trusted; they're always after your man. These were
lessons I heard, over and over again. I also heard the contradictions:
men are weak and want to keep women down. Over time my mother's
bits of wisdom blended into a generic warning: *Beware, beware.*

My mother's lessons were both sad and savvy. I was born in 1961, when my mother was not quite seventeen. My mostly single mother worked hard and never reached middle-class status, except for one brief period during a second marriage, and even that was financed by credit cards. I have been alternately sad and angry about how small my mother's dreams seem, and how unreachable. What she wanted wasn't much: a nice house, maybe with two bathrooms. A husband who had a good job, a new truck to brave the Alaskan winters, maybe a boat for summer trips. No BMWs or trips to Europe for her—just the kind of ease that two incomes could bring.

I wonder about the lessons she tried to instill in me as a teenager. Were they what she perceived to be middle-class or were they just a reflection of her time? I think they were both, because those ideas of domestic security and traditional gender roles were the middle-class goals of the fifties and sixties, and though they never worked for her, she was convinced they might for me. So she told me to be neat, to be friendly, to be feminine. She tried to teach me to dress to draw men, and even in that her class background showed: she suggested Fredericks of Hollywood and blue eye shadow. She wanted me to be a good, if sexy girl, to be popular, and she tried to make me deviate from my costume of flared jeans and black tee-shirts. I refused, knowing even as a teenager that the lessons suggested by my white working-class mother would never catapult her brown-skinned daughter into popularity or Alaska's middle class.

What she told me to do was at odds with what I saw. My mother never fit in with the middle class she longed to be a part of. She was a single mother with a Mestiza daughter. She ran away from the possibility of marriage when I was thirteen and took me to Alaska to make her fortune. She never made it, but I saw her fight. I watched her transform herself from a secretary with perfect hair and nails to a pipeline laborer in Carhartts and work boots. I saw her fight men on the job—both physically and legally. I witnessed her have the kind of friends she thought I shouldn't: former prostitutes, cocktail waitresses and bartenders, gamblers and alcoholics. I saw her fall in love with married men and saw the anguish that followed their inevitable departure. I saw her find a way to support me, with two, sometimes three jobs; to buy a house, the one she still lives in, now sinking into disrepair; and to purchase the only new car she ever owned—a Ford truck that never ran right. I saw all this and vowed to have a different life. The day I got married for the first time, to a young blond man who had just finished a degree in engineering, was one of the happiest days of her life. She thought I'd made it.

It's only now, in my own middle age, that I realize I absorbed all her lessons, contradictory and complex. I fashioned myself into the bad girl, the wild girl, who intrigued the good boys, and got them. And then, when I was married I was the good wife—not the self-effacing fifties model, but the contemporary version, who worked hard and enjoyed a good life, sharing both rewards and difficulties with her husband. I wanted to be part of the perfect couple, and especially in my second marriage, I managed it. In those years, I attained what my mother did not: middle-class status, which I thought rather smugly I had achieved all on my own. To an extent that was true, as my intelligence and education did enable me to become a professor, surely the most middle-class of professions. I was married, but it was always me, rather than my husband, who got the jobs, called the shots. Success was mine.

For years after I left that little house on E Street, I was self-satisfied in a way I now think of as peculiarly middle-class. I had achieved what my mom coveted: marriage, a career with a salary rather than an hourly wage, a lovely house. And like anyone else who doesn't recognize her own privilege, I assumed that what I had was my birthright.

My mother told me that I had it easy. I did at that time, during the stable years of my second marriage. She said, "Lisa, you're married, it's easier for you. You have a husband who loves you and a home and a career. What do I have? Nothing. There's never anything extra. I'm tired of it."

I was smug in my certainty that I had made better choices. I had a husband because I was not a clingy and manipulative woman, in spite of how she tried to teach me to become that very type. I had a house because I worked hard and was responsible. I became who she wanted to be but could not manage to become, and I got that way by rejecting the things she'd tried to teach me, by rejecting her choices.

Or so I thought. For years. Until I hit midlife, was divorced again, moved across the country to a new job and new life, and then, slowly, I began to understand how the lessons of my mother's house are ingrained in me, and how precarious success and security can be.

I was married most of my adult life and during that time I never made a budget or paid bills or in any way managed money. I didn't want to and wasn't good at it. Both my husbands were men who were very careful with money. I got used to having two salaries and few expenses. I got used to a surplus of cash.

When I moved to New Mexico, it was the first time I lived on my own for longer than a few months. My second husband and I had bought a house in the mountains before we divorced, and I kept that beautiful house with a mortgage payment meant for two salaries. My mortgage is more than a third of my monthly salary, but for a while I was okay, and probably would have continued to be fine had I not begun to indulge myself and, like my mother, ignore the consequences. I was free, I was single, I had a good job, and I wanted to live well. I did, and it wasn't until I had accrued so much debt that I simply couldn't pay all the bills that I realized I'd fallen into the same trap my mother had. I was a financial mess.

Like my mother, sometimes my worries launch into melodrama. Soon I was worried I'd lose my house or have to file for bankruptcy. I spoke to a debt counselor, got some things straightened out, but it was clear I simply needed more money. So I took another lesson from my mother, who often worked at more than one job at a time.

I decided to look for a part-time position.

I hated the idea. I loved my leisure time, and felt I'd earned it—the time to write was part of the academic job, after all, a perk we all love. How could I cut into that time with another job? But my financial situation was dire, and I thought of how many people I'd known growing up who'd had multiple jobs. I decided it was a necessary evil.

The first job I got easily. I worked for a private company that tutored students to take the ACT or SAT. It paid fifteen dollars an hour, and seemed pretty good at first.

Soon, however, I realized how utterly spoiled I had become in academia. I had to punch a time card. I had to dress "professionally" and found my usual wardrobe of jeans and casual shirts entirely inadequate. I was asked to cover up my tattoos, and once, when I forgot to wear a long-sleeved shirt on a hot day in October, my boss politely but firmly reminded me that the tattoos on my forearms should not be seen in the learning center again. I remembered what most of the world knows: jobs often suck.

There was a certain method to each lesson at the learning center, and it could not be deviated from. Once I asked the assistant manager if I could change the order of some lessons for an adult student trying to brush up on her grammar: "It makes more sense to start with parts of speech," I said, "rather than punctuation, because how can she learn how to place a comma with a subordinate clause if she has no idea what that is?"

The assistant manager agreed the book we were working from was troubling in its order.

"So I can skip ahead then?" I asked.

She shook her perfectly coiffed head. "No, you can't," she told me. "This is the way we do it here, and you'll just have to follow the order in the book."

It had been a long time since I'd had to answer to a person or method. I chafed in the job.

More to the point, I'd taken the first job I could get, and it wasn't until I started getting paid that I realized I hadn't thought out the situation practically. The pay was much less than I expected once taxes were taken out, and the hours were sporadic, but worst of all, my place of second employment was a fifty-mile round-trip drive from my house, which meant a long commute, and with gas prices rising, it was hardly worth it. I needed something more lucrative. I became a phone dominatrix.

I considered myself very lucky—I worked for one of the oldest fetish phone sex companies in the country. And it was a very informative experience. No matter how much I had heard about what clients wanted and didn't want, I wouldn't know until I did it how much of being a phone domme, or counselor as we were called, was simply chat. Men talked about their lives and their disappointments, about things they couldn't tell their wives. Some things made me sad. Was it really so awful that a man wanted to wear women's panties? Was it really so much of a threat that he couldn't tell this to his wife?

And much of the job was storytelling. I became popular because I could easily fashion a detailed narrative on the spot. It was a natural fit for a writer.

The best thing about the job? The pay. Forty dollars an hour, and I could do it while lying on the couch at home, between writing and grading papers and teaching. Perfect.

I quit the tutoring job and started taking calls more regularly.

And I liked the job. It gave me confidence, because I needed to speak to my callers quite directly and even commandingly, and that directness was something that did not come naturally to me at first. It made me less judgmental; just because I wasn't interested in something sexually didn't mean that no one was, and it wasn't my place to pass judgments on what someone else liked. It taught me that contrary to popular opinion, most people do know the boundaries between fantasy and reality quite well, and exploring fantasies through talk or through porn does not mean that they don't have quite healthy, perhaps very ordinary sex lives. Mostly I learned that the heteronormative world I'd lived in much of my adult life was very narrow indeed.

It was a learning experience, but I thought of it mostly as a job, and having a second job is part of a working-class reality, a reality of my childhood poverty. Money would be tight, perhaps forever, and in the meantime, you work hard and hope to earn enough to keep creditors at bay. That is what I did.

And when people at the university found out and my academic life blew up?

The reactions were class-based, too. Many of the people I worked with were raised middle-class, and they had learned how to handle their money from the example set by financially capable parents. I have talked with other children of poverty and the working class, and I have heard stories of mountainous debt repeated. Our parents were probably in debt, too, and they certainly didn't know how to teach their children about managing money. There is also the issue of two incomes. Although two incomes certainly don't guarantee financial solvency, my colleagues with two incomes have more money coming in than I do, a fact that was confirmed in a department meeting one day when we voted on whether our meager 2 percent raise should go to merit or to cost of living. The few single people in the room voted for the money to go to cost of living. Many of the others spoke about how it was so little money, it really didn't matter where it went at all, but they were voting for it to go to merit. What would likely come out to less than one hundred dollars a month would still make a great difference to me, financially. I knew some of the other people, especially the single people, were also struggling, but it seemed to me many of my colleagues had never known what it was like to dodge bill collectors or to try to figure out which bills you could afford to pay and which you could afford to let slide another month. They simply had no idea. But these things would happen much later.

One day, my mother called to tell me of a dream she had. This is another thing I learned from her—the recitation of dreams. I held the phone in my hand, huddled under a duvet on the couch, trying to stay warm cheaply by burning more wood and using less propane. This has been a reoccurring theme in my life, and I remember the years in Alaska worrying about the price of heating oil and trying to coax more life from the ancient furnace for yet another year. During this call, like every call during the winter, my mother told me the price of heating oil, and how two hundred gallons only lasted two weeks in the deep cold of an arctic winter. I am luckier than her: I snuggled into my blanket to listen to her dream.

"I dreamed I had a rich boyfriend," she said. "He got me a good job, up at Prudhoe." This would be Prudhoe Bay, the oil fields, where my mother herself had worked years ago.

"I never actually saw him," she said. "I only talked to him on the phone. But he got me that really good job." Her voice drifted for a moment, still caught up in her dream of a good job and boyfriend she couldn't even see.

This is my mother's dream, both waking and sleeping, I thought. Not exotic travel or an exotic lover, not even true riches, as if those things are so far out of reach even her dreaming psyche can't manage to conjure them up. What she wants is what she has always wanted: a high-paying job and the health and strength to do it. The man in the dream is not important, not even visible, because she has long ago abandoned the desire for a husband. The important part of the dream is the job.

This is what I return to, my mother's dream, and the lessons she taught me. If you need money, you get a second job, or a third even, the higher paying the better.

This is what I did, and it is ironic indeed that my job reflected her dream: faceless male voices on the phone.

Several months after I become a phone domme, I take a trip home. Fairbanks looks much the same, and so does my mother's house. She tells me she has cleaned up for me, but I can't tell. The big bedroom still holds her clothes, an old Nintendo game she likes to play, and a bed covered with boxes. She has slept on the couch in the living room for fifteen years.

Trips home always worry me. Will I be like this when I am older? I recognize her bad habits in myself. I, too, collect things, not so much because I want to save them, but because I am too busy or too lazy to sort through them and throw them out. I, too, tend to let things pile up, and frankly, it is only the fact that I still have a social life and have to clean occasionally for visitors that keeps me from complete chaos. I see the ways I am like her. And I fear it, and thus I make the occasional effort toward order.

On this visit, I recognize other traits we share. I have my mother's way of talking, of telling stories. And I've always had her anger.

When I arrive, exhausted from an entire day of flying, we still have to clear off the bed for me, find sheets. It is four in the morning. While my mother removes boxes and bags from the bed, I note that this time there isn't even a path from the bedroom door to the closet.

"I had a throwing fit," she says. She'd tried to have a garage sale but it had been rained out, and not only did everything get wet, but not a single person showed up. "I was so pissed," she says, "that I just threw things and broke them. Something fell down, and I said 'Fine, bitch, if you want to fall, I'll help you' and I threw down all this stuff." She seems amused, almost pleased with herself as she tells me this.

In the morning, while she searches for the coffee machine among the items she stores on the kitchen floor, she tells me a long, involved story about fighting for her disabled ex-husband when he went to court. She tells me about the lawyer, how she called his office and called him a dumb bitch and said he was too stupid to practice. As she recalls what she said, her voice rises—she is reliving it, dramatizing the story for me. Her voice gains momentum as she talks.

In the few years before my divorce, my second husband grew tired of my anger. It had only rarely been directed at him, but I hated my job, hated the Midwest, hated the racism and ignorance I felt I battled daily. I would often come home from work and recount stories about the stupid things people said to me, and the ways I responded. When I told these stories, I dramatized them: then she said this, and I said this. I often told him what I wanted to say but didn't, like "shut up, you stupid bitch." My voice escalated as if he were my target. And he would tell me to stop. He'd say, "I didn't do it, so why are you yelling at me?" This puzzled me, because after all I wasn't yelling at him. Couldn't he tell that my raised voice was simply part of acting out the story? Perhaps after ten years of listening to something I was unaware of doing, he was simply tired.

It isn't until many years later, on a spring morning in Alaska when I am forty-five and my mother sixty-three, that I recognize this tendency in myself. This morning, when I am a little hungover from the sleeping pill I took the previous night and am now desperately in need of coffee, I feel annoyance at the raised voice of my mother's story. I wish she'd just stop yelling and make me coffee, since I have no hope of finding the coffee maker on my own. Perhaps yelling is overstating it. My mother's voice is raised in mimicked anger and the excitement of having an audience. I know I do the same thing.

The other thing I recognize is how this storytelling is persona building, which I also do. The story says that my mother is not a fool. That she is tough. That she is not afraid of confrontation. I do the same thing with my stories and have heard others do it, too. These recollections of what we said and of what we should have said are how we give ourselves power in situations when we have little. Much may be wrong with how my mother walks in the world; I've been socialized enough in the ways of academia to know that her yelling and swearing is a working-class way of acting out that will not help her. I know you must let people know you are not meek, but this is not the way to do it. I'm both chagrined that she doesn't know how to do this and filled with an unexpected flood of love: my mother is back. The tough don't-fuck-with-me woman has returned after years of being lost in depression. And I remember what I knew all along—that I modeled myself on her, even when she lost herself, even when I had to be tough for her.

That first day, we talk a lot. After she finds the coffee maker and makes a pot, we clear off a spot on the couch and sit down with cups of coffee. I note we're even dressed similarly, me in a pair of flannel pajama pants and a long underwear shirt and my mother in the pastel sweat pants she prefers and a sweatshirt with yet another picture of a wolf. Why bother getting dressed if we're not going out? We laugh a little at how alike we are in this. I tell my mother about my money woes, how afraid I have been. I tell her what I rarely remember to tell her—how much she has taught me. I tell her I remember how hard she worked, and how I knew I could do that too. And though I hadn't expected to do this, I find myself telling my mother about my third job. It's another trait of hers I inherited: I am often far too open.

I tell her I have a new job that pays extraordinarily well. Then I tell her what it is. "I'm working as a dominatrix, on the phone."

At first, my mother has the expected reaction to hearing such news from her daughter.

"Oh, Lisa," she says. "You'll get in trouble."

But just as quickly she asks, "How much did you say it pays?"

"Fifty bucks an hour, " I say, which is only a slight exaggeration—there are ways to make that much rather than the lower forty-dollar-an-hour base rate.

"It's good money," my mother says, meditatively. "And you don't have to see these guys?"

"No," I say. "I never meet the callers. It's all over the phone, all fantasy."

At that she capitulates. "Well, the money's good, so you might as well do it for a while," she says. "You can quit when you're out of debt."

In the months that follow, when I am punished for doing what I had to do, my mother's lessons will come back to me even more strongly. I'll battle prudishness, the squelching of free speech, and facile moral judgments, but I'll also battle the assumptions of the middle class. I'll be told I should have gotten a more "suitable" second job; I'll be told I should have sold my house and moved into a cheap apartment, or gotten a roommate. Perhaps it is that easy for my judges. Coming from middle-class, two-income families, they have long forgotten economic struggle, if they ever knew it at all. Poverty tests us. I don't trust those that haven't passed that test, for little in my life has shown me they can be trusted.

Nor do I trust the judgments of those who feel they can impose their mores on everyone, who feel that they know what is best for others. I'll see plenty of this too, those who wish to deny women agency by calling the work some of them choose to do degrading, and by suggesting they couldn't possibly have entered into it of their own free will. They do not want to do what we do and that is fine. It may make them uncomfortable or it may even disgust them. But they have no right to tell us what we can and can't do with our voices, our bodies, our lives.

My mother's reaction to my new enterprise surprises me a bit, but it makes sense. She has struggled all her life, and a good job is a good job, as long as it is legal and safe, and this is both. For her, that is all there is to it, and the job which will later cause such consternation and condemnation in my university life is no more to my mother than her high-paying pipeline jobs, though she sees me as luckier since my job involves no physical labor whatsoever, just an active imagination and a facility for words.

That spring morning, I sit on a couch, sipping coffee with my mother, and she laughs. "I bet I could do that job," she says.

I laugh with her. In the year that will follow, my life will explode, and there will be little laughter. I will face a kind of condemnation and hatred I would never expect. I will become "the dominatrix professor," so labeled by media sensationalism, and my life will be irrevocably changed.

But none of that has happened yet. That May morning in Alaska, it is only my mother and me, laughing, talking. Inside, it is dark, cluttered, with precariously piled boxes filling the room, the coffee table a mountain of papers. Outside, the sun shines bright through the new green of the birch trees just bursting into leaf. The world is cluttered with color. And I think of how life is a wilderness we must navigate—sometimes clumsily, sometimes gracefully, and I know that whatever mistakes I might make, I will survive them.

Bumming Work

➤ JUDY OWENS

Finding work as a teenage girl growing up in Appalachia in the 1970s was a near-impossibility. Jobs for teenagers belonged to families who had influence, and other than the small influence my grandparents had from hauling voters to the polls for the Democrats, we had none. I walked along Cumberland Avenue and stopped at every single store and asked if anyone was hiring. Nobody was. I tried for weeks and begged for a job.

Local stores in the East End of Middlesboro, Kentucky, hired neighborhood people, and Avondale Avenue had only two competing groceries on either end of the block: Herald's Grocery on one end and Burchett's Store on the other. There were no openings at either place, and there hadn't been in years.

Herald's was slightly more uptown because it had a deliveryman who drove a battered rust-colored pickup truck and made deliveries in cardboard boxes that once contained a gross of Tide or a lifetime supply of plastic forks. Burchett's didn't have delivery, but was distinguished by a gigantic stainless steel scale to weigh lunch meat. Once it held the baby boy of Mary Sue Wyatt, who dropped out of the sixth grade to have him. That was Mrs. Burchett's version of doting, to lay the baby in the cradle of the bowl that usually held sliced bologna and see exactly how much he weighed.

Herald's was cleaner, had more display cases and a big black cash register stationed on the right side of the door, no doubt an original fixture from the 1930s. The Formica, its off-white surface with little gold flecks floating beneath, offered the store an air of modernity, a calloused foot in two worlds: the poor versus those aspiring to the working class. The floors were made of rough pine slats that creaked under the weight of its patrons.

Earning money was almost out of the question because there was so little of it in our town. Grown people expected kids to help out anyone who was a widow, sick, disabled or crazy for free, and that covered just about everybody. My father's mother, Mammaw Jones, didn't believe in this. When I went to her house, bumming work, she set me to cleaning windows but insisted on paying me. That was opposed to my mother's mother, Mammy Kelly, who had my brother, one of my sisters and me working tobacco for nothing. We started out in the spring, my grandfather, Pappy and I, setting hopeless little plants, all withered and wilted over. My brother Steve and I dug holes and tried to prop the tobacco sets upright, Pappy following behind with a bucket of water and a dipper.

"This'un ain't gonna make it," I remember telling Pappy one time. He filled the dipper from the bucket, baptized the plant and said, "No, I believe he's going to make it. He's going to make it all right."

Most of them did make it, just like Pappy said, and by summertime we were back out in the garden, hoeing weeds so that the broad, brilliant green leaves could rise up to golden splendor in the fall when the men cut the tobacco and stuck it on poles. By the first damp, foggy day in October, when the cool humidity made the leaves pliable enough to handle without crumbling, the tobacco had "come in case," as Pappy would say. We put on two or sometimes three sets of clothes and headed out to the barn to grade and tie.

"There's no place colder than an ol' baccer barn," he said. Mammy would say, "If you're working hard enough, you don't notice the cold." She stripped tobacco and graded it so fast that my brother and I could barely keep up with her, even when Pappy helped out when he wasn't climbing up in the rafters and throwing down sticks.

The tobacco barn had two stories, but there was no second floor, instead a maze of rafters that sticks fit in. These sticks held stalks of tobacco that were stored upside down until they cured. Since that time we've learned much about additives in tobacco, chemicals that the tobacco companies mix in to make smoking even more addictive. I always thought that there was something addictive in the very air that makes tobacco: the sweat rolling off the naked backs of the men with their keen machetes, the blades reflecting beams of sharp summer sunlight. That smell, thrown up into the leaves, was mixed, after the tobacco was hung in the dark barn, with the crisp and sad smell of fall, the death rattle of leaves turning the mountainside from green to brilliant red and amber and pumpkin orange before the dull gray of winter set in. And in that mix was our own breath in the fall tobacco barn, smelling of eggs and sausage and biscuits, and Mammy's and Pappy's breath laced with coffee and PoliGrip.

Inside the tobacco barn, we were all good workers. Mammy graded the tobacco starting at the bottom of the stalk, and pulled off the trash, or leaves nearest the bottom of the plant. Then there were red, yellow and tips.

Each type of leaf was laid onto a wooden, table-like board, with smaller slats nailed on vertically to create compartments for keeping the leaves separated. Pappy was the first one to show me how to tie a hand of tobacco: you took the individual leaves by the stem that would have been nearest the stalk. These leaves were bunched together in your palm, one on top of the other. When your hand was full of leaves, you took another leaf, folded it in half, and wrapped it around the ends to tie them all together. Our conversation most of the day revolved around making a particularly pretty hand. Mammy repeated stories over and over again about what happened when she and Pappy took our tobacco to the auctions, and how the big shots that bid on the tobacco would brag on how pretty our tobacco was. When she told these stories, I would stand up a little straighter and try to tie my hands of tobacco a little tighter and neater, in fear that an important man from R. J. Reynolds would find a defective hand, with my name on it, peering from under the pile, and reject all our summer's work because of it. There may have been people in tobacco barns throughout Kentucky who were tying ugly hands of tobacco, but there never were in ours. If my fingers started getting numb from the cold, and a hand I tied came loose, Pappy just picked it up and retied it without saying anything. I saw this and tried harder the next hand.

Years later, when I was a grown woman, I covered the tobacco auctions for the newspaper in Owensboro. I'll never forget how shocked I was: farmers and warehousemen and county farm agents waited around, and then, wearing tweed sports coats and brimmed hats, the men from R. J. Reynolds and Phillip Morris walked up and down the aisles of the warehouse with an auctioneer and a counter. Farmers stood behind their tobacco and turned over the hands on top with expectation, moving the bundled leaves but eyes affixed on the bidder. The auctioning was so fast that the buyers race-walked up and down the rows of the warehouse. An entire warehouse full of tobacco didn't take an hour to sell.

When the tobacco buyers left, I stood there with my reporter's notebook in disbelief. I followed the buyers from the time they walked through the door until they walked out. Not one of them said a word about a pretty hand. The auctioneer just started his chant, sounding like a cross between preaching a Baptist sermon and calling a horse race at Keeneland. A signal was given and it was over. The whole thing happened without any of them breaking stride. A single word, or even eye contact, with the farmer was rare.

Other than washing Mammaw Jones's windows, I made money shining my daddy's shoes, which paid a quarter. My daddy inspected the shoes after I shined them, and was quick to remind me that he could get them shined by a professional for a dime, so he'd better not find any missed places for the kind of money I was making.

When I was in high school, I wished hard that I could have a real job. During the summer just before school was out, I walked up and down the streets of Middlesboro, stopping in stores and asking them if they needed any help. There was only one fast food restaurant then, a regional chain called Clancy's with a logo of a cartoon English bobby. These days, work like this would be dismissed as a "McJob," but in Middlesboro at that time some members of the merchant and professional classes pushed to get such jobs for their children. Wives of blue-collar workers also took jobs in fast food, so there were few opportunities for someone like me. Lunch counters, like the one at Woolworth or at Lee's Drug Store, had waitresses who started when they were in high school, and there wouldn't be any openings until somebody died.

My family, which survived on my father's salary as a truck driver and my mother's income as a teacher's aide, tried to fill my need to work. Mammy taught me to crochet, and one day, while she showed me some new stitches, she told me the story of the Valentine pillows. She had visited a lady downtown who made little heart-shaped pillows out of satin and crocheted a top for them, then inserted a ribbon through the crochet that stood up like a crown. Mammy bought one of the pillows so she could copy the pattern, but couldn't figure out how to get the ribbon to stand up.

While my grandmother looked the part of the sweet little Southern lady, she salted her tales with profanity. "I went back to that woman and asked her if she would show me how to put the ribbon in, but the old bitch wouldn't show me," Mammy said. "So I took the thing home and I worked and worked with it, and I couldn't get it to stand upright. About two o'clock in the morning, I fell asleep, and I'll be damned if I didn't dream how to put the ribbon in. I woke up and threaded it in there just like the dream, and it went in perfect."

That January she showed me the secret of threading the ribbon, and together we made Valentine pillows. I sold them at school to teachers and even to some students for ten dollars apiece. Though this was a fortune, she let me keep all the money.

Then, a miracle happened. Mammy heard that Herald's Grocery was looking for a cashier. I walked down to the store and talked to the lady. She hired me right on the spot. I was thrilled to learn I would start work the next day. I showed up just like she told me to, and I remember how surreal it felt to walk behind the counter. The lady showed me the cash register and how to work all the buttons and how to code the items. I tried to do a good job for her so she wouldn't be sorry she gave me a chance. I took a bottle of Fantastik and cleaned the counters and shelves with a paper towel when we didn't have customers so she would see what a good worker I was. My first pay day, my mother cashed my check and I went to the Tack Room, the fanciest women's dress store in town, and picked out three outfits that I would have never dared to ask for and put them on layaway.

The next Monday I went to work. When the shift was over, I walked home. There, the phone rang, and it was the lady who had hired me at Herald's. She said, "I won't be needing you down at the store. I sold it and the new people are taking over tomorrow."

I was mortified. I hadn't told anybody about the layaway, and I didn't know how I would get it out. Finally, when my daddy came home from work, I told him.

"Dad," I said. "I lost my job today. They sold the store and the new owners are going to run it." I remember swallowing hard before the worst part. "I put this stuff on layaway, some clothes for school, and now I can't pay to get them out."

My younger sisters were cackling and laughing. "Judy lost her big job," Susan said, in a mocking voice.

Donna chimed in: "Judy had her a big job but she lost it."

Dad said, "The layaway, it was stuff you had to have for school anyway, wasn't it? Don't worry about it. I'll get it out for you."

He went into the living room, and I heard him telling my mother: "They knew they were selling out when they hired her."

The year I graduated from high school, I was not able to find a paying job. Finally my mother told me if I raised a garden and put it in the freezer to hold down the grocery bill for the coming fall, she would use her paycheck to help me go to school.

In the spring of my senior year, I picked and froze strawberries from my grandmother's strawberry patch. Her patch was wonderfully mature, located just past her front yard, on a small sloping knoll that rose and fell again over the steep hillside. I would go out there in the morning, tiny mirrors of dewdrops on the ragged-edged leaves, to pick the berries, some blushing pink, some brilliant rose, some damaged a little bit where the slugs had gotten to them or they had rotted a little after a rain. I remember the gentle morning spring air, the civilized little berry patch, and the enveloping wildly green crags of the rugged mountains. These were the hills where I was born, like all my family, since they came to the Cumberland's two hundred years before. This was the place where I belonged, in spite of all the hardship.

My daddy opposed my going to college and told me I would starve out before he would help me. In a way, he was right. After that summer, I would be starved out. Starved for the family and the place I was leaving behind.

After my first semester in college, I signed up on campus for the student work program. I asked to work in the library because that was the place I felt most at home—the marble stairs, the woody, musty smell of the book stacks, and most of all the cool silence. I was horrified when I was assigned to work in the copy service. All day every day while school was in session, students, faculty and staff lined up before the large, open window of the copy service. It was a noisy and angry place.

Mary Verrill, the chief librarian, showed me my job. There were two copy machines—a new one and an older one with a peculiar rounded glass. She said, "Only use this one when you are copying single pages, not books. If you try to use this one to copy books, pressing on it could break the glass, and I would have to hold you responsible."

I was a speed demon on the copiers, taking orders and running copies as fast as I could. In those days, all the interlibrary loans had to be copied one page at a time. Someone from Special Collections would bring an entire book truck down, and in my spare time, I was asked to try to make a dent in the copying for articles to be mailed.

One day, the normal copy machine was broken, so the only one I had was the one with the rounded glass. A middle-aged, self-important man came to the window, pushed past the other patrons and insisted that he had an emergency and had to have pages from a book copied right away. I told him I was sorry, that I could only copy single pages that day because the other copier was broken.

The man marched away from the crowd, turned the corner and came through the "employees only" side door into the copy room and started for the copier. In a slow-motion, adrenaline-flushed moment, I saw a Coke bottle that someone had left in the copy service window, grabbed it with my left hand, spread my legs in a crouched stance ready to kick his groin and slam the bottle over his head.

Something in my eyes must have told him to stop. He did. But he went to Mrs. Verrill's office and reported me.

When I was called in, Mrs. Verrill was sitting at her desk. She had a chair beside it and she asked me to sit down. "Tell me what happened today at the copy service."

I struggled to find the words to describe the feelings I had for my job. The deep desperation I felt when I walked the streets of my hometown and no one would hire me at any price to do anything. My daddy's words about my starving out. How much I depended on my job to pay for my education, which my mother and my mentors had repeatedly and emphatically told me was my only path to a different life.

It never entered my mind that the student work program was a collection of made-up jobs where students, aside from a few repetitive tasks that the secretaries did not want to do, were not actually expected to do anything.

My position at the copy service window was not a *make-work* job to me. The outcome of my entire life could turn on it.

But in my family there were no words for feelings. We didn't say words like "desperate." "Afraid." "Terrified." "Confused." Those ideas were reserved for characters in books and people on TV.

In the mountain culture, our feelings were folded into three main categories: grim acceptance of whatever backbreaking, thankless job we were destined to do; alcoholism when we couldn't cope; and sarcasm about anyone who expressed any other feelings.

So what I said was: "Mrs. Verrill, you told me that I had to protect the copy machine and that I would be responsible if something happened to it. You told me that the machine with the curved glass would break if I tried to copy a book on it. That man tried to make me copy a book on the curved glass, and I was responsible for stopping him. That's the job you gave me, and I was trying to do my job."

Mrs. Verrill looked back at me. She paused, and then she said, "Judy, you're right. That is what I told you. But if this happens again, what I would like to see you do is just say, 'Mrs. Verrill told me that you could not use this machine. If you do use it, I'll have to tell her.' That's all you have to do, and you'll be doing your job."

I didn't lose my job at the copy service and if that man ever had his book copied, I don't know how.

Money was always an issue while I was a student, and so was food. The first summer I was on campus I stayed in a studio apartment with my brother. We would buy one box of Rice-A-Roni and cook it in an iron skillet, dividing it six ways so we could have one serving each to eat a day. One afternoon as I was walking home, I noticed somebody in our apartment complex was grilling a rib-eye steak on a hibachi. My eyes watered and I had a gnawing feeling like being in love except for the mean low growl in my stomach. I looked around, and seeing no one, I snatched the steak with my bare hands. It seared the tips of my fingers. The pain was so fast and exquisite that at first I couldn't tell if it was hot or cold. I raced around the back of the building and ate the whole thing in two or three big ripping bites, like a wolf.

In my senior year, though, I dropped out, partially because of chronic money problems and also because of a romance gone sour. My first full-time employment was with my hometown newspaper, writing obituaries. Eventually I was promoted to writing feature stories. This job represented the ultimate position for a writer in my hometown. Encouraged by the consistent praise I received, I applied for other newspaper jobs that gave me more responsibility. During the ensuing fifteen years, I worked as a staff writer for three of Kentucky's four largest newspapers. My writing took me to murder trials, a biker's funeral, coal mine strikes, business buy-outs and even tobacco auctions.

While I was covering a murder trial for the Lexington, Kentucky, newspaper, one of the attorneys asked me why I didn't go to law school. I thought about it and decided to try. It would give me an incentive to finish my bachelor's degree. After a year of study, I scored well on the LSAT, and so, at age thirty-two, I resigned from the newspaper and entered law school. My writing carried me through two law journal articles, a moot court board competition and a mock trial contest.

I left legal practice years ago to work in politics and later in academic administration. During that time, I began my most difficult writing challenge: the effort to tell my own story. I was surprised at how awkward I felt, as though I was learning to write for the first time. Some early Sunday mornings, right at dawn, I went upstairs in the old mission-style house I had bought, with only a pen and a notepad. There on the blank pages I conjured up the old barriers and my efforts to surmount them. I recalled old hurts, crushing setbacks and unexpected blessings just when I needed them. Sometimes the memories were so painful that I felt physically sickened as I wrote. Sometimes I wrote blindly as I sobbed. Every time, though, I looked back at the page, I was surprised and pleased by what it reflected and revealed.

Earning my place among the educated class was easy compared with settling there. Despite the humble and generous encouragement I received from my extended family, there was an unexpected result from my success. My education severed me from my family. The more they claimed to be proud of my accomplishments, the less frequently I was invited to family get-togethers or holiday dinners. Before the last Thanksgiving dinner planned by my mother and siblings, my mother called to tell me about it and to tell me that she was sorry that I was not invited, but my sister did not feel comfortable with me there.

Back in 1996, Mammy Kelley asked if I would serve as her executor. I agreed, and in 2000, she died. The night before the final hearing to close out Mammy's estate, I dreamed about us making those pillows, and I was filled with a feeling of pride and satisfaction. Before the court hearing I had to go to the bank, and I was prepared for a confrontation. But it was unbelievable. Everything went very smoothly, as though I were a graceful dancer and every motion choreographed. The extra hour I had allowed for haggling with the bank was suddenly empty. I drove by my mother's office to see if she wanted to get lunch, but she was gone. I decided to drive up the hill to Mammy's house.

When I drove through the dark hollow and into the bright light of Mammy's yard, I thought I would cry my eyes out, but I didn't. I felt her hand in everything I saw: the fuchsia-colored rhododendron, the old-fashioned red rose along her gateway trellis, the porch addition that she had tried to make look like Tara using columns made from plastic drain pipe. "Look at these—they were cheap and you never have to paint them!" she'd said when she put them up.

I didn't feel like crying. I just felt so full of her—so full of everything she was and everything she had meant to me. I remember how crazy and strong and funny and mean and generous she was. I remember her competing values. She liked the very latest stuff, but only for the very cheapest price, which led to odd concoctions like a silver skillet clock that she had me paint aqua in the early 1960s. I remember her outrageous earthiness, with her most vivid descriptions reserved for men and money. "I can't look up a cow's ass and tell you how cheap butter is going to be." About sex researchers Masters and Johnson: "I never dreamed I'd see the day when people would have to watch TV to find out what their ass was for." My mother's boyfriend wearing shorts: "He pranced all over this yard like a peach-orchard boar." I remember the evolution of her house during my lifetime, from the Little House, a one-room outbuilding with its quilt frames, a pot-bellied stove with that warm, sulfur coal-burning smell, the Maytag wringer on the front porch, the place where she kept a fire outside, where we would make a gnat smoke, and sometimes can vegetables outside. All that changed. She got a big new electric stove with an overhead vent. She remodeled and had the potato bin taken out because the wood was rotting and because that's where Pappy and my uncle Bobby hid liquor.

Gazing across that impossibly green mountain and her idle garden and the flower beds that were waning without her care reminded me of her determination to be a force—whether it was sleeping with a shotgun across her lap during the Union Wars, or fighting off gnats, or scraping hogs in the fall or outsmarting the woman who tried to hide the secret of threading the ribbon. She could bake the most delicate biscuits, with so many layers that they made phyllo look like Melba toast, but then turn around and fart loud enough to peel paint. I touched the doors to her house, but of course they were locked. Then I went back over to the Little House, and I couldn't believe it—it was open.

I walked through all her sewing notions and scraps for quilts that were organized in boxes labeled "Polky Dots" and "Whites." I walked straight through to the back. There, laying right on top of a mountain of weed-eater instructions and Butterick patterns and quilt pieces made out of polyester, was a scarlet red heart-shaped pillow and matching, as only she could, an orangey-red crocheted top with a white border.

I picked up the pillow, and as many patterns and sewing notions as I could carry, ran outside and threw them in the trunk of the car like a thief.

Stink Jobs

~ MAUREEN GIBBON

When I was fifteen I got a job on a chicken farm. I was, by turns, a chicken carrier, a chicken puller, and a chicken stuffer.

Most of the time, I carried chickens from the coop out to the truck. I carried the birds by one leg each, hanging upside down, three to a hand. Sometimes I pulled old chickens from their cages and handed them off to someone else to carry. When a new flock got delivered to the farm, the whole process got reversed: I carried chickens from the truck into the coop. Once in a while, I got to be a stuffer, meaning I was the one who tucked new chickens into their cages. That was the best job. It's a lot easier to put a chicken into something than it is to take it out.

Nothing about the job was really hard except the smell of the chickens and their shit. It worked its way into my clothes and hair. When I came home from work, my mom made me strip out on the back porch so I wouldn't bring the stench into the house. She threw my work clothes—tight Lee jeans, skinny tank top and flannel shirt, a bandana for my hair—right into the washing machine, and I headed directly to the shower. But I made $3.50 an hour for carrying chickens, which was good money for a teenager in rural Pennsylvania in 1978.

At my next job I waited tables and earned $1.10 an hour plus tips, which usually came out to be three or four dollars an hour. I came home from that job stinking, too—of french fries and cigarette smoke—but my mom didn't make me strip down on the porch. She kept my coat out there, though, because of its smell, and I still took a shower as soon as I got home.

Those were some stink jobs. They were so redolent they worked their way into my spirit and my psyche—or whatever the thing inside a person is called.

My parents treated me differently when I got that job waiting tables. If I was going to school and work, I was an adult, at least in some ways, and they left me alone. Work was work, and if I did it, I had certain rights. That meant I was my own boss at sixteen, and I did what a lot of country kids did: I partied hearty. A carload of us would go driving around to buy off-sale beer, and then we'd park somewhere in a field and drink it all up. Sometimes I went to school stoned, while other days I took pretty robin's egg speed and wrote as fast as I could in one of my notebooks about the dark purple mountains outside my math classroom. A couple miles west and south, the Appalachian Trail went through my town, so the mountains were *right there*. When they weren't dark purple, they were green, and when they weren't green, they were bluish black.

Of all my jobs, waiting tables lasted the longest, and there were some parts of it that I liked. I liked the way I had to think all the time and make my actions as efficient as possible. I didn't even mind doing dishes, at least not breakfast dishes. I liked the way the plates felt and how I could bang them around a bit without breaking them. I especially liked the heavy coffee cups with their thick sides and lips. Those cups always felt solid in my hands.

But mostly I just hated working at the restaurant. I hated getting yelled at by the cook in front of customers; she and her niece ran the place, and they were usually in a rage over something. I hated the dirty backroom where the other waitresses and I scraped plates and washed dishes. It was lit most of the time only by a fly-zapping bug light, and old newspapers covered the floor. I hated the filth and disarray that existed everywhere that customers couldn't see and in some places they could. But I think I mostly hated the feeling of hours going by in a place where people were angry nearly all the time.

My mom listened to me complain about the place for a while, but then she told me to shut up.

"If you hate the job that goddamn much, then quit," she said. "I can't stand to listen to you night after night."

My father must have been taking a break from his drinking that night because he was around to hear what my mother said to me. He came into the living room then and told me he didn't want me to upset my mother anymore.

"If I hear you talking about this again, I'll slap you so hard you'll have something to complain about," he told me. "Do you understand?"

I said that I did. I never talked to either of them about my job again. And I didn't quit.

I had another, more ambitious side to me, so in addition to buying weed and beer, I also used my waitress money to pay for college applications and my SAT test. To prepare for the test, I planned to give up smoking dope for a week beforehand, but I broke down on Tuesday and smoked a couple joints. Still, I went into the test as clearheaded as I could be, and I wondered if my score would be high enough to get me into Barnard College, which was where my English teacher told me I should apply when she found out I wanted to go to school in New York City.

Or maybe my poetry would get me into Barnard. I'd been writing poems ever since sixth grade when Mrs. Clark, my English teacher, told me she liked something I'd turned in for class. The summer I was fifteen, my poems were good or promising enough to get me into the summertime Pennsylvania Governor's School. There I wrote a poem about picking pears—my first job, the one I had when I was thirteen—and my teachers praised it. They told me they liked the way I worked through a metaphor about the ball-and-socket joint that joined a pear to a tree. That's when I got the first real idea that I could be a writer.

After Governor's School, though, I had to come back home and start eleventh grade. Even though I kept my drinking and drug use secret from my mother, she saw me getting more and more depressed that fall when I was waiting tables.

"I see you going downhill," she said. Then she told me to talk to my guidance counselor about going to college early and skipping my senior year in high school. Even though my mom only had a high school diploma, she always said to my brother and me, "When you go to college . . ." She made me believe in it.

That was how the ball got rolling. I talked to my counselor, my tenth-grade English teacher brought me an application for Barnard, and my French teacher took me to the interview Barnard required of early admission applicants. I bought a black dress for the interview, and shoes that hurt my feet. The main thing I remember from the day is that the interviewer used a word I didn't know.

"So you would say you feel stultified in your present environment," the interviewer said when she asked about my school and my hometown.

Stultified. I figured it meant something like stunted or stagnant, but I wasn't sure. Someplace in my mind, I didn't really like the dead-end sound of it. I think I didn't want to believe it about myself. I felt stronger than that.

"It's not so much that I feel stultified," I said carefully. "It's just that I know I would do better somewhere else."

When I got home I looked up the word. That's when I saw that stultify meant *to render useless* or *to cripple*. I had answered the question in a way that made sense, but it was true: my hometown was crippling me. I stayed home from school at least once a week, and I was doing too many drugs and drinking too much. I was generally running wild, but I was also running aground.

Barnard did admit me that spring. I got accepted. But the news was almost meaningless, because there was no way I could possibly afford to go, even with my parents' help. Tuition alone was more than $7,000 per year, not counting money for housing and food and books. It might as well have been a million dollars. Still, something inside me changed the day I got the slender envelope containing my acceptance letter. I stopped smoking dope. I still drank, but I didn't want the cloudiness marijuana brought. I rejected it over and over when friends offered it, and I also rejected the idea of it. I wanted something different, even if I didn't know how to go about getting it.

One night I was lying on the sofa after coming home from the restaurant. It was about eight o'clock at night, but I was tired enough that I was drifting off to sleep, even though my mom was running the vacuum cleaner in the same room. In spite of the hum of the Hoover, I heard the phone ring and my mom answering.

"She's asleep," my mom said, and I knew she was talking about me. The rest of the conversation didn't make sense.

After my mom hung up, she told me, "Wake up. That was the Barnard financial-aid office. They're making you a financial-aid package."

"What did they say?"

"I don't know," my mother said, upset. "I couldn't understand everything they told me. You're going to have to call them."

When I telephoned, I talked to someone who was so nice on the phone, that I couldn't believe she was really talking to me. When she outlined the terms of the financial-aid package Barnard was offering, I couldn't believe that, either. Barnard was offering thousands of dollars in financial-aid and work-study money. Because of a phone call, I was going to college.

In that way, I got a ticket out of my hometown.

A few months later I bought an actual ticket on the Bieber bus line. I shipped all of my junk to Barnard, got on the bus, and took myself to college.

Before I got to Barnard, I didn't know I belonged to a social class. Growing up among the Pennsylvania Dutch farmers and coal miners, I knew there were different kinds of people, and I knew there were families with names that signified a whole type of living and behavior, but I did not know those things went into making up social class, or that my family belonged to the weave of our small town in just as clear a way as the Moyers, the Zerbes, and the Zimmermans.

Both my parents came from Edwardsville, Pennsylvania, in Luzerne County—the heart of anthracite coal country. My Welsh great-grandfather, David Gibbon, was president of the Edwardsville charter of United Mine Workers of America in the year 1900; I know this because I have a copy of the certificate from the UMWA that "doth grant this charter to" my great-grandfather. My grandpa Tom Gibbon worked in the mines for a couple of years before he became a plumber; a copy of a payroll slip for my grandfather from March 1939 says he earned $5.74 for one day of work at the Kingston Coal Company, minus six cents for "Old Age Tax" and $1.05 for "Lamp Rent." The Kingston Coal Company sold my Lithuanian great-grandmother Sarah Martinaitis her home in 1936 for a down payment of fifty dollars and a total price of two thousand. On the Slovak side of the family, my maternal grandmother worked first in a laundry and then as a pieceworker in a sewing factory, while my grandfather worked as a meatpacker.

But I didn't know any of this in 1980. I took a bus to New York City and arrived at campus in my "good" jeans, secondhand sandals from my mom, and a shirt from Hills, a discount store near my hometown that was kind of like K-Mart. As a seventeen-year-old freshman who'd been carrying chickens a couple years earlier, I didn't know there were things like prep schools and trust funds, but my classmates quickly gave me a nose full. For instance, one day when I was riding in an elevator in my dorm, I made an idle comment about something in my tote bag. The young woman riding in the elevator with me said excitedly, "You went to Choate?"

I didn't understand what she was talking about at first, and then I did. "I went to public school," I said. "I said 'tote bag.'"

"Oh, I thought you said 'Choate bag.'"

"Did you go to Choate?"

"I went to Miss Porter's."

I was ready to go on talking about the differences between private and public schools, about her experiences at Miss Porter's—whatever the situation called for. But the young woman turned and faced front, signaling the end of the conversation. I felt awkward, but I got the sense that the other girl felt even more awkward. I didn't know anything about what distinguished Choate from Porter's, but I did know the loudest, most obnoxious girl in my French class—the one Monsieur Nowak had to reprimand in class—had gone to Miss Porter's. (I now know the 2007–8 fees for tuition and boarding at Choate Rosemary Hall were $39,000. At Miss Porter's, they were $40,000.)

Another classmate of mine taught me a lesson at the start of a spring semester when I was standing in line waiting to talk to someone at the financial-aid office. This particular young woman entered the room, dropped a mink coat onto a chair, and jumped to the head of the line. She turned to all of us standing there and said, "It will just take a second."

A mink coat? In the financial-aid office? I knew everyone in that line must have been thinking the same thing. None of us said a word, though, including me. But inside I seethed.

At Barnard, I didn't know what to study. Math and science were out of the question, and I felt out of place every time I ventured onto the third floor of Barnard Hall, where the English Department was housed. The intense young women there all seemed to have artfully arranged hair and striking outfits that paired vintage sweaters with impeccable skirts— or vintage hairstyles artfully paired with impeccable sweaters. Whatever the equation was, I couldn't achieve it, not with my blocky body, just as I could never achieve the polish even ten-year-old girls had on Madison Avenue, waiting for the M4 bus to take them home after a day of private school at Brearly, Dalton, or Spence.

Since I couldn't match the sartorial sense or dramatic demeanor of Barnard English majors, I ended up in the Anthropology Department, where I wasn't intimidated by wardrobes, and where reading ethnographies was almost like reading novels. Though I couldn't have put it into words at the time, I think studying things like acculturation, or individuals who had to keep a foot in two cultures, appealed to me because it was my own story. On one of my trips home, my mother told me that at first she worried that I'd change when I went away to school and somehow come to think I was too good for her and my father.

"But you didn't change like that," my mom said. "You're the same as you always were."

I didn't tell her I tried to change.

But some things just wouldn't budge. Even though I left my hometown, it was in me all the same. In one of just a couple of English classes I let myself take at Barnard—Fiction I with Professor Elizabeth Dalton— the stories I ended up writing nearly all revolved around those early jobs of picking pears and waiting tables. I couldn't stop myself from writing about work.

Those stink jobs were mine.

By my senior year at Barnard, I was both grateful and bitter about the school that gave me an education. At my graduation, when all the athletes got recognized for their participation in sports, I wondered why the college couldn't somehow recognize students like me, young women who knocked themselves out juggling classes and one or two or three jobs, just so they could pay for tuition or buy books and food. But after lunching on the stale sandwiches the college provided for new graduates and their families (families who had just forked out $40,000-plus for their daughters' educations), I figured out the answer to my own question: for working students like me, the recognition was the diploma itself. We'd been allowed a place at the table, and if we didn't have time to participate in sports or campus activities, well, that was the bargain.

And would I have wanted to forgo my college job anyway? I started working at the Academy of American Poets at seventeen, addressing envelopes and typing up letters for $4.50 an hour, and I stayed there all through my college years. Because of that job, I met and heard many writers read, including Richard Hugo, Lucille Clifton, and Louise Erdrich. Those years, work wasn't just where I earned a living—work was where I learned and lived.

After graduating from Barnard, I supported myself by teaching high school English in Brooklyn. I liked the job and my students; I taught everything from the *Odyssey* to *Things Fall Apart*. But within a year I was applying to graduate school. I wanted a master of fine arts. My waitress and pear picking stories got me into the University of Iowa Writer's Workshop.

I loved Iowa. I could afford to live without roommates—unheard of for a New Yorker. I took a writing workshop with Jim Salter my first semester. I took French classes because the Workshop gave you that kind of freedom. And right before I graduated, I wrote a story that somehow seemed different from everything I'd written in the past. It was called "The Work in Tulpehocken County," and it was a story about a young woman who worked on a chicken farm, an orchard, and a restaurant.

Day after day I sat in a study carrel at the Iowa City Public Library and wrote sentences and recast them. I felt like I was learning how to write in the truest voice I'd ever used, and it felt like I was learning a new language. I kept Alice Munro's "Turkey Season" in my bag at all times, and that story was a kind of talisman to me. If Munro could write about a character who cleaned turkey innards, maybe I could write about carrying chickens. I was also able to write my way into the piece because I was in Elizabeth Tallent's workshop at the time, and I felt understood and championed by her. When I stopped writing, I had a piece about forty pages long.

But I didn't know how to go any further with it. It was too long to be a short story and not long enough to be a novel. Maybe if I had some more time in school or more guidance, I could have done something more with the piece, but when I graduated in 1989, I put it and all my other writing away.

"The Work in Tulpehocken County" stayed tucked away for about four years, until I wrote a collection of short stories. The collection didn't sell, but I got enough encouragement from agents and editors that I decided to try to write a novel. By this time I was living and teaching in Minnesota, so I rented a lake cabin in the northern part of the state for my summer vacation in 1995, and I started writing. A lot of my motivation was financial. I knew the only possible way I stood of getting free from the grind of high school teaching was to sell a book.

I didn't know how to write a novel, especially how to begin one, so I did what I could to make the process less threatening: I took short stories that dealt with the same characters, and I looked for ways to put them together. Sitting at a table that was shoved up against the stove, I pillaged all my old stories. I cut them up, I melted them down, I sewed them together—I don't know what metaphor to use. That's how *Swimming Sweet Arrow* started. The book was a mess for a long time, until I followed a friend's advice and let the voice from my Iowa City story, from "The Work in Tulpehocken County," take over and narrate the entire novel.

Vangie Starr Raybuck, my working-class narrator, made me able to write my novel. Her voice kept the novel focused and urgent. I didn't know she was going to change my life.

Swimming Sweet Arrow is an explicit coming-of-age story. When I was writing the book, I figured the sexuality in the book would draw attention—hell, I hoped it would draw attention. But what I mostly did was focus on honestly telling Vangie's story, in her voice. I wrote as viscerally about the jobs my narrator Vangie held as I did about the sex she had.

Once the book was published, some people roundly criticized the graphic nature of the novel. A coworker called me a pornographer, and one local reviewer said my characters were "poor and aimless" and "losers." Other people liked the honesty of the book. I was compared to Kate Chopin in one review, and another christened me "the Anaïs Nin of Minnesota." All I can say is that I wrote a book from which there was no turning back. I quit my job teaching high school. I won a prestigious grant, a grant for which Joy Harjo was one of the final judges; I often envisioned her standing on the other side of a canyon, calling to me to step out into the air, telling me a bridge would form beneath my feet if I trusted. I bought a house "up north" on ten acres of land, complete with American toads, big bluestem grass, and black bears. I got a job at the local newspaper in my new hometown and covered everything from the shenanigans of the county commissioners to the prize-winning pigs at the county fair. I married. My father got sick. I turned forty. I kept writing.

Now when people ask me what *Swimming Sweet Arrow* is about, I say, "Sex and drugs and rock and roll." It's a silly answer, but I've given up on saying anything else. People can read the book or not, and they can like it or not. I'm proud of it, and I'm glad I wrote it. And I think my narrator is anything but aimless. She got different jobs, each a little better than the last, and she worked hard. She didn't attempt to make a bad relationship better by having a child. To me, Vangie is a star. I know she set me free.

There is one other thing my novel about working-class life helped me achieve: it got me my current job teaching writing at a small college in northern Minnesota. For this tenure-track position, I had to have at least one published book at the time of hire, and Vangie filled the bill. And I think I'm pretty much in the right place. As a result of writing assignments I've given in my college classes for the last two years, I know I've taught any number of first-generation college students. And because I asked my students to write about work for a process analysis paper, I also know they've held or are holding the kind of jobs I once had. Many of my students have worked in restaurants, while others have worked in lumber mills and factories. This past semester, I learned in class discussions that one of my students worked on a turkey farm, while another worked on a pheasant farm.

I told those students, "I can relate."

Sails with Good People

⤙ HEATHER SELLERS

Doubt is not a pleasant state of mind, but certainty is absurd.
— VOLTAIRE

Many years ago I arrived at the department Christmas party in the pleasant Silver Fox Shores subdivision, held in the home of my former department chair. I knocked on the door. I was right on time, as I always am, and as I always am: absolutely uncertain.

Keep knocking? Walk in?

I stood in the foyer, and looked around for someone I knew. For a way in to the room. I took off my down jacket and accidentally dropped it on the floor. It landed like a pillow and wrong, like a sigh, a terrible fuchsia *plumpf*. At this moment, the host appeared.

And patted heartily on the back a tall tan man, who'd also drifted into the foyer. Three of us, suddenly sharing air space. Me. The tall, tanned-in-winter man, the portly department head. Both of them in heathery sweater vests over holiday bellies.

My coat lay on the parquet between us like a small hot-pink down-filled human corpse. I wanted to kick it aside, disown it, and thereby distance myself from every single mistake I've ever made.

My department chair looked at his fellow man, and then at me. My chair said to me, "He sails with good people." He thumbs-upped his friend and they smiled and nodded in unison.

These are kind men.

The tan man who sails with good people reached out his hand while my own arms pasted themselves against my body, against my will, as if shellacked.

And simultaneously this sentence, *he sails with good people,* plunge cut, like a Sawzall fitted with the rip blade, in a cartoon, a circle in the hardwood floor on which I was standing and whoosh, I dropped right down, out of sight, presto, I was one hundred miles below the party falling faster and faster, arms pasted to my sides. I gasped for air, deep in the earth below the department chairman's pseudo-French home on Fox Run Way.

He sails with good people.

He sails with good people?

Above me, a hand, outstretched, moving toward me in slow-mo, for the *how do you do?*

Not always so well.

This is not about the sailboat, the blunder, the club, the boy's club, the secret club, the yacht club, or the fact that my department chair knows perfectly well what my name is, how to introduce two people—it's not about old resentments, hating the rich.

There are more interesting and more invisible principles of poverty and class operating here, luffing in the opening line: *he sails with good people.*

My mom didn't pay our light bill, and several times each year of my childhood the electricity was turned off. The oil man didn't refill the reserve; we could conserve, she said. She had a witchy pointer finger and she used it.

We huddled. We slept with her for warmth. She said, "Isn't this kind of fun? We're on the frontier."

Yikes.

I slept like a parenthesis. Kept my mouth shut.

The water was shut off by a man with a long silver rod with a little frowning mouth at the end. The garbage went uncollected. Orange stickers stuck on our front door—*dispose of the junk in the yard or else.* I went to fifteen different schools before I graduated high school. We lived in trailers and other people's apartments; we called people who weren't related to us "Uncle Roy" and "Grandma Hazel." When we got our mail, she often liked to put it, undisturbed, directly into the trash. Trash makes things hush. This unopened mail in the garbage, pristine envelopes comingling with coffee grounds and tuna cans and wadded paper towels—about killed me.

Sometimes, after weeks of buildup and letdown and overflow and darkness, we finally bagged our house trash, our littlest movable trash—tissues and coffee grounds and notebook paper and waxy generic fish sticks boxes, and drove it all out to the county dump near Okahumpka.

I gripped them by their necks and flung the black plastic bags into the pit.

My mother wept in the truck.

I held my nose.

I worried body parts somehow had gotten in to our trash; I worried we had put them there ourselves.

While I flung the terrible fleshy-weighted bags into the stinking hole, my brother destroyed the detritus on the edges of the pit. The laziest worst most abandoned trash of all. Not even in the pit with its kin. A festering box springs. Milk jugs. A green vinyl upholstered side chair, psycho-slit: my brother plucked gold moist foam out of it, flicking the bits up into the air, tricking seagulls.

They think it's food. Ha ha. Suckers.

"We are upper-middle-class, in the middle, but I would say the upper-upper section of the middle upper," my mother would say. "I just don't waste money on junk made in China." She said we lived within our means: that was our big secret. That's why our lives looked so different. We were responsible and not living on credit. We marched to our own drummer. We were not sheep.

We bought our food at a series of day-old and wholesale outlets. She knew where to find pecan wheels, three dozen for ten cents, veal patties, six for a quarter.

She seemed clever and quick; she never worked for long. She was thin. She loved coffee cake and angel food cake and all cake, especially breakfast cake.

My mother's constant caution: Do not tell anyone anything ever.

They'll take you from me. I will lose you, and you will live in an institution and you will not do well there.

It's unspeakable, what happens in those places. She'd been to one. On a tour. Some kind of tour.

The rubber room, my brother said. Heh heh.

Worse, she said. *Much* worse.

When *Sails with Good People* is introduced to me in this awkward, thumbs-up way, in this foyer, with its groomed wood squares, and he reaches out, and that soft long arm, with its cushiony professorial hand, is coming to me, coming at me, it's this past life that flashes before my eyes as I drop.

We didn't starve; poverty doesn't really work like that, with clear cordoned-off areas. There were weeks I was hungry every night. Poverty's messy, foggy; you still have fun.

We could have a bowl of puffed cereal anytime, bought from the Nut House in dusty plastic sacks tied with string. My brother loved the Nut House policy he said he'd read on the wall of the warehouse, *ten percent infestation* allowed by law.

She said: *Do not tell anyone anything ever.*

My brother flicked me on the head regularly in those days. He treated me the same way he treated trash.

We were hungry.

We were turning on each other.

The poverty I'm talking about is *poverty of the imagination* and that's the definition of mental illness.

Both of my parents are mentally ill.

I am not even close to calling the department chair mentally ill or academia insane; he's not and it isn't.

But it's possible to sail with good people and never really be in actual water, moved by actual wind. Yet be under the impression you are making great progress, at terrific speed, Godspeed. For example, my current department wants to increase its "class diversity." It wants people who do not sail with good people to come be with people who do; this is supposed to be good for everyone involved. It's good but it's also very hard and confusing for everyone involved.

When those of us from outside the college-bound class enter the homes of our suddenly new peers, we are bound by uncertainty: how to behave, how to feel, how to think, how to be?

What academia and mental illness and *Sails with Good People* have in common is certainty.

Mental patients typically have reasons for what they do, and if you can get your head around it, their actions usually make a kind of sense. It is sureness, certainty, they have in common, in contrast to our trashy constant doubt, insecurity, wonder, and alarm.

Our ship was going down. My brother was sent away for petty theft and grand theft; then my father, for slower, waxier, middle-aged versions of the same crimes. I was crystallizing at home, with my mother, who said I was the most important thing in her life. She also said I had to try to get over my emotional problems; my propensity toward histrionics was going to make life difficult, very difficult for me.

My family is mentally ill; we all thought *I* was the nut. I didn't see the men trying to break in to our house; I didn't see the reasons to leave in the middle of the night. I didn't ever see the sinister soldiers—imposter soldiers—steering the convoys that my mother enjoyed following, all the way to the Space Coast. We always came back from these runs as we came back from the normal full-price grocery store, beautiful Publix: *empty-handed.* I was always thinking *it's time to start getting ready for dinner.* I felt plain and dumb and I didn't fit in. I thought it was okay that I was crazy but not okay to turn out like them.

I vowed to always do the opposite of whatever they would do, in any situation. This is a dangerous, primitive way to make a self.

My mom was bankrupt, she had very little to give, she was struggling to stay alive. She couldn't leave the house without checking that the doors were locked, six, seven, eight times, getting in the truck, backing out of the driveway, and pulling back in, leaving the engine running while she again checked. Then she couldn't leave the house. Next, she couldn't talk, couldn't move—she was turning to a wax version of herself in her bed. Then, people were trying to get in the house. She pasted herself against the walls in the kitchen, the hallway. We had to keep the lights off so they wouldn't know we were in here. We had to walk on our knees, stay below the window line. Her soul was a subsistence farm, her sense of a self a ghost town. *Don't tell anyone anything, not ever* was how she was keeping us alive.

Paranoid schizophrenia is one of the poorest counties in the nation. Though it was never my address, for a long time, it's where the mail came.

When you grow up with the mantra—*don't tell anyone anything ever*—

there is only one career path available to you: *tell everyone everything always.*

At a typewriter my father stole from Martin Marietta before he was fired, I set up at the end of the kitchen, on the floor, as far as I could get from my mother and brother but still see them.

They talked at great length with great certainty about things they knew nothing about.

Academia: it feels like home.

I typed out the conversations she and my brother had. I wrote everything down. Writing them down, I felt like I was pinning them like butterflies, mounting them for close study.

The electric typewriter vibrated under my fingertips like it was alive. It *was* alive. We were both electrified.

"You better not be typing what I think you're typing," my mother called to me occasionally. Like you holler to the neighbor's dog: "Stop that barking."

My sweet wild handful, Fred, my father, is from Somerset, Kentucky, between Mammoth Cave and the mental institution. He likes to tell people he is from Possum Trot. He's not. But it makes him sound like *he* sails with good people. It's so pleasing to say, why not wedge into every possible conversation?

My father likes to talk about how greasy and rubbery possum is, in the pan and in the mouth; his mother cooked it some and he did once. (My first publisher, based in Kentucky, wanted possum cooking out of my first book—too much of a stereotype. I said no, it has to stay in. The possum was the only thing I fought for in that book.)

My father likes to hold forth. But it's not long before he's weeping.

My father's dad was a coal miner *as a child*, but it was brutal beatings more than the dark hard work that drove him out of his house and hollow at age fourteen. His grandmother Mallie, whom I was lucky enough to meet, sat on the porch of her shotgun shack with no teeth, smoking a pipe, looking really pissed off, and she was. The women and the children in this history were beaten and broken by the men in this history, and my father's mental illness and alcoholism was how he coped with the blows. The booze was his body of water, what held him, and the illness was how he sailed, his inspiration. He believes he is free. He's fond of this creation.

My mother's hallucinations and mania kept her busy—in cycles, she was out and about. My father rarely left the house. He ordered expensive steaks and shrimp in the mail on credit; he prodded me to cook, cook, cook, and clean up. He believed the homeless drug addicts to whom he gave thousands and thousands of dollars were fixing the roof, completing the game room addition. That *I* was the one stealing his tools. He drank around the clock and couldn't keep his hands to himself or far from weaponry, but because he liked the idea of a big dinner, variety meats and lobster, prime rib, biscuits and greens and desserts, and he didn't have my mother's urge to drive us over bridges into deep water (*Save yourself! Don't worry about me!*), it was more relaxing to live with him than with my mother and so we did and we got hit and we learned the key to uncertainty: how to escape while standing right there, how to be in two places at once. Right and wrong, hurts and doesn't, love and hate, loyalty and pain. It's that bi-location trick that every artist has to learn, somehow.

Like my mother, my father was certain I was mentally handicapped. "You got to be more like me," he would say. "You gots to try to be free."

I tried and I didn't try.

Back in the foyer of the chairman's lovely home in the leafy subdivision, it's true I have missed a beat, and it's possible I have glowered, or made a strange noise, but I do pull it off, in the nick of time: I shake hands with *Sails with Good People* and I have to trust he can't see the dump buzzards circling around my head. (They haven't heard the screaming. They're not listening for it. This is academia. The walls are padded with dusty books and good intentions.)

I shake hands with him, long, full, shaking, my palm damp as ripe fruit.

Can he tell where I have been?

Can he smell a rat?

I tell *Sails with Good People* my name, while my balding department chair stands there, inexplicably, dumb, and as I do I bend down to pick up my dropped coat, still between us like a bad idea. And as we haven't quite let go of each other's hands, when I bend down, down by his shiny skinny shoes, and it hits me: I am the opposite of everything I expected—not the poor girl, not the distant, benevolent professor I intended, either. I'm something in between and that's where I need to be in order to see. And I discover that as I bend down I am pulling him. I am pulling him down. And grinning.

First Class Back to the Summer of Love

❧ JUDITH ORTIZ COFER

Someone smashes a cigarette butt on the outside of my window ledge. I tap on the glass with my fingernails to let him/her of the blue-black nail polish know that there is a life being lived within these ancient hallowed walls of academia. He/she presses his/her nose to the glass trying to see in. I let down the blind against the humanity—oh, the humanity. I return to my fat folder of "Visions of America in the New Millennium," the essay assignment I have given my Multicultural American Literature class. After reading about life on the rez, the barrio, the ghetto, the Chinatown; about the Japanese internment, the Black Power movement, the Chicano Renaissance, the Puerto Rican Diaspora, I asked them to give shape to *their* personal vision of America, and to write a brief history of their time, and how their experiences shaped their individual American identity.

"I grew up in a suburb of Atlanta. Life was not always easy. My mother sat around watching reruns of *This Old House* and my father was married to his job at CNN, at least that's what my mother said about him. I hardly ever saw him. On weekends my mother shopped at Lenox Square, or took long walks at the Botanical Gardens, while my father did his second job, as he called it; he was a slave to 'lawn maintenance.' My vision of America may be different from that of the African Americans, the Native Americans, the Mexican Americans, and the Lesbians and Gays in your class, Professor Cofer, but that doesn't mean that I have not been oppressed. In high school I was the lonely bookworm . . ."

I put that one down and pick at random from the pile.

"All through high school I kept a secret. I lived alone. Both my parents were sent to prison for selling drugs, and my grandmother got custody of me. But one day she just up and left for her sister's in Alabama. The message on my cell phone said 'You a big girl now, Shakilla, I had two babies when I was your age. You can take care of yourself. Check comes every month and food stamps; you know how to sign my name. Too old for this. Going home to Alabama to die in peace.' She left some numbers where I could call other kin I never met. Never used them. Got this Hope Scholarship all on my own. My vision of America in the new millennium is that you still look out for yourself, nobody's going to get your back. I'm going to be a lawyer, make money, maybe get my folks out."

Another afternoon, I am at my desk, writing. I should be reading student papers. Instead, I'm trying to work on an essay I promised a fellow writer for an anthology she is editing. She has requested a meditation on class in America and how I overcame economic and social class limitations to become a writer and a professor. The topic makes me a little bit dizzy. It's the travel malaise I sometimes experience when I try to enter that treacherous time-warping wormhole to the struggles in my past that now seem like either boasting (see how I have suffered more than you, my fellow Americans) or family gossip. I may just write a poem on the sepia hue and the warping on my office window, caused by generations of cigarette smoke. It's rather intriguing to see the lovely faces of the young through my glass darkly. Now that the smokers have moved to the lawn of this neo-classical temple where Literature and Classics are housed, I have turned my chair to face the window to catch the last rays. The late afternoon sun has called the students to lie on the ground and warm their skin like iguanas in blue jeans. A lie-in for narcissism. They are protesting winter. They want to heat their blood for the Friday-night mating dance.

Turning back to face my blank sheet of paper, I notice a shadow moving across the opaque glass on my office door, someone politely letting me know that he is waiting for me to leave my office so he can dust, mop, empty the trash basket. If I decide to stay until midnight, he will have to either await my pleasure, or come back early in the morning on a weekend to pick up after me.

"No, Josh," I say to Josh #1. "I said I *lived* through the Woodstock era. I said it changed my life, as it did many others of my generation. I had friends, a little older than I, who went to Woodstock." (*Yes, I say to myself, it is possible to be a little older than I am, Class. Hard for people born in the '80s to believe that I was not in a soup line during the Great Depression.*)

Josh #1 speaks the name of the place reverently. *Woodstock.* He sits to my right, absorbing what's left of my 1960s-era aura. He stares at me as if beneath my disguise of a middle-aged woman who should be addressed as Professor, there is perhaps a wild young thing once called by the name of a flower or the title of a song (*Professor Blossom? Professor Brown-Eyed Girl?*), one whom he doesn't dare yet imagine dressed in gauzy see-through Indian garments, starry-eyed, dancing ecstatically at the sacred festival. Josh reads my poems for signs and clues of my alternate existence. He cannot believe I have not written about the most significant event in rock and roll history. I will only answer direct questions on the subject of the '60s (a decade I am covertly researching in order to be one step ahead of them), and only because it serves me as a pedagogical hook, a way to get their wandering attention fixed on an optical illusion while I inject poetry into their veins. It's also refreshing to be seen as the old hippie as opposed to the multicultural representative and expert on oppression, American style.

Josh is being sponsored as a dreamer by his single-parent father, a lonely rocket scientist somewhere in Texas, an expert on photographing the surface of the moon and Mars, who adores his only child. I met the elder star-gazer during parents' day for honors students, and I know that my idealistic Josh #1 is one of the lucky ones. He will be allowed to follow the wanderings of his imagination with the safety net of unqualified love always beneath him, a nice change from many of my other younger students, whose career goals were programmed in with their pre-school alphabet lessons by their helicopter parents. Even my Josh #2 is in pre-law, an enthusiastic member of every major student organization. He is the best poet in my class, but I will not tell him that he is a natural-born writer, unless he asks. He will get his law degree with an emphasis on minority issues. His mother is a prominent political figure and an activist, and so she is his entrée into the elite law firms and political life in Atlanta.

I have not met this busy woman. I only know that my best poet, Josh #2, is doomed to succeed in following someone else's American vision.

"With your help I am going to find your friends at Woodstock, Professor Cofer, and post the pictures on my Web page. It will be a collage made up of group photos, each person digitally enhanced. My father says it can be done. I've found a high school yearbook picture of you in 1968 on the Web, Professor Cofer! Can I put it up too?"

Ay, ay, ay bendito. I will not tell them that even digitally enhanced neither Josh nor anyone who visits his psychedelic Web site will be able to really see who I was then. What they may expect to see is their teacher in pupa stage, someone training toward correct grammar, and guiding them through the intricacies of their native language. If they could fit in my one-woman time machine, and drop into my life in the late '60s, they would find themselves in the immigrant's limbo that was my reality then. Back then, I did not know, could not realistically hope, that I would become an American woman, much less a writer and teacher. Like many Puerto Ricans of their generation, my parents were "trying out" America. As U.S. citizens, we have the option to be undecided as to what we will be: Puerto Ricans or Puerto Rican–Americans.

Our future was negotiated at the kitchen table. Any day my parents could declare that they'd had enough of *la lucha* in the cold, foreign city, and go back to their familiar hardships in Puerto Rico. No, I don't think my students would recognize the insecure girl I was then. I am so assertive in the classroom (perhaps as a result of my deeply ingrained fear of being outed as an impersonator), that they cannot possibly imagine I was once the silent student in the back of the room. By making myself invisible I felt safe from the humiliation I had witnessed and experienced over "broken" English. I chose not to volunteer to speak until I had the necessary number of words in English, until I shed my fear of sounding "dumb" because of my thick accent and my stumbling over difficult sounds. I was the unobtrusive sponge on the bottom of the ocean, taking it all in, waiting until I felt adequate in volume and weight, until I had presence.

I touch Josh's arm lightly to let him know I appreciate his attention to my potentially glamorous former being, but I will not let him derail the class discussion toward the date tattooed on his arm and in his tender heart.

In my undergraduate creative writing class, I had assigned them to research the decade that most interested them, and to place themselves or someone in their lives at a particular moment in time. It could be expressed in either prose or poetry. Many of them chose the '60s.

It is Josh #1's turn to present to the class.

"August 1969. The day the souls of 600,000 American youths were lifted to a higher plane. Jim Morrison's songs were my time-machine to this long ago moment that changed the history of rock and roll forever." He leans toward me, heat-seeking. I move my chair a bit farther from his. Touching students even by accident is risky business in this era when an inappropriate facial expression or eye contact or the lack of it can be cause for an inquisition—but I can always claim culture made me do it.

Latinos are such touchy-feely people. Public displays of affection are so prevalent among us that to others it must seem a genetic trait. But touching one another is a privilege we give ourselves in my culture. The right to give and expect affection and comfort on demand. At least this is the way it worked in my family and community. Never more so than in the year when my family's hopes for peace and prosperity in America began to give way to the dark months of senseless assassinations, riots, and a war that was dividing and subdividing us; there was dissent between the leaders and the people, parents and children, the races, men and women, gays and straights. Everyone had a fight to pick. My parents feared losing their tenuous claim to a life in this country, and they feared losing control over us. So they clung, passing their fears to us through words and touch, and we were all afraid together.

By 1968 Paterson was an urban disaster. Racial turmoil had been building in our city, and it peaked as the assassinations of Martin Luther King Jr. and then, incredibly, of Robert Kennedy took over the headlines, and we were at the throbbing epicenter of the crumbling structure: 45 Park Avenue, our ironic upper-class-sounding street address located in the middle of one of those American neighborhoods that are like seawalls, encrusted with all that the waves wash onshore. We lived in a house originally owned by Italian immigrants, later by Jewish immigrants of the post–World War II years, and eventually subdivided into apartments to house the Puerto Ricans, Dominicans, African Americans, the ever-changing ethnic and racial multitudes. The danger of such a volatile mix came to a head during the riots in Newark and Trenton that spilled over to neighboring cities like Paterson.

While the middle-class offspring of America grew their hair long and shaggy, marched for peace, racial and gender equality, and the other privileges they believed belonged to all Americans, in my family we kept close to home, and we held our intense kitchen-table councils, where we children were told to walk straight to school and back home, and where our civil liberties (which we didn't know we had) were curtailed further each time there was a drive-by shooting by rival gangs or a looting of nearby businesses reported. No going out after dark, no bringing friends over, who might turn out to be false friends, troublemakers "casing the joint" to invade our home and violate us when Father was away. My mother embarrassed me by trying to hold my hand when we walked downtown to shop on Saturdays. Her fears went with us and came home with us. She kissed us and hugged us when we left for school in the morning as if we were going to be separated for years. My friends teased me about my clingy Puerto Rican mother and over-protective father, but I knew this was not normal behavior even for my relatives. Paranoia burrowed itself into our psyches that year, a parasite that would remain in our systems, feeding off of our insecurities, forever. It went south with us in our exodus from Paterson the year of the Summer of Love.

"Come on, Baby / light my fire," I quote from Josh's piece. "Let us begin by discussing what line breaks do to the music of a poem. No, Josh, Josh is not plagiarizing Jim Morrison unless he publishes this poem. This is an exercise in form, remember? We will compose original poems for the next assignment. No, Josh, Morrison's lyrics do not belong to the people. They are copyrighted. I don't think Josh meant to accuse you of stealing, Josh. Can we get back to line breaks? I suggest we read this poem, or song if you will, as it appears on the page. We can discuss copyright laws later. Jennifer? Yes. Jennifer Kelly. Oh, Jennifer Reingold? I'm sorry. Jennifer, go ahead. Jennifer Kelly dropped the class? Okay. I'll make note of that. So, Jennifer, what effect does breaking "Light My Fire" into three-word lines have on us? You don't know Jim Morrison's music? Can we get Josh to post an answer to your question on our e-mail list?"

Sorry, my dear students nostalgic for a glamorized past. No. Woodstock made a minimal impression on me. The only person I knew who had actually been to Woodstock was an undersized boy everyone at St. Joseph's School in Paterson called Billy the Bud. It became his claim to fame. I heard him tell his tale three times, and each one escalated in drama to the point where he claimed to have been airlifted in a helicopter after he tasted some of that "bad stuff, man—tainted LSD." Maybe it was true that the experience transformed him; his overdue secondary sex characteristics kicked in soon after. He grew a red beard, which got him suspended. He became a popular guy.

Woodstock meant little to my family and consequently to me.

We were not involved in popular culture; we were involved in *la lucha*. Our discussions started and ended in the kitchen of our Paterson, New Jersey, apartment. Our father brought the news from the world to us and translated it to Spanish for Mother. And the only news that interested them had to do with our finances, our personal safety, and my brother's and my education. All else was mainstream chatter, background noise.

By early 1969, the talk in the barrio was focused on the tensions and conflicts in the streets, schools, and factories; the unrest we saw in black and white on our televisions touched everyone's lives in living color one way or another: businesses shut down in "dangerous" neighborhoods— the Italian brothers who owned the American grocery store on our street were particularly aloof with their Latino customers, and kept an unfriendly eye on us while we shopped. I no longer enjoyed the flirtatious banter they had carried on with me and other *muchachas* who were sent in for the odd item (our parents bought their soul food from the Island at the bodega), such as a carton of L&M cigarettes for my mother, or a loaf of Wonder Bread, which I preferred over the hard, crusty loaves of *pan* my family ate. I had a crush on the nephew, who worked at the Italian brothers' store part-time, and he had encouraged my interest, if only to practice his flirting skills.

But the Year of Little Love in America, 1968, had created an atmosphere of suspicion among us that even I, at fifteen and trying hard just to be normal, just to be liked and fit in, could not ignore. When I felt eyes on me in the store, it wasn't an admirer's gaze. I was being watched as a potential troublemaker. This feeling of "looking suspicious" in stores, airports, and other public places has stayed with me. I learned that to certain people, I do not look innocent or trustworthy. In fact, as someone who works for the airlines explained to me, I bear a general resemblance to the composite sketch of the female terrorist all security personnel are trained to notice. In 1968, before the feminist movement had made us women more equal to male criminals to discerning eyes, I must have fit the profile for the juvenile delinquent's girlfriend. I trace my social paranoia to that time: the year I stopped believing that it was the new reconfigurations of my body that were attracting the attention of men. It is a dismaying sense of disappointment I still experience when I realize that I am being assessed and measured by a clerk in a store where I may be lingering too long in the aisle of designer bags that, in her mind, I surely cannot afford. The only benefit to this mercantile profiling is that I get to pay for my purchases faster than the trusted customers who must catch the eyes of scurrying cashiers since they do not have employees following them.

Another Friday afternoon, and the halls are practically empty. We the academic elite observe the social Friday as well as any third-world country. Our business of leading the examined life for the sake of Western civilization ends early. I hear the custodian revving up the waxing machine. The smokers are scattering toward their tribal longhouses to light their fires. I catch a final glimpse of the late-day sun illuminating the columned facades and cupolaed rooftops on this university campus where I have found my intellectual home-place. I am safely ensconced within the ivory tower and I feel at home among my stacks of papers, my books, and my generation after generation of students. My future turned out to be a place I could not envision in my childhood or early youth, because no one in my family had attended college, much less imagined one of us making a living that did not involve *la lucha*. I believe I earned the price of every brick in my little turret. Yet I am always aware that I will have to work harder than the other members of this club to prove what I know and what I can do, mainly because I just don't look the part of the university professor. And when I step outside, I am once again the suspicious outsider. I put on "privilege" in the morning like a fine winter coat that protects me from inclement weather, but it is a borrowed garment, like those men's jackets and ties that some fine restaurants keep in case a customer walks in "inappropriately dressed." I have to walk outside in my own skin, which to some people still represents, if not a threat, a bit of a challenge.

I hear the custodian moving around and around, doing his slow waltz with the floor waxer, down the hall toward my end of the building. I stuff my students' essays in my take-work-home book bag that will look pregnant (I refuse to buy a bigger one; to me it is like buying a larger size in clothes, an accommodation for more fat, more work, encouragement to fill the vacuum). The size of the bag's belly predicts my immediate future: a weekend of grading visions of America, and because I am an obsessive writer, of thinking about my own essay or poem, influenced, as it will inevitably be, by the comparison and contrast of my past to my present, of the visions of America I had, the ones I encounter, and the one I must constantly revise as I live.

The black man polishing the marble floors of this Hitchcockian hall of endless numbered doors nods solemnly at me as I tiptoe out, letting him know that I respect the lake effect of his work by my caution, my restraint. I will not be jocular, nor falsely wish him a good weekend. His movements are a waltz back and forth in measured, elegant, swaying sweeps he makes his own silent dance. What does he think about? *My* brain does not allow me to rest even in repetitive movement. I take no pleasure in the Zen of ironing or the Tao of cooking. The only time I am still (more or less) is when I'm writing. But, if this man has achieved tranquility in this, his solitary task done outside philosophy, I envy him. He nods in my direction without smiling. I nod back at him, neither of us attempting to lock eyes in some pretense of mutual understanding. He is not looking at me anyway; it takes his full attention and weight to operate his heavy machine.

I have left the first few lines of a poem lying on my desk. I will start whatever I am writing as a poem, and I will follow it to my subject: fact and fiction, myth, images, memories. The poem will always lead me to the truth. I have invented and reinvented myself in lines; in poetry I have created a refuge where I can distill my painful memories and make bittersweet liquor out of my most painful and/or joyful discoveries. It is the dissection of these images in straightforward prose that makes me a bit queasy. Memory is as malleable as any of the raw materials I use to make my art. Time changes the past's colors and textures, sometimes softening them like butter on a lens, and other times warping the reflections, turning remembered scenes into funhouse images. Poetry allows me to defend my artifact, my made thing. The truth. I want to be able to claim with Virginia Woolf, "This is how I shape it."

In 1968 America went wild. Martin Luther King's assassination ignited riots in cities across the nation. Then Robert Kennedy's senseless murder left even my politically alienated family stunned. Father decided that we could not stay in Paterson since he was away several months each year on tours with the navy, and he feared for our safety. My parents spent a great deal of time arguing as to where we should move. My mother wanted us to return to her mother's house in Puerto Rico; Father did not want us to interrupt our education in English. He had come up with a "temporary" solution. We would move to Augusta, Georgia, for a year or two, until things calmed down in Paterson. His two brothers were stationed in Fort Gordon with the army, and we had teenage cousins there. My brother, then twelve, and I, fifteen, threw fits. We did not want to move away. Not that we loved our socially limited lives in Paterson, but Augusta sounded like a foreign land. And it was. We left our familiar war zone of the inner city just before the Summer of Love, and headed south toward a new American life we could not imagine.

In Georgia we had to explore a different landscape and we had to relearn spoken English with new inflections, acquaint ourselves with another set of customs and boundaries. We became aware that there are many Americas, and Georgia is as different an America from New Jersey as a peach is from a mango, and that saying we were from New Jersey and thus Yankees was at times a more socially awkward admission than explaining our ethnicity. Race in the South is a subtle system little understood by outsiders, and it was with a mixture of dismay and relief that I found myself neither in the center nor quite on the margins of turmoil and tensions of the Civil Rights era in the Deep South. There were not enough brown people here to make us players of any significance. I could stay silent and invisible until I knew if I wanted to remain in this America.

I am a cosmic distance from the New Jersey Puerto Rican girl who channeled her parents' fears and their all-consuming sense of being strangers in a strange land. I have lived in the Deep South most of my adult life with my family, and I have learned to see the beauty of the place where my husband and daughter feel most at home. I have learned how to navigate the complex nature of race and class relations by maneuvering through the labyrinth daily. Who and what I am to others changes by a simple act of leaving my office building on a traditional university campus where I enjoy all the rights and privileges and the attendant irritations of being a chaired professor in English. In English. Who would have believed it'd be possible in my Paterson days? If my parents had moved us back to the Island in 1969 instead of to Augusta, would I have led a parallel life in Spanish? Maybe.

The difference is that those of us who achieve some measure of success out of class almost never *believe* our identities are real. I cannot ever simply relax and enjoy. I must keep acting like the scholarship kid, a way of being that allowed me to get the education I needed to be whom I could be, and that still helps me achieve my goals. I believe my "malady" is called the impostor complex. I work at everything twice as long and hard as I need to. I joke in class about "losing my English" when I make a mistake, and I suffer agonies after a lecture or a reading, or even a simple conversation, when I think I have revealed my English-as-a-second-language ineptitudes—a wrong usage, failure to respond to cultural clues or to laugh at a joke because I am missing some crucial allusion—keep me awake some nights. Fighting phantoms is part of my parents' negative legacy, as is the feeling that I cannot rest. *La lucha* is forever, even now that I am living in the America I chose, and doing what I want to do. I always have to remind myself that, like Don Quixote, dusting himself off after battling windmills, reclaims his dignity by proclaiming "I know who I am, and who I may be if I choose."

But I don't really believe it. I can't.

Trip Around the World

～ KAREN SALYER MCELMURRAY

Ten students and I are sitting around a rectangular table, sizing each other up. I smooth the legs of my standard professorial attire—black pants, white shirt, minimal cat hair—and tell them it's my third year at this small liberal arts college in central Georgia. *Them?* Six women and four men, ages twenty-two to forty-five, variously from Wisconsin, rural Georgia and Alabama, New York, D.C. MFA students in our graduate program in creative writing. One is a former DJ and actor. Another just left D.C. corporate life. One tends bar at a Midwestern cowboy place. Another is a former powwow jingle dancer. The young woman from upstate New York confides that she has just converted from Catholicism to Judaism. *Welcome,* I say at last, *to Prose Forms and Theory.*

Since Prose Forms and Theory is a little vague to me as a course for creative writing students, I have planned to teach this particular semester a bit differently. We're going to take a look at some forms and styles of prose of some current writers, but we're also going to look at the lives of those writers. Why are they artists of the word? I want my students, by the end of the term, to write an essay which explores why they, themselves, write in any particular way, in any given genre. To examine where the desire to create came from in their lives, and how, even at this early stage, they make this thing called art.

We'll begin tonight, I tell them as I dim the lights, by taking a look at a film, *The Rough South of Harry Crews,* by independent filmmaker Gary Hawkins. The documentary chronicles the writing life of a rough-living, hard-drinking Florida novelist and essayist and short story writer, author of some twenty-seven books. Crews, a dirt farmer's son from South Georgia, has also been a marine, a boxer, and a body builder. There are interviews with literary critics in the film, and there are conversations with a cast of folks from Georgia including Crews's mother and his fellow Southern writer Larry Brown. His writing life, fired by his childhood's Pentecostal religion and by sheer will, has kept Crews alive.

When I flip the lights back on, I just plain admit it. I'm a groupie when it comes to this Hawkins film. I'm right at home when Crews tells us that the folks in Bacon County, Georgia, had little, lived rough, and dreamed dreams right out of the Sears and Roebuck catalog. The red dirt fields of Georgia aren't exactly the mountains of Eastern Kentucky, but they're close. I hand out a sheet with quotes from the film that must serve as prompts for their first nonfiction pieces. *Ritual ways of doing keep us safe. Cut thin nights. I woke in my daddy's arms,* Crews remembers, *with the sweet smell of whiskey and sweat.*

The film, I tell the class, is about the most important part of the writing life, one that isn't a workshop or craft discussion, one that has nothing to do with the publication of manuscripts. *Transcendence.* Along the dirt roads of Bacon County, Crews finds what he calls "ritual ways of doing that keep him safe." A conjure woman from his childhood doesn't save him from infantile paralysis, but she does show him the magic of blackbirds and snakes that might just "spit in his mouth" and change his life forever. Spirit is at work here, I tell these students. It's how my friend, the poet Alice Friman, describes the creating of a poem. *A ghost in the bones.* What, I ask the students, transcends even us when we put words down on a page?

As we begin a discussion, a few students are intrigued by Crews and his Mohawk and his jar of moonshine and the "special considerations under the Lord" that he finds in circus freaks and conjure women. Others nod and say that the film reminds them of home, while some are uncomfortable with toothless dirt farmers and Southern accents so thick they say it's hard to understand the words. Still others are cynical about power in something as ordinary as a flock of blackbirds. The student from New York doesn't, she says, find one more portrayal of hardscrabble existence particularly useful.

My childhood wasn't Bacon County, Georgia, hardscrabble in the way Crews's was, but generations on both sides of my family are working-class. Of the women in my family, none but myself have gone to college

and some, on my mother's side, not even to high school. My father's father was a Standard Oil Service station man, and my mother's a coal
miner. My father and his brother dreamed big, and my uncle Darnell
went to college to study chemistry and became a teacher at Eastern Kentucky University. My father joined the air force, and after that stint he
went back to school on the GI Bill, then took a job teaching high school
math in Harlan County in Eastern Kentucky.

Harlan. For some the word means coal mine disasters and union wars
and some of the worst poverty in the United States. I remember seeing a
family of thirteen children walk up the road mornings to school past our
trailer park. *The Esteps.* My mother spoke disdainfully of this family,
talked about how black their faces and hands and nails were from coal
dust, the same dust she feared contaminated the walls and floors of our
trailer. I went to the same grade school, Lynch Elementary, that the
Esteps did, and my memories of that place are of oiled board floors and
turkey and gravy lunches from Meals on Wheels. At singing circle, a
mop-headed boy sang the theme from *The Beverly Hillbillies* and I remember, with a funny taste in my mouth, how the teacher would get him
up front, give him a toy guitar, and let him lead us in verse after verse. *A
poor mountaineer, barely kept his family fed.*

We weren't exactly poor, but we were trailer park people nonetheless.
My mother and father and I lived in Cumberland, a tiny town one over
from Lynch, where there was a lot on a back street my mother liked as
well as she'd like anywhere not her own parents' home in Floyd County.
High school teaching salaries were low, low enough that my father
signed us up for commodity cheese and peanut butter and his mother
kept me clothed all the years up to high school with homemade dresses
and hand-me-downs.

My father taught at Lynch East Main, a high school smack dab in the
middle of Harlan. My father's stories today are about names of people in
Lynch, changed from Italian or Polish or Czechoslovakian, names made
Smith-and-Jones simple for the lines for coal scrip or welfare. He still
tells a story about a boy, his favorite trigonometry student, who got blown
up at the face of a mine his first day on the job after he graduated. He
urged his students to want more. Applications to University of Kentucky.
Football scholarships. Jobs in the big city of Lexington. I remember my

father's slashed tires in the driveway one morning. *The Esteps,* my mother said.

Some late Friday afternoons after my father finished teaching, we drove north, home to Floyd County. We passed towns like Middlesboro, Pineville, Whitesburg. We took back roads, Highway 119 or 23 and one stretch called Straight Creek, an unusual section of highway that ran along a creek as straight as a chalk line for thirty-five miles. On one ride home, rain cascaded down as our car snaked up and around the mountains and we stopped for soda crackers to ease my stomach. *Reckon it'll let up any?* The store's owner cut slices for us from a round of deep yellow cheddar and offered us tomatoes so ripe they glistened. My mother, fearing stains on our clothes and stray crumbs and dirt of any variety at all, vetoed those tomatoes, and later my parents' angry voices collided as we eventually straddled the top of Pine Mountain, 2,500 feet of it. Rain fell more quietly as we stopped beside the road and my father held the back of my head as I vomited into a paper bag. We looked down past a trash-strewn hill and into a valley so deep and wet-green and far away, I shivered.

You come by it honest, my Granny Baisden, my mother's mother, would say. My love of all things spiritual. When I was a child, I tried to read the Bible cover to cover, checked out *Fox's Book of Martyrs* from the public library. I read about as many women saints as I could. By high school, I was drawn to the meditations of Thomas Merton, the prison diaries of Dietrich Bonhoeffer. I loved Frazer's *Golden Bough* and the studies of sacred places by Mircea Eliade. To this day I'm drawn to anything that describes power of the transcendent variety. Rudolph Otto, in a book called *The Idea of the Holy,* describes mysterium tremendum—awe, ecstasy, revelation—and in my teaching, over the years, I have been fascinated with how to impart this very experience to the creative writing classes I teach. I've read them essays about the power of love and the human heart. We've listened to Nusrat Fateh Al-Khan and written about our pasts. We've sat on a dock on an October night and tried to describe the moonlight. *Transcendence,* I tell them, *must reach for that moonlight and make it as ordinary as the work of our hands.*

Eastern Kentucky *was* a hardscrabble existence, one that my mother escaped when she married my father, the air force man who bought her an engagement ring in Morocco, married her, took her away from home. *Kansas. Lexington. Harlan County.* We moved from place to place, then finally to a subdivision house in Frankfort, the state capitol, where my father worked for the Kentucky Department of Education. When we made visits east, my father would bring us to Dwale while he took off for the next county to visit his own mother and father, a visit and a house to which my mother preferred not to accompany him.

During visits to Dwale, I still remember my mother's distaste as she tiptoed down the hill, in and out of the dirt ruts and stones of the path that led to the outhouse. At home, our floors were so pristine, neither my father nor I had ever walked on them in our outdoor shoes. We had to shower in the garage to keep the bathtub clean. I still remember the feel of my mother's hand at night, the gloves thick with lotions she wore to bed to try to heal her hands, so chapped from housework they bled. *Don't touch anything in there,* she'd say when we visited the outhouse in Dwale. She'd stand by me while I looked down into a hole that led to lime and decomposition, to all the vile things she preferred to forget from her own childhood. I loved standing there, listening to magpies in the stone pear tree in the bottom land.

Her father, my grandfather called Pa, worked in the mines in Martin and David, tiny towns in the next county, up until I was much older and he filed for black lung benefits. He'd head out with a dinner pail before daylight, leaving us to days of visiting with my granny and my mother's two sisters. It's my Granny Baisden I remember most. She raised or canned or made everything the family ate, and I remember her, in a cotton sunbonnet, hoeing one more row of potatoes or beans in the hot sun in the bottom down from the house. Mornings she'd wake me and my mother where we slept in the bed in the front room. *Morning this morning, fine morning,* she'd say, her face all creased and toothless, her teeth in a canning jar in the kitchen where she'd next go to make us all homemade biscuits and sugar syrup I'd stir up with butter on a plate. I'd watch her hands folding that light dough, up and over, watch her make pie crusts with meringues that could float all the way up to heaven. I'd sit out in the side yard, afternoons, and watch her maneuver work shirts and overalls through the tight rollers on the wringer washing machine. Her hands were strong and freckled from the sun, palms orangey from sulfur water from the well as she reached in, took the clothes back out, put them through again.

Evenings, I'd sit with her on the front porch that overlooked the bottom land, and she'd take down her long, braided hair, let me play with her combs and pins. She'd show me how to pretend the white porch chairs were cars. I planned all the places I'd go, the roads I'd someday take to foreign places in the world she'd never see. Who'd have thought of Thailand, Nepal, India, all those places I'd someday go, ones that meant nothing then, next to the bottom land and the pear tree and that house in Dwale, all the world both of us then knew.

It was my father who took me to church on Sundays on those trips home. Lick Fork Missionary Baptist Church sat on the side of a road I'd jog on, twenty years later on visits to Eastern Kentucky. It was a small, whitewashed building full of benches and the preacher's voice. He was red-faced and short-sleeved and sweating as he held his hand against his ear and told-sang-shouted his sermon for the day with an almost sexual frenzy, words about hell and devotion to Jesus Christ Our Lord and doing good with our neighbors. Men and women knelt in the front below the preacher and prayed, all together. People ran circles around the church's insides, shouting—*Oh Hallajamondia, Hallajamondia*—waving their ecstatic arms to God. *Praise Jesus. Praise Him.* And sometimes someone would fall out in front of the pulpit, her body quivering with the power of God. Hands fell on this person, that one, anyone visited by the power of the Spirit, the power of the Holy Ghost.

Later, outside, the brothers and sisters gathered around chairs set out here and there on top of the hill near the church. There was a washbasin, an aluminum one like the one my Granny Baisden washed dishes in. This one or that one, Brother Clifford or Brother Howard, took a seat and untied his boots, peeled off his socks, waited his turn for the metal pan. I remember the thick-nailed toes, the rough heels. Hands reaching into cool water, touching those feet, their calloused and yellow hides. *Foot washing.* A sign of humbleness. Loving one's neighbor like one's self.

At home, feet were dirty things, laden with grime and toil and stench. At home, we took our shoes off and barely touched the floors on our prescribed paths to television, to bed, to the door out. At Lick Fork, I watched towels dry the feet of strangers. Small, remembered acts of devotion.

A few weeks into my Prose Forms class, I meet with all my students, one by one. I've had some of them already in nonfiction writing workshops, so we talk about both essays on their writing lives for Prose Forms class, and about their nonfiction in general. One student is writing about his cross-country journey, a Hunter S. Thompsonesque van ride through the small towns and valleys of the South. Another is writing about both her decision to leave a job in finance and her fascination with Prader-Willi syndrome, a genetic disorder causing constant feelings of hunger. I am holding some of my conferences in a local Tex-Mex restaurant, and I'm sitting there nibbling at a burrito when the student from upstate New York comes in, orders her own taco salad, and takes a seat.

The student and I, since the first night of class, have been experiencing some unease. She smiles tightly in class when I talk about "the writing life," and has more than once referred to such a topic of class discussion as "simplistic." I've been, I admit, inwardly cringing, for weeks, about her first-night comments about hardscrabble lives, and about transcendence itself. I've heard it rumored that she calls me "the leader of a school of transcendence." And all that stuff about art. Art, she maintains, is like any other trade. Why not, she asks us in class, speak of the transcendent value of plumbing, the transcendent value of drywall?

She divides the lettuce and cheese in her salad. "I don't think that's it," she begins. "I'll be honest," she says. "My problem is the topic itself."

"What do you mean?"

"Why I write." She leans forward into the table, peers at me. "I'm just a student," she says. "Not an artist. How am I supposed to know anything about the writing life? About why I write?"

Not to mention, she goes on, all this business about human hearts and transcendence. She wants the nuts and bolts. She wants to get in there and unravel stories, rip them apart.

"I'm here," she says, "to learn about craft."

My face feels warm, salty-warm. I am somewhere between shame and anger. We sit quietly.

"I've worked with someone like you before," she says. "A mountain writer, when I was at college. She likes the same things you do."

We eat and I now feel unaccountably sad. What things do I like? And maybe she's right. What, I wonder, *is* all this business about transcendence anyway?

In grade school when we lived in Frankfort, we were studying a chapter on genealogy. We had to tell the class about our families, and there was a paper to fill out with questions. *Our mother's maiden name. The story we heard repeated most often at the dinner table.* Dinner table stories? We fought there, over who got the fattiest ham slice, over who my father flirted with at the office. I raised my hand and asked permission to come up front, tell my teacher privately what my mother's peculiar name was. *Pearlie Lee Baisden.* A good mountain name, but one I was sure my peers would laugh at, just as I knew they laughed at my odd-turned way of speaking, the long *i*'s of mountain-speak that I still had, from when we lived in Harlan. *Night. White. Bright.* A nasal, long *i* that I held in on my tongue, sour as communion crackers and grape juice. I was ashamed. Of the names we still held for things, at home. *Rack.* Meaning coat hanger. *Smelled of.* Meaning had a scent. *Gommed.* Meaning tangled up.

By the time high school came, I was ashamed of my dresses, the homemade ones with rickrack and lace, fresh-made by my father's mother, my Granny Salyer. I was ashamed of the clothes I had to wear to school, hand-me-downs from my own mother's high school days, back in Floyd County. I was ashamed of the way my mother stayed home all the time, hiding from the world out there, the clean, middle-class world of Frankfort, so desirable, yet jarringly different from the one she'd grown up with in Eastern Kentucky. She never went to church, hid when the church ladies from Graefenburg, my father's Baptist church, came calling. I was ashamed of the way, on Sunday mornings, when I accompanied my father to church, he nervously clipped his nails, cleared his throat, of the way, on Sunday afternoons, we stayed away from my mother, hiding out at his office. Somewhere in the mix was another kind of shame. The church we went to now was middle-class, complete with announcements about youth group trips to Florida, Lottie Moon offerings for African children. During church services I heard echoes of Lick Fork in my head. *Praise Him. Praise Jesus.* I was ashamed, thinking of how tame the church world was now with its sculpted lines of pews, its carpeted floors, its smart sermons. At night once, I believed I heard the voice of God, coming through my bedroom window, just for me. *Daughter, I have need of you.* His voice was long-voweled with Eastern Kentucky–speak, just like my own.

I grew up, moved away to other towns, states, countries. But shame, some variety or other of it, followed me like a shadow, like a drift of coal dust. At Berea, where I went to college, I was in my element, in some ways. Berea is a school "for mountain youth" where education is paid for by student labor. At my job in Crafts and Weaving, I sewed stuffed animals and wove placemats. Our crafts industry, along with Berea's pottery and broom-making and Appalachian heritage museum, was a tourists' hot spot. We were hillbillies. Poor mountaineers. I sat there, furious and ashamed, when a group came through the crafts shop one day. *Do you children really not have shoes?* a woman asked me.

In graduate school, at the University of Virginia, I felt totally out of my element. I'd earned my points at Berea, but could not now adequately apply theoretical language to the books that had been my salvation, back in my parents' house. In my first creative writing workshop, I began to write stories that hinted at both my childhood and Eastern Kentucky. *I appreciate this quaint story,* a peer wrote, *about a little mountain hamlet.* When, at last, I won a fellowship for my stories, I received many congratulations from the other writers. *It's good that this went to someone who really needed the money,* one person said. I continued to write stories about baptisms and fortune tellers and quilts with names like "Trip Around the World." *What you're writing,* one person said in my workshop. *It isn't fiction yet.*

That was true. I was in-between worlds. *Fiction. Nonfiction. Childhood and now.* I was somewhere between the mountains that often hurt in my memory and the life I was now living. I was translating my life into stories that did not yet possess a soul.

After graduate school, I spent some months in England and France, but found myself most alive as my traveling companion and I traveled east, first to Greece, where I was thrilled mornings by the sounds of the muezzin's call to prayer. *Thailand. Nepal. Malaysia. India.* Oils and curries. Funeral pyres and sadhus. We traveled north and south. *Kashmir. Jaipur. Rajasthan.* The hot months before the monsoon season left us sleepless and exhausted. I ate water-thin dal and picked bits of filth from my rice. I loved the feel of my own sharp hips and ribs.

Soon I was reduced to something thin and brittle. I had visions so palpable I could hold them in the palm of my hand. A leper with his fingers eaten away. A sadhu with a swollen scrotum, ringing a bell in a marketplace. A blind man at a train station who told me he'd seen God and time and that he could give me both. An ear cleaner on the steps of a temple assured me I'd hear like before if I sampled his skills. And in the deserts of Rajasthan, heat so keen I watched it shine on the desert sands at night. Here, I told my friend, everything is real. *Unconcealed.*

At night, as we slept in hostels and cheap and good guest houses with the blood of street junkies on the walls, I dreamed often of Eastern Kentucky. I dreamed of praying in the church at Lick Fork. I dreamed once of a bridge spanning a creek and on its other side, my grandmother's house and on the porch, my Granny Baisden and my mother. They beckoned to me.

In order to go home again, I heard a voice tell me, I had to learn how to pray.

Praying is, in fact, something I haven't done very much of in years. Not really.

I've prayed for this or that outcome. *Please, oh please, let this turn out this way.* There've been the aphorisms from my childhood that I sometimes say, like prayers, at sunset. *Red sky at night, sailor's delight.* There are always mealtime blessings at my father and stepmother's new home in Shelbyville, Kentucky, prayers of thanks during which we hold hands. *Thank you, Lord, for bringing us this food today.* And at my mother's, now that she is living alone, back in Eastern Kentucky, there are bitter charms, stays against disaster. *You can't trust love, not one bit of it.* And if there are other prayers, times I travel back to Eastern Kentucky, they are ones said over the dinner table at my aunt and uncle's trailer, up Mining Hollow. *Forgive us, Lord, for our sins against you. Teach us, Lord, to live in thy loving ways.* Out the window of that trailer, you can see the grave of their son in the family cemetery.

And yet it is via Eastern Kentucky, or the Appalachian mountains themselves, that I have at last learned to genuinely listen those times I tilt my head up to the sky and wait. In the fall of 2006, I taught a class in Appalachian literature as a corollary to the classes I teach in the creative writing program. I arranged films, photos, food, oral history projects. I picked a range of books—novels, stories, poetry—and I called upon all the names I love from prominent Appalachian writers. *Denise Giardina. Lee Smith. John Ehle.* In short, I began to summon my own past and to tell my students stories of my own childhood. I remembered again the coal tipples at Martin, the ones we'd drive by on trips home to Floyd County. I remembered the particular taste of wild greens. *Cressy. Mustard. Poor man's bacon.* I took out the quilts I'd inherited from my father's mother and I touched this square of cloth, that one, pieces from junk stores she'd visited, pieces from my grandfather's shirts, ones cut from the dresses made for me when I was a child. The names of those quilts stirred my heart. *Cathedral Window. Trip Around the World.*

The heart, says Deborah McCauley in a book called *Appalachian Mountain Religion,* is "one of the most significant and telling recurrent themes in mountain preaching." It is the heart, "broken . . . tender . . . a heart not hardened to the Spirit," that is important in mountain faiths. And, most significant for me, McCauley says that, for mountain faiths, "rational belief alone . . . what makes sense to the head, is woefully inadequate." There I was again. Back in Lick Fork, at church. Back in other church houses I'd been to in the mountains, ones that were tender. Soft as the laying on of hands. But fierce and unabashed, full of visions of angels and Spirit. I remembered when my great-grandfather died, and the funeral they had for him. A service at some church house, maybe in Dwale. All the windows were open to the sound of bees and wind and summertime. And inside, rapturous voices called up to God. *Lordy. Lordy.* Hands waved. My great-aunt Essie ran up and back, mourning and weeping, then threw herself across the body of her daddy. *Lord,* she cried. *Take me. Take me.* As I read now about tender hearts and hands, about the faith of the mountains, I feel again how I felt that long-ago day. As if the dark arms could reach down, scoop me up, make me disappear.

And yet, when it comes to matters of the heart, how to convey that in the classroom, in the study of the text, the manuscript itself, without some sense of shame? If I teach from the heart, will I hear what I've sometimes heard before in the halls of academia? My colleagues hint that matters of the heart are precious, touchy-feely, of less consequence than intellect and analysis. Deborah McCauley, again in her text *Appalachian Mountain Religion,* confirms just that schism. Mountain people, who base their faith on the heart, on grace, on inspiration of the Holy Spirit, met an influx of missionaries and revivalists during the Great Awakening of the mid-1800s. Visions and tongues and the Holy Spirit began to seem barbaric. Emphasis on grace and knowledge of the heart took a back seat to social action, individual achievement, and rational interpretations of religious experience.

Patricia Foster, in an essay called "The Intelligent Heart," writes that "the heart is the source, the goods, the first principle from which everything else is made." It is that heart, spirit, source, goods, and first principle that I long for both when I lead workshops and when I read drafts of my students' stories. For me, it is by far not enough to discuss characterization, setting, plot. It is not nearly enough to write a story or a poem or an essay with the publisher, the magazine, even the audience in mind. I want my students, first, to locate the intentions of their writing. The story must have "an about," a purpose that begins with understanding "heart," both of writer and act of writing, of story and the story's *why.* A story must understand itself and language must translate that understanding—a process that, on my best of days, is what I mean by transcend. "Story," says Foster, "must act as a catalyst for thinking and feeling [and] the congruence of both elevates the story to the status of art." Division of heart and mind translates into a schism of spirit and language.

"I'm trying to sort it out," Foster wrote me recently. "Exactly what's happened with my students of late. The ones who don't seem interested in the darker conflicts of the human spirit, the emotional range of familial and cultural incidents, the hard work of trying to forgive self and other. I do hope to write about this determined resistance to the inner life of story, to the inner life of either self or another." I, like my friend, am finding this true, this perplexity about interest in the human spirit, no less a larger world. Transcendence, my Prose Form and Theory student told me toward the end of that particular class. She'd tried it, and it just didn't work. *Transcendence.* Is it something we try? Or is it a gift, an unexpected wonder that lies at the heart of the best of our words and, I hope, the best of what we have to teach. Is true poverty, as Heather Sellers says in her essay in this collection, one of imagination? Of spirit and heart?

One fall, a few years back, I traveled with a friend to Atlanta to hear a reading by poet Robert Bly and to see a performance by Sufi dancers. On the drive, I kept hearing lines of Bly's—ones about mystery—that haunted me. *The toe of the shoe pivots in the dust . . . the man in the black coat turns.* We were late as we took our seats in the upper tier of a darkened auditorium in the Emory Center for the Performing Arts, and we'd missed the poet. What we saw was light on a stage and a circle of trousered men in long white and gold coats—the Sufi dancers. Their long coats swayed and the dance was silent except for the whoosh of cloth and that dizzying circling, over, over, faster and faster until their coats belled out. I remembered the way women danced in the church houses I'd visited when I was a child. *The dizzying circle of those women as they summoned the spirit.* The six men turned and turned in dance, and something—a translation of memory I'm still waiting to understand—traveled out and settled in the palms of my hands.

An Angle of Vision

✎ JOY CASTRO

As formerly poor women now working as writers in and out of the academy, the gifts we bring—not only to the readers of our work but also to the institutions that currently shelter us—are an angle of vision and the will for change.

When I took my first teaching job, I was startled by all the food. Everywhere, food: good food, free for the taking. At department meetings, the chair would lay out a spread. At division meetings, a similar spread, with wine. At lunchtime talks, no one brought brown bags; dozens of pizza boxes stood stacked on the table outside, and students helped themselves. After evening lectures and readings, there were always receptions with cookies, hors d'oeuvres, piles of cut fresh fruit, washed strawberries—even, sometimes, tapas. There were permanent lines in the budget for these things.

This astonished me. For the first time in my life, at twenty-nine, I was earning a salary that put me above the minimum wage; I could buy all the food I wanted with my own money. Yet here was this perpetual buffet, free, for people who did not need it.

It was not the first time academia has amazed me. As a sixteen-year-old heading across the country, a first-generation college student at a country-club college, I didn't know a lot of things. I didn't know how to play tennis or how to ski. Carless, fresh from factory work, I didn't know that kids my age drove their parents' hand-me-down Volvos and convertible Mercedes. I didn't know the words *paradigm* or *paradox* or *essentialism*. When at seventeen I dropped out, I didn't know I was just another at-risk retention statistic; that domestic violence rates leap by a factor of five when families live below the poverty line, as ours had; or that children in low-income homes are raised in ways that render higher education and professional achievement difficult because of deep attitudes parents convey about one's worth and the right to speak up. And I didn't know that the word *testimony* could mean something besides the scary, throat-pounding experiences I'd had in courtrooms, lawyers' offices, and judges' chambers. Testifying didn't feel like power, though it and the cops did get my brother removed from the abusive and poverty-stricken home I'd run away from. It didn't feel like power. It felt like terror, like telling, like telling on my own mother, like lifting up the veil on the violence and hunger and pathology she'd tried so hard to hide, a veil that schoolteachers and classmates and even the other Jehovah's Witnesses were content to leave hanging there, even after they knew. That veil of poverty and dysfunction hung there like a vertical safety net, keeping them comfortably on their side, while we and the trauma we suffered were effectively invisible.

"You save yourself or you remain unsaved," I read in *Lucky,* Alice Sebold's memoir, as I prepared to teach it in a senior seminar for English majors at that college, where I later earned tenure, where I chaired my department from a corner office with windows and a beautiful rug.

You get used to things. I was at my first institution for ten years, and I called catering to order fine dinners for our visiting poets, our job candidates, our senior English majors, and I signed the invoices when they were sent to me. It was no longer jarring or strange.

So it is easy for me to empathize with my colleagues and students. If I, who have known hunger and food stamps, dry pancakes for dinner for nights on end, who stole food as a hungry child—if I can grow accustomed to plenty, if what once astonished me can become routine, then I can understand the obliviousness of my colleagues who have never known want.

The flaunting of privilege and the connections privilege draws among gender, race, and class are not new. In the Europe of the 1200s, only the head of the household could urinate in the great hall, where people dined, his phallus a marvelously literal, visible signifier of privilege. Centuries later, such manifestations of linked privileges are much rarer, and those that remain are subtler.

But at my former institution, where my office trash disappeared in the night, emptied by the hands of a woman I never saw, the nexus of class and gender privilege remains writ unusually large: Wabash College is one of the last three remaining all-male private liberal arts colleges in the country. "Why do women like Wabash men?" asked the front of the red tee-shirt of a student in my introductory creative writing class. In a pun that explicitly links masculinity to institutional wealth, the back of the tee-shirt read, "Because we're well endowed." And they are: Wabash has a 370 million–dollar endowment for an enrollment of 850 young men—per student, it's one of the highest endowments in the country, and the institution remains adamantly all-male. "Co-Ed Never," reads another tee-shirt. All of the trustees are men, and most are white; one described board membership as "the most exclusive men's club in Indiana." Wabash's president, dean, CFO, and deans of advancement, admissions, and student life were all white men when I left, and white men comprised 74 percent of the faculty. The thick crimson carpet that unspooled across the wooden floor of my historic building, thicker than the carpeting of any home I've lived in, was vacuumed each night by invisible women, and then tromped on each day by hundreds of young men.

For a woman coming from an impoverished background, a woman who took the first job offered in a tough market, it was a very strange environment, a place where the intersections of male privilege and class privilege were constantly foregrounded, where my own twinned vulnerabilities of poverty and femaleness were repeatedly drawn to my attention.

For several years, I struggled to pass as a native, fell silent when I had no cultural capital to contribute to the conversation, which was most of the time. People called me shy, and I thought of myself that way. But I wasn't. Rather, I was incognito, unknowable—strategically so, and it was a strategy born of shame and desperation, of the felt sense that who I really was would disturb people too much to let me stay. I was a stranger in a strange land, a trailer-trash girl from a fucked-up background whose test scores and polite smile and diligence let her slip inoffensively upward.

The classroom was fine, a space of clearly delineated topics, a conversation I could prepare for. So I prepared, and prepared, with the determination that got me through my junior year of college, twenty, nursing a new baby, living in a sketchy barrio on WIC and food stamps, getting straight As. That kind of doggedness I brought to my preps, my grading, my articles about leftist-feminist writers, the experimental short fiction I published about Latina waitresses, housecleaners, minimum-wage shop-girls.

But there was no way to prepare for the other part of academic life at my institution, the part that, as a grad student, I had been spared: the dinner parties, receptions, and cocktail hours, the social life where people chatted off the grid—and, weirdly, as I soon learned, not about ideas at all, but about vacation plans and good restaurants and cultural activities and *So, where did you grow up?* With massive student loans to pay, my vacations were staying home with my son and husband, and our restaurants of choice were Taco Bell and Subway. My discretionary income and spare time went to the "cultural activity" of therapy, where I was still working through the symptoms of post-traumatic stress disorder.

Where I grew up, and how, and that I ran away at fourteen—those were off-limits. Everything true about my background was shocking, vulgar, fodder for tabloids: abuse, rootlessness, broken families, weird religion, prison. I didn't want to seem unseemly, didn't want anyone's pity, didn't want to scare or repel anyone with the monstrous background I carried, the monstrous anxieties that still plagued me. I certainly did not "authorize [my] desire," as Emma Perez writes in *The Decolonial Imaginary,* "through third space feminist practice by deliberately fashioning a sexed body for public consumption." Instead, I deliberately fashioned a sexless, undistracting body for classroom and committee meeting consumption.

The tenure track in a small community is a tightrope. I worked hard to reveal nothing, not to fall, to just keep placing one foot in front of the other, eyes on the prize of tenure and tuition remission for my son.

I was entering my fifth year of college teaching before I learned that all my departmental colleagues had a woman.

For four years, I'd wondered in frustration and despair how my colleagues were able to entertain so freely, their houses immaculate when we arrived, while our own hundred-year-old, un-air-conditioned, badly heated house—with a growing son and a blond collie-lab mix who lived indoors—was always considerably more chaotic. Each weeknight, I worked late after dinner, grading and preparing for class, and my husband worked full-time, so the laundry, cleaning, and yard work were left until the weekends. I was exhausted, my husband was exhausted, and the house was still a mess, unfit for throwing the dinner parties that were a staple of social life in our small town. We did manage to host a couple of dinners, but they left me drained, not glowing. Old feelings from childhood flared up: I felt ashamed of my family's dirtiness and guilty that I couldn't work hard enough to fix it.

Oh, yes, my older male colleagues told me on the ride to the state park where our annual retreat was held, they all had women who came in. Their wives all worked—those secondary kinds of jobs women often take in deference to the family's true careerist—so they all had women who came in once a week or oftener to clean.

For me, it was a light bulb, a paradigm shift. My colleagues weren't cleaner, purer, more scrupulous people by nature. They hired help.

I felt queasy at the prospect, though. When I was growing up, my mother cleaned houses, so did my aunt. My relations were the women people had. To now be a person who hired such a woman put me on the wrong side of the equation, away from what felt familiar, safe, and comfortable.

My husband and I tried, but it felt weird, and a housecleaner was an expense we ultimately found we could not afford. We gave up. Our house went back to being lower-class messy, and we failed to reciprocate the generous invitations we received.

Jumping class comes at a price, and the price is not belonging. Within academia and the publishing world, I often find myself occupying a space of painful ambiguity. I don't fit, don't know the rules—didn't know until this year, for example, that you're supposed to send your agent an extravagant gift when he or she lands a book deal for you. (Who knew? Where I come from, people don't get presents for doing their jobs.) So I trip up, make mistakes. In this ambiguous space of not belonging, I waver between shame and guilt, my alliances unclear.

Once I went to dinner with two editors who were publishing my work. They were nice women. I liked them, and I was excited to be in a big city trying sushi for the first time. Over dinner, talk turned to the professions of our cousins. (Siblings are boring, said one editor; everyone talks about

their siblings.) The two women's cousins were art gallery owners and attorneys and things I can't remember now, and then it was my turn. At the
time, I wasn't in close touch with my extended family, but I offered what
I knew.

"My girl cousins are all secretaries," I said, "and my guy cousins are either cops or the guys who drive the wrecking trucks around after cops."

Both women burst into laughter.

"Oh, you've got to use that!" said one. "It's absolutely priceless." They
kept repeating what I'd said and breaking into gales of laughter.

I felt weird: confused and embarrassed—but yeah, okay, I could see
how it was funny. I smiled along gamely, feeling ashamed for my cousins,
who surely did not know, as I had not, that their hardworking lives and
labor were a matter for mirth.

My brother, a mechanic, had no such ambivalence. When I confided
my confusion and discomfort about the incident, he didn't hesitate.

"Well, fuck you very much," he said, as if addressing the two editors
directly. "I'm glad you find our family so *funny*. I'm glad we could *amuse*
you."

My brother's clarity is undimmed, his allegiances clear; he stands on
solid ground. His friends work construction and renovation. They and
their wives drink beer and smoke cigarettes around their toddlers, which
makes me uneasy. They're scathingly smart and politically informed, but
their humor also concerns bodily functions, which I stopped finding hilarious decades ago. Forcing weak smiles about anal leakage, I feel up-
tight, a snob.

I love my brother, and I like the people in my brother's circle, but I
don't fit there, even when I sit around their campfire drinking beer. I
don't fit anywhere.

For me as a writer, each choice to disclose true information comes
with the anxiety of betrayal, whether I reveal things about my poor family, whom I love, or the rich institution that sheltered me, where many
people were kind and generous.

"Oh, you've got to use that!" laughed the editor. And now I have.

Happy to be a visiting writer at Vanderbilt University, where one can
safely hazard that the majority of students do not come from backgrounds of poverty or working-class labor, I opened my reading by hold-

ing up a water glass from the cushy Nashville hotel where the university was housing me.

I don't drink out of such glasses, I said, and neither should they. I'd recently seen on TV a hidden-camera exposé of hotel maids using toxic chemical cleaners to wipe out the glasses and then setting them back on the counters, unwashed, and putting the little covers on them to indicate that they were clean. The TV show remarked in horror on the practice. Were the maids stupid? The camera zoomed in close to the large-lettered warnings on the bottles full of blue liquid. Could they not read?

I don't think it's either one. For sure, those women don't squirt Windex on the glasses their children drink from at home.

It's not ignorance. It's not illiteracy.

"No," I told the audience. "That's class rage."

For formerly poor women in the academy and publishing, our challenge is how not to let our rage become toxic, how to use it to clean things up for real.

At my own institution, it was strange to be so frequently the only one in a committee meeting arguing for my point of view. In my first year on the Visiting Artists Series Committee, I couldn't understand why we charged local citizens for events by big-name visiting artists when our budget covered all the costs. The committee chair voiced the committee's traditional argument for charging local citizens fifteen and twenty dollars a ticket: that people wouldn't *appreciate* the arts if they didn't *pay* for them. The rest of the (all-male) committee smiled patiently as I tried to explain a position that had never before been voiced at that table: If someone has never *been* to a ballet or a live theater performance, how will he or she *know* to appreciate it?

It took some doing, but our old policy did change. Wabash's auditoriums are now regularly packed, and our sharing of the arts with the larger community resulted in better town-gown relations. Looking back now, everyone agrees we made the right choice.

And we made the right choice to fund and teach in Indiana's first Clemente Course, which offers a college-level curriculum free to poor people. It was the right choice, when I took students to England for a fully funded study trip, to invite as chaperone not another faculty member, as was customary, but our department secretary; and it was the right choice to offer free creative writing workshops through the public library and at the domestic violence shelter.

As women coming from the condition of poverty, we bring an immediacy, an urgency to the table. We cannot falsely imagine that, because our suffering has ended, it does not go on and on. As accustomed as we might become to the presence of sufficient food, we cannot forget, as Toni Morrison writes, that "the function of freedom is to free someone else."

Friends had urged me to write a memoir, but I couldn't. I knew the market was glutted. I couldn't bear to open those wounds, that shame, the terror, only to have my tale trounced by reviewers sick of sob stories, of writers they called narcissistic, attention-seeking. Attention was a thing I didn't want.

But my silence about my background ended when, the summer before my tenure year, my father shot himself. It was too big to conceal. The dirt. The drama.

My memoir appeared in 2005: *The Truth Book,* ironically titled after the book used with new converts by Jehovah's Witnesses, the religion I'd been adopted into at birth, a complicated religion that practiced racial and ethnic equality, which my assimilating Latino father hungered for; a religion that prohibited any desire for material objects—that forbade, at that time, going to college; a religion predicated on severe gender hierarchy, so that it was a mark of godliness for a woman to be silent and submissive, as I was raised to be; a religion that preached ignorance of the body, that children were to be immediately obedient to adults in all things, that men were the unquestionable heads of the household, and that sexual molestation was only actionable if it had been witnessed by two neutral adult observers; an evangelical Christian sect that has historically appealed to the poor and working-class by promising us beautiful houses on a paradise earth, as soon as the apocalypse wipes away all the worldly people.

The thought of having this book, the story of my trashy, messed-up life, my hurt young female body, available to my middle-class, mostly male, mostly white, often quite privileged colleagues and students, was unnerving.

My son, who's now nineteen, a college junior, has not read my book.

A wise child with good boundaries, he says he knows it would make him sad. He wants to keep intact his image of me as the mama he has always known: his protector, brave, in charge.

My students and colleagues felt, of course, no such compunction, and I had to confront the fact that many of them—and I might never know which—would see me in that other, vulnerable way: young and poor, living in trashy places and wearing the clothes kids ridicule, and violated in body and spirit. Weird. Visible.

To write my book, I had to reinhabit, without shame, that place of shame, of trauma, of anguish and silence. I had to give it a voice.

To put my art into the world as memoir, I had to be willing to stand as the living, visible representative of the text, the body at the front of the room.

To be a writer is to claim a voice, a hard thing for anyone schooled to silence. To publish autobiographical work is to be the word made flesh in front of audience after audience, formal when you tour and informal when you return home to your community, which views you with new eyes. You, who have suffered so from being the helpless object of the male gaze, the inadequate object of the classed gaze—"You live *there?*"— you step deliberately now into the spotlight, your scars as visible as your competencies. You step into the light on your own terms now, you claim the mic, telling the story you have come here to tell.

Suggested for Further Reading

Allison, Dorothy
> *Bastard Out of Carolina.* Plume, 1992.
> *Cavedweller.* Plume, 1998.
> *She Who.* New York: Penguin, *forthcoming.*
> *Skin–Talking about Sex, Class & Literature.* Firebrand Books, 1994.
> *Trash: Stories.* Plume, 2002.
> *Two or Three Things I Know for Sure.* Plume, 1995.

Alvarez, Julia
> *Once Upon a Quinceañera: Coming of Age in the USA.* Plume, 2008.

Anzaldua, Gloria
> *Borderlands/La Frontera: The New Mestiza.* Spinsters/Aunt Lute, 1987.

Angelou, Maya.
> *I Know Why the Caged Bird Sings.* Random House, 1969.

Buss, Fran Leeper
> *Dignity: Lower Income Women Tell of Their Lives and Struggles.* University of Michigan Press, 1985.
> *Forged under the Sun/Forjada bajo el sol: The Life of Maria Elena Lucas.* University of Michigan Press, 1993.
> *Moisture of the Earth: Mary Robinson, Civil Rights and Textile Union Activist.* University of Michigan Press, 2009.

Castro, Joy
> *The Truth Book: Escaping a Childhood of Abuse Among Jehovah's Witnesses.* Arcade Publishing, 2005.

Chavez, Lisa D.
> *Destruction Bay.* West End Press, 1999.
> *In an Angry Season.* University of Arizona Press, 2001.

Childers, Mary
> *Welfare Brat: A Memoir.* Bloomsbury, 2005.

Cisneros, Sandra
> *Caramelo.* Vintage, 2002.
> *The House on Mango Street.* Vintage, 1991.
> *Loose Woman.* Knopf, 1994.
> *My Wicked, Wicked Ways.* Knopf, 1992.
> *Woman Hollering Creek.* Vintage, 1991.

Cofer, Judith Ortiz
    Call Me Maria. Scholastic, 2006.
    An Island Like You: Stories of the Barrio. Puffn, 1995.
    The Latin Deli: Telling the Lives of Barrio Women. W.W. Norton, 1995.
    The Line of the Sun. University of Georgia Press, 1989.
    A Love Story Beginning in Spanish: Poems. University of Georgia Press, 2005.
    The Meaning of Consuelo. Beacon Press, 2003.
    Reaching for the Mainland and Selected New Poems. Bilingual Press, 1995.
    Silent Dancing: A Partial Remembrance of a Puerto Rican Childhood. Arte
        Público, 1990.
    Terms of Survival. Arte Público, 1995.
    The Year of Our Revolution: Selected and New Prose and Poetry. Piñata Books,
        1998.
    Woman in Front of the Sun: On Becoming a Writer. University of Georgia Press,
        2000.
Dovalpage, Teresa
    A Girl Like Che Guevara: A Novel. Soho Press, 2004.
    Muerte de un murciano en La Habana. Barcelona : Editorial Anagrama,
        2006.
    Por culpa de Candela. Floricanto Press, 2008.
    Posesas de la Habana: A Novela. Pureplay Press, 2004.
Dunbar-Ortiz, Roxanne
    Red Dirt: Growing Up Okie. University of Oklahoma Press. 2006.
Ehrenreich, Barbara
    Nickel and Dimed: On (Not) Getting By in America. Holt, 2008.
Giardina, Denise
    Storming Heaven. Ivy Books, 1988.
    Unquiet Earth. Ivy Books, 1994.
Gibbon, Maureen
    Swimming Sweet Arrow: A Novel. Little, Brown & Co., 2000.
    Magdalena. White Pine Press, 2007.
Goldstone, Dwonna Naomi
    *Integrating the 40 Acres: The Fifty-Year Struggle for Racial Equality at the University
        of Texas.* University of Georgia Press, 2006.
Harjo, Joy
    How We Became Human: New and Selected Poems. W.W. Norton, 2004.
    In Mad Love and War. Wesleyan University Press, 1990.
    She Had Some Horses. Seal Press, 2005.
    The Woman Who Fell from the Sky. W.W. Norton, 1996.
Hays, Sharon
    Flat Broke with Children: Women in the Age of Welfare Reform. Oxford University
        Press, 2004.

Hernández, Daisy, and Bushra Rehman, Editors
Colonize This!: Young Women of Color on Today's Feminism. Seal Press, 2002.

Hoffman, Nancy and Florence Howe, Editors
Women Working: An Anthology of Stories and Poems. Feminist Press, 1979.

hooks, bell
Bone Black: Memories of Girlhood. Holt, 1997.

Iceland, John
Poverty in America. University of California Press, 2006.

Jordan, June
Soldier: A Poet's Childhood. Basic Civitas Books, 2000.

Karr, Mary
The Liars' Club: A Memoir. Viking Penguin, 1995.

Kennedy, Michelle
Without a Net: Middle Class and Homeless (with Kids) in America. Penguin, 2006.

Kotlowitz, Alex
There Are No Children Here: The Story of Two Boys Growing Up in the Other America. Random House/Anchor, 1992.

Lareau, Annette
Unequal Childhoods: Class, Race, and Family Life. University of California Press, 2003.

LeBlanc, Adrian Nicole
Random Family: Love, Drugs, Trouble, and Coming of Age in the Bronx. Scribner, 2004.

López, Lorraine
Call Me Henri. Curbstone Press, 2005.
The Gifted Gabaldón Sisters. Grand Central Press, 2008.
Homicide Survivors Picnic. BkMk Press, 2009.
Limpieza. Grand Central Press, forthcoming.
Soy la Avon Lady and Other Stories. Curbstone Press, 2002.

Lorde, Audre
The Cancer Journals. Spinster's Ink, 1980.
Zami, A New Spelling of My Name: A Biomythography by Audre Lorde. Crossing Press, 1982.

Lubrano, Alfred
Limbo: Blue Collar Roots, White Collar Dreams. John Wiley & Sons, 2003.

Mason, Bobbie Ann
Clear Springs: A Memoir. Random House, 1999.

McCarriston, Linda
Eva-Mary. Triquarterly, 1991.

McElmurray, Karen Salyer
Motel of the Stars. Sarabande Books, 2008.

Strange Birds in the Tree of Heaven. University of Georgia Press, 2004.

Surrendered Child: A Birth Mother's Journey. University of Georgia Press, 2006.

Mitchell, Richelene

Dear Self: A Year in the Life of a Welfare Mother. NID Publishers, 2008.

Montes, Amelia María de la Luz

María Amparo Ruiz de Burton: Critical and Pedagogical Perspectives. University of Nebraska Press, 2004.

Moss, Barbara Robinette

Change Me into Zeus's Daughter: A Memoir. Simon and Schuster, 2001.

Nguyen, Bich Minh

Stealing Buddha's Dinner. Vintage, 2007.

Short Girls. Viking, 2009.

Olsen, Tillie

Silences. The Feminist Press, 2003.

Yonnondio: From the Thirties. Bison Books, 2004.

Pancake, Ann

Strange as This Weather Has Been: A Novel. Counterpoint, 2007.

Pruett, Lynn

Ruby River. Grove Press, 2004.

Rahman, Aishah

Chewed Water: A Memoir. University Press of New England, 2001.

Rank, Mark Robert

One Nation Underprivileged: Why American Poverty Affects Us All. Oxford, 2005.

Register, Cheri

Packinghouse Daughter: A Memoir. Harper Perennial, 2001.

Sellers, Heather

The Boys I Borrow. New Issues Poetry and Prose, 2007.

Chapter After Chapter: Discover the Dedication and Focus You Need to Write the Book of Your Dreams. Writers Digest Books, 2006.

Drinking Girls and Their Dresses. Ahsahta Press, 2002.

Georgia Under Water. Sarabande Books, 2001.

Page After Page. Writers Digest Books, 2004.

The Practice of Creative Writing: A Guide for Students. Bedford/St. Martins Press, 2007.

Spike and Cubby Ice Cream Island Adventure. Holt, 2004.

Shipler, David K.

The Working Poor: Invisible in America. Vintage, 2005.

Summer, Lauralee

Learning Joy from Dogs Without Collars. Simon and Schuster, 2003.

Tea, Michelle, Editor

Without a Net: The Female Experience of Growing Up Working Class. Seal Press, 2004.

Tokarczyk, Michelle M., and Elizabeth A. Fay, Editors
  Working-Class Women in the Academy: Laborers in the Knowledge Factory.
    University of Massachusetts Press, 1993.
Wilson, William Julius
  The Truly Disadvantaged: The Inner City, the Underclass, and Public Policy. The
    University of Chicago Press, 1990.
Wilson, William Julius
  *There Goes the Neighborhood: Racial, Ethnic, and Class Tensions in Four Chicago
    Neighborhoods and Their Meaning for America.* Knopf, 2006.
Zandy, Janet
  Hands: Physical Labor, Class, and Cultural Work. Rutgers University Press,
    2004.
Zandy, Janet, Editor
  Calling Home: Working-Class Women's Writings—An Anthology. Rutgers, 1990.
  Liberating Memory: Our Work and Our Working-Class Consciousness. Rutgers,
    1994.
  What We Hold In Common: An Introduction to Working-Class Studies. The
    Feminist Press, 2001.

Contributors

DOROTHY ALLISON grew up in Greenville, South Carolina, the first child of a fifteen-year-old unwed mother who worked as a waitress. Now living in Northern California with her partner, Alix, and her teenage son, Wolf Michael, she describes herself as a feminist, a working-class storyteller, a Southern expatriate, a sometime poet and a happily born-again Californian. Awarded the 2007 Robert Penn Warren Award for Fiction, Allison is a member of the Fellowship of Southern Writers. The first member of her family to graduate from high school, Allison attended Florida Presbyterian College on a National Merit Scholarship and, in 1979, studied anthropology at the New School for Social Research. She is the author of a chapbook of poetry, *The Women Who Hate Me* (Long Haul Press, 1983); the short story collection *Trash* (Firebrand Books, 1988), which was awarded two Lambda Literary awards and the American Library Association Prize for Lesbian and Gay Writing; and the novels *Bastard Out of Carolina* and *Cavedweller.* Allison has a forthcoming novel, *She Who.*

JOY CASTRO writes fiction, poetry, creative nonfiction, and critical essays. Her memoir, *The Truth Book,* was named a Book Sense Notable Book by the American Booksellers Association in 2005, and her work has appeared in *Quarterly West,* the *North American Review,* the *Mid-American Review, Chelsea,* the *New York Times Magazine,* and other journals and in the anthologies *Breeder: Real-Life Stories from the New Generation of Mothers, Without a Net: The Female Experience of Growing Up Working Class, Faith and Doubt, White Ink: Poems on Mothers and Motherhood,* and *A Ghost at Heart's Edge: Stories and Poems of Adoption.* She teaches literature, creative writing, and Latino studies at the University of Nebraska–Lincoln and creative writing in the Pine Manor College low-residency MFA program in Boston.

LISA D. CHAVEZ was born in Los Angeles and raised in Fairbanks, Alaska. She has published two books of poetry, *Destruction Bay* and *In an Angry Season,* and has been included in such anthologies as *Floricanto Si! A Collection of Latina Poetry, The Floating Borderlands: 25 Years of U.S. Hispanic Literature,* and *American Poetry: The Next Generation.* Her creative nonfiction has been published in *Fourth Genre,* the *Clackamas Literary Review,* and other places. She lives in the mountains outside of Albuquerque.

MARY CHILDERS is the author of *Welfare Brat,* a memoir about growing up in the Bronx in a family in which five out of seven children dropped out of high school. As she had hoped, the widely reviewed book has given her a platform for working on literacy and aspiration with lower-income youth and adults. Mary has a Ph.D. in English literature from the State University of New York at Buffalo and held numerous visiting teaching positions before becoming an administrator. Having served as the director of equal opportunity and affirmative action at Dartmouth College and the associate dean of arts and sciences at Brandeis University, she is now the Dartmouth College ombudsperson and a consultant who provides discrimination prevention training. Her current weekend writing project is a memoir tentatively entitled "Reeling in the Halls of Privilege."

SANDRA CISNEROS is a novelist, short story writer, and poet. The only daughter in a family of six brothers, Cisneros was born and raised in Chicago, Illinois, and has degrees from Loyola University and the University of Iowa. She is the author of the poetry collections *My Wicked Ways* and *Loose Women,* as well as the short story collection *Woman Hollering Creek and Other Stories* and the novels *Caramelo* and *The House on Mango Street.* Cisneros is the recipient of many awards, including the prestigious MacArthur Foundation Fellowship. She lives in San Antonio, Texas, where she is president and founder of the Maconodo Foundation, an organization of talented and passionate artists dedicated to community-building and nonviolent social change.

JUDITH ORTIZ COFER is the author of *A Love Story Beginning in Spanish: Poems* (2005); *Call Me Maria* (2006), a young adult novel; *The Meaning of Consuelo* (2003), a novel; *Woman in Front of the Sun: On Becoming a Writer* (2000), a collection of essays; *An Island Like You: Stories of the Barrio* (1995), a collection of short stories; *The Line of the Sun* (1989), a novel; *Silent Dancing* (1990), a collection of essays and poetry; two books of poetry, *Terms of Survival* (1987) and *Reaching for the Mainland* (1987); and *The Latin Deli: Prose and Poetry* (1993). Her work has appeared in the *Georgia Review,* the *Kenyon Review,* the *Southern Review, Glamour,* and other journals.

TERESA DOVALPAGE was born in Havana, Cuba, in 1966. She is the author of *A Girl Like Che Guevara* (2004) and *Posesas de La Habana* (2004). Inspired by New Mexican traditions, she wrote the play *La hija de La Llorona* (*The Wailing Woman's Daughter*), staged by Aguijon Theater in Chicago in 2006. Her novel, *Muerte de un murciano en La Habana* (*Death of a Murcian in Havana*), was a runner-up for the prestigious Herralde Award and published by Anagrama in Spain in 2006. Her articles and short stories have appeared in *Rosebud, Hispanic Magazine, Latina Style, Latino Today, Puerto del Sol, El Nuevo Herald, Caribe,* and *Revista Baquiana.* Her web site is http://www.dovalpage.com.

MAUREEN GIBBON is the author of *Magdalena,* a collection of prose poems published by White Pine Press in 2007; *Swimming Sweet Arrow,* a novel published by Little, Brown in 2000; and the new novel, *Thief,* which will be published by Farrar, Straus & Giroux. A graduate of Barnard College and the Iowa Writer's Workshop, she was awarded a Bush Foundation Artist Fellowship in 2001 and Loft McKnight Artist fellowships in 1992 and 1999. Her writing has been translated into French, German, Norwegian, and Spanish and has appeared in the *New York Times, Playboy,* and on nerve.com. She lives in northern Minnesota, where she teaches writing.

DWONNA GOLDSTONE grew up in Moline, Illinois, and received her B.A. in American studies from the University of Iowa. After earning her MAT in secondary English education from Brown University, she taught high school English and coached ninth-grade girls' basketball and track in Fairfax County, Virginia. She attended the University of Texas, where she received her Ph.D. in American civilization in 2001. Her book, *Integrating the 40 Acres: The Fifty-Year Struggle for Racial Equality at the University of Texas,* won the 2006 Coral H. Tullis Memorial Prize for the best book on Texas history. Dwonna is an associate professor of African American literature at Austin Peay State University in Clarksville, Tennessee. She lives in Nashville with her four dogs—Langston Hughes, Satchel Paige, Butterfly McQueen, and Charlie Parker—and is working on a collection of essays about growing up black in Moline.

JOY HARJO is an internationally known poet, performer, writer, and musician of the Mvskoke/Creek Nation. She has published seven books of acclaimed poetry, such as *She Had Some Horses, In Mad Love and War, The Woman Who Fell From the Sky,* and her most recent, *How We Became Human: New and Selected Poems,* from W. W. Norton. Her poetry awards include the Arrell Gibson Lifetime Achievement Award, Oklahoma Book awards, the American Indian Festival of Words Author Award from the Tulsa City County Library, the 2000 Western Literature Association Distinguished Achievement Award, a 1998 Lila Wallace–Reader's Digest Award, the 1997 New Mexico Governor's Award for Excellence in the Arts, the Lifetime Achievement Award from the Native Writers Circle of the Americas, and the William Carlos Williams Award from the Poetry Society of America. She is the Joseph Russo Endowed Professor at the University of New Mexico, and when not teaching and performing she lives in Honolulu, Hawaii, where she is a member of the Hui Nalu Canoe Club.

LORRAINE M. LÓPEZ is from Los Angeles, California. She is an assistant professor of English at Vanderbilt University in Nashville and associate editor of the *Afro-Hispanic Review.* Her work has appeared in *Prairie Schooner, Voices of Mexico, CrazyHorse, Image,* the *Cimarron Review,* the *Alaska Quarterly Review, StoryQuar-*

terly/Narrative Magazine, and *Latino Boom.* Her short story collection, *Soy la Avon Lady and Other Stories* (Curbstone Press, 2002), won the inaugural Miguel Marmól prize for fiction. Her second book, *Call Me Henri* (Curbstone Press, 2006), was awarded the Paterson Prize for Young Adult Literature, and her novel *The Gifted Gabaldón Sisters* was released in October of 2008 from Grand Central Publishing. Her new story collection, *Homicide Survivors Picnic,* is forthcoming from BKMK Press.

KAREN SALYER MCELMURRAY, who has been a landscaper, a casino employee, and a sporting towel factory worker, is in her current life a writer and a teacher of writing. She is the author of *Surrendered Child: A Birth Mother's Journey,* described by the *Atlanta Journal-Constitution* as "a moving meditation on loss and memory and the rendering of truth and story." The book was the recipient of the 2003 AWP Award for Creative Nonfiction and a National Book Critics Circle Notable Book. McElmurray's debut novel, *Strange Birds in the Tree of Heaven,* was the winner of the 2001 Thomas and Lillie D. Chaffin Award for Appalachian Writing. Her work in both fiction and nonfiction has also received support from the National Endowment for the Arts, the Kentucky Foundation for Women, and the North Carolina Arts Council. An assistant professor in the Creative Writing Program at Georgia College and State University, McElmurray is the creative nonfiction editor for *Arts and Letters.* Her newest novel is *The Motel of the Stars* (Sarabande Books, 2008), and she hopes, in the next year, to begin a new memoir about her travels in India and Nepal and the end of a love affair.

AMELIA MARIA DE LA LUZ MONTES is an associate professor of English and ethnic studies at the University of Nebraska–Lincoln. Currently, she is the director of the Institute for Ethnic Studies. Among her scholarly publications are a coedited anthology, *Maria Amparo Ruiz de Burton: Critical and Pedagogical Perspectives,* and "Tortilleras on the Prairie: Latina Lesbians Writing the Midwest" (*Journal of Lesbian Studies*). Her most recently published short fiction includes "Amigdala" in the *River City Journal,* and "R for Ricura," in *Circa 2000: Lesbian Fiction at the Millennium.* Her current writing projects are a memoir entitled *The Diabetes Chronicles* and a critical book, *Corazon y Tierra: Latinas Writing on the Great Plains and Midwest.* Montes was born and raised in Los Angeles, California.

BICH MINH NGUYEN is the author of *Stealing Buddha's Dinner* (Viking Penguin, 2007), which received the PEN/Jerard Award. Her essays have also appeared on the *PBS NewsHour* with Jim Lehrer and in anthologies including *Dream Me Home Safely: Writers on Growing up in America* and *The Presence of Others.* Her novel *Short Girls* is forthcoming. She teaches at Purdue University.

JUDY OWENS is a lawyer, writer, and policy expert on matters that pertain to rural communities. Owens is a graduate of the University of Kentucky and the UK College of Law and has received national recognition for her writing about rural education, social services, and other issues, including the National Education Writers award for coauthoring an analysis of how poor literacy impairs Appalachian schoolchildren. In 1989 she was nominated for the Pulitzer Prize for a series of articles about how low educational attainment engenders poverty. Judy's creative nonfiction essays have appeared in the *Lexington Herald-Leader, USA Weekend,* and *Southern Exposure.* A twelve-part series of her work appears on the Web portal the *Daily Yonder,* supported by the Kellogg, Annie E. Casey, and Nathan Cummins foundations. She is currently at work on a memoir.

LYNN PRUETT is the author of the novel *Ruby River.* Her short stories and essays have appeared in numerous publications. She has received fellowships from the Kentucky Arts Council, Sewanee, Squaw Valley, and Yaddo. On the faculty of the low residency program at Murray State University, she lives in Lexington, Kentucky.

HEATHER SELLERS is the author of a collection of short fiction, *Georgia Under Water,* three volumes of poetry, two books on writing, and a textbook for the creative writing classroom, *The Practice of Creative Writing.* Her children's book, *Spike and Cubby's Ice Cream Island Adventure,* is set in her home state, Michigan, where she teaches fiction, nonfiction, and poetry at Hope College. Her memoir-in-progress is titled *Face First.* It is about her experience with face blindness (prosopagnosia), a rare condition that makes it difficult to identify people visually.

ANGELA THREATT's fiction and creative nonfiction have appeared in *New Stories from the South: The Year's Best, 2007; The Truth about the Fact: A Journal of Literary Nonfiction; Gargoyle;* and *Stanford University's Black Arts Quarterly.* Her essays are forthcoming in the anthologies *Thinking Class: The Adjunct Experience* and *The Hip Hop Jam: Messages and Music.* She was a 1998 Hurston/Wright College Award finalist and a 2005 Virginia Commission for the Arts fellowship finalist. She has an MFA from the University of Maryland, College Park.